RAPTURE READY....OR NOT?

15 REASONS THIS IS THE GENERATION THAT WILL BE LEFT BEHIND

TERRY JAMES

First printing: June 2016

New Leaf Press, P.O. Box 726, Green Forest, AR 72638
New Leaf Press is a division of the New Leaf Publishing Group, Inc.

ISBN: 978-0-89221-742-7
Library of Congress Number: 2016906859

Cover design by Diana Bogardus
Cover photo of Alex White by Andrew Edwards, www.andrew-edwards.com

Unless otherwise noted, Scripture quotations are from the King James Version (KJV) of the Bible.

Please consider requesting that a copy of this volume be purchased by your local library system.

Printed in the United States of America

Please visit our website for other great titles:
www.newleafpress.net

For information regarding author interviews,
please contact the publicity department at (870) 438-5288.

New Leaf Press
A Division of New Leaf Publishing Group
www.newleafpress.net

This book is dedicated to James Michael Hile
— a friend like no other.

Acknowledgments

Rapture Ready . . . or Not? 15 Reasons This Is the Generation That Will Be Left Behind is, I believe, the product of Holy Spirit direction. Primary acknowledgment goes to my Lord Jesus Christ, without whom there would be no *Blessed Hope* of Titus 2:13.

Again, as in all my books, I owe so much to Angie Peters, my editor of more than two decades. The Lord foreknew my many deficiencies within the writing process, of course, so put Angie in my life at just the right time — so that I would be publishable down through the many volumes we have produced. My deep love and thanks to Angie. She is my daughter in my heart.

Dana Neel is another of my daughters/close family members who helps me in the writing and in so many ways, the number of which is impossible to count. The enormous contribution made to this book through her research acumen and other input is incalculable. My profound love and thanks to Dana.

To Todd Strandberg, my partner and close associate in our www.raptureready.com website, my love and gratitude for inviting me to join him many years ago in his cyberspace mission to disseminate God's prophetic Word in these last days. Thanks, Todd, too, for writing an introduction to this book.

To Jim Fletcher, my friend of many years, and an editor and writer of the first order, who was instrumental in bringing this book to publication, my deepest gratitude and affection. Thanks, Jim, for the kind and generous foreword.

To Margaret and our sons, Terry Jr. and Nathan, and daughter-in-law Kerry, to my mother, Kathleen James-Basse, my brother Robin James, and to Jeanie and John, all my love and devotion, which goes deeper than I will ever be able to express.

To the reader of *Rapture Ready . . . or Not?* my prayerful hope is that the most important matters contained between these covers will turn your spiritual attention to the Lord of heaven, who, I'm convinced, is on the very brink of calling all who believe in Him for salvation into the clouds of glory.

Contents

FOREWORD BY JIM FLETCHER

When people ask me how I know we are living in the last days (and they often do), I answer that the intensifying pressure on Israel is the surest sign. Throughout Scripture, a final scenario is repeated: The Jewish state will be alone and defenseless . . . except. . . .

The difference of course is that the God of Abraham, Isaac, and Jacob will come to the aid of His people, and with His help on the Day of Battle, the final prophetic agenda will commence and eternity will be ushered in.

There is, however, a "twin" prophetic signpost that accompanies Israel's role: the sweeping apostasy of the worldwide Church. Never in my life until recently did I believe I'd see the American Church lead the way, but that is indeed the case. Even the evangelical community, with its leadership increasingly turning on Israel, leaves Bible-believing Christians chagrined.

One of the biggest targets for scoffers is the Rapture. Increasingly vicious attacks on this teaching are in full swing.

Added to this particular gloom is a global convergence that is marked by terrorism, economic disaster, natural catastrophes, and ineffectual leadership in the West.

For starters.

And yet, God always provides a ray of light in every generation, no matter how thick the darkness. Such a ray of light is my friend Terry James, who has for decades watched the prophetic clock and been faithful in teaching the message of the Rapture.

His latest masterpiece — and I don't use the word often — is *Rapture Ready . . . or Not?* I cut my publishing teeth back in the day, editing Terry's books, and each new manuscript was a big event. It has been a wonderful thing to read his latest book, and I would urge you, the reader, to help promote it by recommending it widely. I certainly will.

In this latest effort, Terry manages to make an exhaustive list of topics absolutely fascinating, as only he can do. He lists 15 reasons why we are on the brink of that great "snatching away."

For example, in chapter 9, Terry points to Christ's warning in Matthew 24 that in the last days, deceivers would come, including those who claim to be Christ. Terry lists a staggering number of such people in the last several hundred years, from colonial times until now. Such depth of research, and his uncanny ability to analyze the culture in light of Bible prophecy, make Terry, I think, the premier researcher in the prophecy community today. The above-mentioned list brings Christ's prophecy into a modern, colorful image that makes the prophecy highly relevant for our times.

In chapter 4, he spotlights how George Orwell and Aldous Huxley helped fulfill Bible prophecy (you'll have to read this book to learn how!).

It all adds up to a new classic in the Bible prophecy field.

One last thing about Terry James and his teaching: he is one of the kindest, most Christ-like men I've ever known, and he fervently — *fervently* — wishes to see all people come to know the Lord. His specialty is making the Rapture understandable, logical, and perhaps most importantly, *real*.

I wholeheartedly recommend *Rapture Ready . . . or Not?* to you and anyone who means something to you. This is a book for the ages.

It has been my joy to know Terry for over 20 years. I greatly look forward to spending eternity with him.

— Jim Fletcher
Director, Prophecy Matters

INTRODUCTION BY TODD STRANDBERG

It is commonly taught that Bible prophecy is a fringe belief that only a select portion of the American population acknowledges and accepts. In actuality, a large percentage of the public attests to having a basic understanding of Bible prophecy. A recent poll by the Barna Group found that 41 percent of American adults believe that we are living in the end times.[1]

To some degree, Hollywood has helped spread the knowledge of Bible prophecy. In 2013, four major movies were released that covered the subject. We have also seen a host of documentaries on prophecy; the History Channel alone normally produces a new one each year.

Most people know that the last days include wars in the Middle East, earthquakes, Armageddon, the Antichrist, the Rapture, and the number 666. But if you ask them about the details and order of events, things get fuzzy quickly.

The word "Armageddon" has wide recognition, but I doubt that 5 percent of these people would know it's an actual location in Israel, and far fewer could point it out on a map. Since I've never seen the liberal media give fair coverage to prophecy, I can understand why prophecy knowledge is so thin. What makes *Rapture Ready . . . or Not?* so important is its focus on the end-time topic that matters the most — the *pre-Tribulation Rapture.*

I have long stood with those who believe the Rapture will occur before all other end-time events. The Rapture can easily be boiled down to one easy-to-understand argument: There just simply cannot be a Rapture

1. Jeff Shapiro, "Poll: 4 in 10 Americans Believe They Are Living in the End Times," Christian Post, http://www.christianpost.com/news/poll-4-in-10-americans-believe-they-are-living-in-the-end-times-104423/.

surprise if you know it's coming at the midpoint, pre-wrath, or end of the Tribulation:

> For this reason you also must be ready; for the Son of Man is coming at an hour when you do not think He will (Matthew 24:44; NASB).

In order for the Rapture to be a surprise, it must take place before the Tribulation starts. It would be absolutely absurd to apply this premise to any other view.

During the final hours of the Tribulation, two-thirds of mankind will die from the various judgments. And those who come to faith after the Rapture will be under constant threat from the Antichrist. Keeping these things in mind, I cannot understand how any believer can be oblivious to the nearness of the Lord's return. The pre-Trib Rapture is the only position that makes sense.

One of the most common criticisms against end-time teachers is that they are too fixated on negativity. People are offended by what they perceive to be doomsayers who go around trying to scare people by saying that the Rapture is imminent and the Tribulation is about to begin. They also accuse us of saying the world is about to end — which the Bible does not claim. Nor do we.

These critics rarely go after our real reason for promoting Bible prophecy. They mostly argue that there should be a time limit on our message — that we doomsayers have been beating the last-days drum for so long, it's time for us to give it a rest. They often cite recently failed predictions as proof of our folly.

The Lord Jesus knew that there would be a two thousand-year gap between His First Coming and Second Coming. But He never once implied that we should place Bible prophecy on a back burner. Jesus said end-time watchers need to be on constant alert because He would intentionally choose a time frame when most Christians are not expecting His return.

What makes our foes all the more angry is their belief that Bible prophecy is some kind of big money-making business. I've read countless articles that whine about how men like Hal Lindsey and Tim LaHaye have become rich by selling millions of books, DVDs, movies, and bumper stickers.

The field of Bible prophecy has produced some best-selling books, but I don't think it's accurate to describe it as a cash-cow industry. The largest prophecy ministry I know of has an annual budget of less than $3 million. Most word-of-faith organizations need to take in $50 million a year just to qualify as a big league player.

What makes interest in Bible prophecy so vital is the constant progression of prophecy itself. If Israel had never been reborn as a nation, I might not have as much enthusiasm for prophecy as I do now. Many other predicted events have also occurred in our generation. It would be foolish for us to ignore them.

Many prophecy teachers see the time before and after the Rapture as the Great Divide. Today, we need to rely totally on faith to believe in God. Once the Rapture takes place, there will be no doubt about the reality of God's supernatural realm. What makes *Rapture Ready . . . or Not? 15 Reasons Why This Is the Generation That Will Be Left Behind* such a vital book is that it provides people with proof that they need to rearrange their priorities. Because the signs presented in this book point to the soon arrival of the Tribulation hour, we need to have an end-time mindset.

This time in our history reminds me of the 2003 fire at The Station nightclub where 100 people were killed and 200 were injured. A set of pyrotechnics for the rock band Great White had accidentally ignited flammable sound insulation foam in the walls and ceilings surrounding the stage. Once the fire started, it only took one minute before the entire club was filled with deadly black smoke. The vast majority of people initially stood around watching the fire grow for the first 40 seconds; at that point it only took 10 seconds for someone to move from the front of the stage close enough to the exit to ensure survival.

A video documenting this event can be seen on YouTube. What makes the footage remarkable is that the moment the person who is filming the event realizes he is in grave danger, he quickly moves to safety. The most striking part is when he turns the camera around as he is fleeing the building only to show a tangled mass of people piled on top of each other, desperately trying to get to safety. People perished in that fire because they didn't understand the intensity of the danger at hand.

Today there are simmering fires all around us. We don't know how everything will transpire before we reach the flashpoint, but we have enough warning signs to cause us to look for the ultimate exit — the Rapture.

I recently traveled through the Dallas, Texas, airport, and I marveled at the hordes of people busy engaging in various activities. Businessmen were on their way to meetings to make new deals, military members were on the move to take on new assignments, and others were traveling to meet friends and family. I could only wonder how many of these people comprehended the travel destination that matters the most — the Kingdom of God.

Someday, the Rapture will become the most important topic of the time. It will be so spectacular that even the airports in America will likely shut down while people try to make sense of what happened. Since our most important destination is the Kingdom of God, everyone needs to ask himself or herself if he or she is Rapture Ready . . . or not. After reading this book, you will be able to answer that question for yourself.

In my Father's house are many mansions: if it were not so, I would have told you. I go to prepare a place for you. And if I go and prepare a place for you, I will come again, and receive you unto myself; that where I am, there ye may be also (John 14:2–3).

— Todd Strandberg
Founder of raptureready.com

PREFACE

Instantaneously, I stood before a throng of cheering people who appeared to be in their mid-twenties. Young men and young women looked at me with expressions of absolute jubilation projecting from the most beautiful faces I've seen before or since. Their hands were thrusting at full arm's length above their heads while they looked into my eyes. I knew theirs was a cheer for some immense victory. They were bidding me to join them — or so I thought at that eternal moment.

But everything turned dark again, and I heard someone say, "I had to hit him with the paddles."

"What paddles?" I asked.

"Your heart stopped and I had to use the defib paddles," the man's voice said.

In what seemed mere moments, I heard a strange sound, the same one I had heard immediately before standing in front of that cheering throng. It was a blip sound, like that of going from one computer application to another.

I instantly stood for the second time before the same wildly cheering young men and women, their hands again thrusting upward, as if expressing victory. They laughed and jumped up and down while looking into my eyes with pure delight projecting into my core being, causing an inner warmth I had not known before that moment.

Things started darkening around me again, and I said — whether audibly or not, I don't know — that I didn't want to leave. I wanted to stay with them — wanted to join them.

But I was again on the gurney, or hospital cath-lab table. "What are you doing?" I asked the people who were working feverishly on me.

"They're trying to save your life," came the voice from the one who had said he had to use the defib paddles.

Then it happened again. I heard the electronic-sounding blip. Immediately, for the third time, I stood with the beautiful young men and women. This time I joined them while they continued to look into my eyes and wave their hands high above their heads.

This time we were running, and they were looking over at me while we ran. Toward what, I don't know. We were moving swiftly, with no effort whatsoever, toward something wonderful — toward the reason for this "victory lap."

The darkness came again, and I was again on the table. I didn't want to be there. I wanted to be with the group I had somehow gotten to feel a visceral part of during my three trips to . . . where? I don't know.

It was Good Friday, April 22, 2011, and I was said to be dead on arrival, and then was clinically dead — flatlined — on two other occasions. The interventional cardiologist told me that 95 percent of people with the "widow maker" never make it to the cath lab. Of those who do, he informed, only 50 percent live. Then he wanted me to look at the picture of my artery and what he had done to remove the blockage that had stopped my heart.

I told him I couldn't see it. I'd been totally blind since a retinal disease took my eyesight almost 20 years earlier.

"You should see where I've just been," I tried to tell the doctor and the others who had just pulled off a medical miracle. They were too busy to listen.

My case was so unusual, and the "miracle" of my recovery was so astounding, that the cardiologist association of my state gave me the "Cardiologist Patient of the Year Award," which still sits on a shelf in my office.

There isn't a day that passes that I don't think deeply on the reason for my experience — my trip into that realm, suspended somewhere between life and death, that could only be described as being on the periphery of heaven.

Although there are reasons beyond my ability to know why I was allowed that Good Friday trip to be with those cheering, young, heavenly beings, I have been given over the months since some answers as to what the experience was about. I intend to share that knowledge here. Not only do I *want* to share what I know the experience involved, but I *must* tell you, because I am absolutely required to do so. It is my commission from God in heaven. The purpose is that important.

My commission is to tell you that there is coming — *and very soon* — one specific tick of the clock's second hand that is going to convulse every culture, every society, every individual on planet earth. God has spoken it. It will happen. That instant of time will be the event that is one of the most derided, the most mocked, of all biblical truths. It will come without any immediate forewarning. But, it will not happen without a great number of prophetic signposts that presage its occurrence.

As a matter of fact, those signals are literally pulsing all around us at this moment. The very atmosphere is electric with the heavenly siren call to be alert. Something of earth-shocking impact is about to happen.

Multiplied millions of people across the world will disappear in less than a microsecond. The aftermath of the sudden vanishing in America in particular will produce carnage that staggers the imagination. Those left behind will face problems that will make any situations they are presently experiencing seem like nothing by comparison.

Beware and be aware: believe it or not, it is going to happen. According to the signals that warn of its horror-filled aftermath, the Rapture is about to rip civilization as no other event since the Flood of Noah's day.

This is the distinct impression permanently engraved into my spirit on that Good Friday, 2011.

The crowd's cheering, my spirit-impression tells me, is for the message I have been disseminating for many years through books, speaking engagements, broadcasts, and articles on our website, www.raptureready.com. However, the young, heavenly cheerleaders were mostly praising. They weren't praising me, or the others who present the message of the Rapture in all its truth — although that was part of the reason they cheered. They were praising God that this astonishing event is on the very brink of bringing the vast body of believers into the Father's house, just as God's Son, the Lord Jesus Christ, promised. Their jubilation was heaven's validation of the view of the Rapture that proclaims that believers in Jesus Christ — alone — for salvation will be brought instantaneously into His blessed presence *before* the most horrendous time of human history breaks upon a world ripe for judgment. Be assured: Rapture ready or not, these things are about to take place!

(My book, *HeavenVision: Glimpses into Glory,* is the entire account of my Good Friday 2011 meeting with the cheering, heavenly beings.)

CHAPTER 1

THE END ISN'T *NEAR*
. . . IT'S *HERE!*

Reason #1: A sure reason that this is the generation that
will be left behind is the many scoffers who ask in derisive,
scathing tone: "Where is the promise of Jesus' coming?"

We have all seen a cartoon of the little, balding, bearded prophet in a long robe, holding a sign that says "The end is near!" His message, I'm absolutely convinced, is passé — out of date.

A sure signal that the end is not near, but that it is already here, bombards my email inbox constantly. Hardly a day passes that I don't get at least one message from which I receive scriptural assurance that the last of the last days are upon this generation.

It is not the emails from Christian-haters mocking us for believing in something as foolish as Christ's return and other prophecies that are the most cutting. The emails that scoff most are from professing fellow believers in Christ. These emails are usually from those who almost without exception begin with a statement something like: "I used to believe in the pre-Trib view of the Rapture, but I've since stopped listening to what men (prophecy teachers like you) say, and read for myself that the Bible teaches believers will go through the Tribulation."

These then berate me for teaching that the Rapture will save Christians from the horrific things prophetically scheduled to precede Christ's Second Advent. They then most often say I'm leading people to hell with my false teaching. I've never figured out just what they mean in saying I'm leading people to that terrible, eternal place by teaching the pre-Tribulational Rapture. They also charge, with hostility in their words, that we who teach the pre-Trib Rapture are causing believers in Christ to be in danger of not recognizing the Antichrist when that "beast" of Revelation chapter 13 comes onto the world scene. This accusation, I understand — on the intellectual level, at least. The indictment is, however, groundless.

In either case, the angry, mocking tone of my accusers gives me absolute confidence that we who teach, preach, write, and broadcast that Jesus will call His Church (His Bride) into heaven before that most terrible time in human history is on the biblical mark. This angry opposition also lets me know that we are in the last days for certain.

The prophecy that provides such profound assurance was given through the Apostle Peter, one of Christ's closest disciples.

> Knowing this first, that there shall come in the last days scoffers, walking after their own lusts, and saying, Where is the promise of his coming? for since the fathers fell asleep, all things continue as they were from the beginning of the creation (2 Peter 3:3–4).

Today's mocking of and scoffing at Bible prophecy in general and of the Rapture in particular is a very strong indicator of where this generation stands on God's prophetic timeline. There are, however, much, much stronger assurances that this generation is on the very cusp of the moment when millions will vanish in less than a microsecond of time. They will then join their Savior and Lord above planet earth for the entrance into heaven where Christ has prepared their eternal homes (John 14:1–3).

The Rapture is an event that has always been imminent — that is, it could occur at any moment. There are no signals given that will announce its taking place except for the words from heaven every believer of the Church Age — living and dead — will hear when Jesus shouts, "Come up here!" (see Revelation 4:1).

Jesus spoke about this unknown moment in time. It was prophesied through the Apostle Paul. The Rapture will happen in the twinkling of an eye (1 Corinthians 15:52). Jesus said:

> But of that day and hour knoweth no man, no, not the angels of heaven, but my Father only (Matthew 24:36).

How, if Jesus said that only His Father (God) knows the time of the Rapture, can I make such an audacious statement as "There are strong assurances that the end is here, now — that the Rapture is very near"?

The following chapters will, I hope, make clear why the generation alive today will likely suffer billions left behind, as the novel series by Tim LaHaye and Jerry Jenkins put it. That is, most people on earth will not go to be with Jesus Christ when He calls, "Come up here," (again, see Revelation 4:1). Those billions will instead be left behind on a planet ripe for God's judgment and wrath.

It gives no pleasure to inform of this coming era of horror that most alive at the time will endure when the Rapture occurs. The prophetic truth from God's Word, nonetheless, is something I have been commissioned to forewarn. To fail to do so would bring dishonor to the Lord I serve. To do less than sound the siren would bring judgment that would adversely affect my own life, according to God's own Word.

> Son of man, speak to the children of thy people, and say unto them, When I bring the sword upon a land, if the people of the land take a man of their coasts, and set him for their watchman: If when he seeth the sword come upon the land, he blow the trumpet, and warn the people; then whosoever heareth the sound of the trumpet, and taketh not warning; if the sword come, and take him away, his blood shall be upon his own head. He heard the sound of the trumpet, and took not warning; his blood shall be upon him. But he that taketh warning shall deliver his soul. But if the watchman see the sword come, and blow not the trumpet, and the people be not warned; if the sword come, and take any person from among them, he is taken away in his iniquity; but his blood will I require at the watchman's hand (Ezekiel 33:2–6).

Chapters that follow present a mountain of evidence that the time of God's judgment and wrath looms heavily above the world at this very moment. Indicators are in every direction that the wind-up of human history is very near.

It is proper to say the end is *here* — not just *near* — because of the words of God Himself. Jesus — who *is* God — had answers in addressing

His disciples' question: "What shall be the sign of thy coming, and of the end of the world?" (Matthew 24:3).

He gave a list of such signs, then said, "And when these things begin to come to pass, then look up, and lift up your heads; for your redemption draweth nigh" (Luke 21:28).

Jesus had just given specific conditions and events that would mark the time leading up to His *Second Advent* (the moment He will return in power and great glory as given in Revelation 19:11–14).

> And I saw heaven opened, and behold a white horse; and he that sat upon him was called Faithful and True, and in righteousness he doth judge and make war. His eyes were as a flame of fire, and on his head were many crowns; and he had a name written, that no man knew, but he himself. And he was clothed with a vesture dipped in blood: and his name is called The Word of God. And the armies which were in heaven followed him upon white horses, clothed in fine linen, white and clean.

The Lord Jesus Christ is called "the word" in this Revelation account and in John 1:1:

> In the beginning was the Word, and the Word was with God, and the Word was God.

His written Word promises all of Christ's disciples (those who are born again — John 3:3) that they will be kept out of the most terrible time of human history (see Revelation 3:10). That was the horrendous era He had just described to His immediate disciples who asked Him the question: "When shall be the sign of thy coming, and of the end of the world?"

Jesus will return in power and glory as *King of kings and Lord of lords* during man's most deadly war — Armageddon. He gave many signals or signs of what would lead up to this glorious return to put an end to war. He told His disciples — those immediately surrounding Him at the time and all of His disciples to follow down through the centuries — to look up and watch, because He will be about to gather them to Himself when the prophecies or signs He and the prophets gave for that most terrible time of history begin to become evident.

That time of horror will be the seven years leading up to His return to planet earth. It is referred to as the Tribulation. Jesus promised He would come to rescue believers when the signals or signs of that soon-to-come seven-year period began to become obvious.

There is misunderstanding and confusion because of erroneous teachings about Christ's promise to keep those who have been born again out of the time of Tribulation.

Much of the error revolves around the teachers' claim that Christians (all born-again believers in Christ) will be kept "through" that time of Tribulation. The Christians alive at the time the Tribulation begins, these teachers say, will go through those seven years of horror, but God will supernaturally protect many of them. Exactly which of these believers God will protect and which He will allow to become martyrs — and why — the errant teachers fail to make clear.

The resurrected and ascended Christ spoke to John the Revelator, telling the prophet to write the following to all believers of the Church Age (Age of Grace):

> Because thou hast kept the word of my patience, I also will keep thee from the hour of temptation, which shall come upon all the world, to try them that dwell upon the earth (Revelation 3:10).

This is referring to the time of *Tribulation.* God's prophetic word uses the Greek word *ek* (the verb meaning "out of") in indicating that believers will be kept "from" the time of the last seven years of history immediately preceding Christ's Second Coming. All will be kept "out of" the very hour of Tribulation. Believers who live during the Age of Grace will not go through even one second of that time of "testing" (Tribulation).

Jesus Christ gave that promise to John, who recorded Revelation while exiled on Patmos in the Aegean Sea. Jesus was in His resurrected, ascended form when He gave the promise. That God-given guarantee that believers of the Church Age will be kept out of the very time of God's judgment and wrath was given by the same Jesus decades earlier, while He was still alive in human flesh — before His crucifixion.

Matthew recorded the words Jesus spoke while He and the disciples sat overlooking the Temple Mount from atop the Mount of Olives in Jerusalem. Jesus first made the statement about the time of His coming to again intervene in the affairs of mankind. These words by the Son of God are most important in considering the fact that believers will be kept from the seven years of Tribulation.

Jesus, in answering the question about the time of His coming again, first said:

> But of that day and hour knoweth no man, no, not the angels of heaven, but my Father only (Matthew 24:36).

He was saying that His coming will be at an unknown moment. At the time He made the statement, He was yet in human flesh, and had not yet died, arisen, and ascended into heaven. He chose to become a man, and, for the time He was within human history's time constraints, He chose to put aside some aspects of foreknowledge. Only His Father knew the time Jesus will again intervene at the end of days. Now ascended to the Father's right hand, He certainly knows the time when he will come to call His Church — all believers — to Himself (see Revelation 4:1; John 14:1–3).

Immediately after telling His disciples that only the Father knew the time of Christ's return, the Lord said:

> But as the days of Noah were, so shall also the coming of the Son of man be. For as in the days that were before the flood they were eating and drinking, marrying and giving in marriage, until the day that Noah entered into the ark, and knew not until the flood came, and took them all away; so shall also the coming of the Son of man be. Then shall two be in the field; the one shall be taken, and the other left.
>
> Two women shall be grinding at the mill; the one shall be taken, and the other left. Watch therefore: for ye know not what hour your Lord doth come (Matthew 24:37–42).

Jesus followed up the exhortation to be watchful with a second exhortation, reinforcing the first:

> Therefore be ye also ready: for in such an hour as ye think not the Son of man cometh (Matthew 24:44).

Seminaries have long taught that Jesus' words here refer to His *Second Advent*, the time of His return at Armageddon, when He will then destroy God's enemies and set up His thousand-year reign in Jerusalem. This prophecy by the Lord, however, cannot allude to that time of Christ's return with His Church and the armies of heaven. His prophecy here refers to His coming at least seven years earlier, to call His Church into the air to be with Him as given by the Apostle Paul in 1 Corinthians 15:52–55 and 1 Thessalonians 4:13–18. More about this in due course.

The Gospel account of Luke further enlightens this most important prophecy by Jesus while He sat, teaching His disciples, looking down on the soon-to-be-destroyed Jewish Temple.

Jesus said further about the time of His next major intervention into human history:

> Likewise also as it was in the days of Lot; they did eat, they drank, they bought, they sold, they planted, they builded; But the same day that Lot went out of Sodom it rained fire and brimstone from heaven, and destroyed them all. Even thus shall it be in the day when the Son of man is revealed (Luke 17:28–30).

This foretelling by the Creator of all things is stunningly clear. Jesus was telling His disciples — those immediately surrounding Him and all believers who would follow down through the centuries — that He is coming at an unknown time when things will be exactly like they were during the days of Noah and of Lot. Everything will be going along pretty much as normal in societies and cultures of the day, just like things were going along normally up until the very day judgment began falling, destroying the antediluvian world by water and Sodom and Gomorrah by fire and brimstone.

This is a profoundly precise prophecy by God Himself, giving very strong indication of when He will begin to bring human history to a conclusion. Remember what He later says as recorded by Luke:

> When these things begin to come to pass, then look up, and
> lift up your heads; for your redemption draweth nigh (Luke 21:28).

In both cases — that of Noah's day, and that of Lot's day — the cultures and societies had reached certain tipping points that made God say "enough is enough." Of course, God is omniscient — that is, He knows all things from beginning to end — so He wasn't taken by surprise. But His cup of wrath was filled to the brim with the wickedness and violence of His creation called "man." The tipping point happened at the end of Noah's preaching of coming judgment for 120 years while he built the big boat, the ark. He no doubt underwent much ridicule for his project and his message. The time came when Noah went into the safety of the ark, and God's deadly judgment fell.

Lot must have spent years trying to bring some degree of lawfulness and even godliness to the people of Sodom. He was no doubt mocked, ridiculed, and despised, even though God had him in a place of prominence, because the Scripture says he sat in the city gate — a reference to leadership in the city's governance. The tipping point was reached in the Lord's holy balance of things, and Lot was taken out of Sodom. Fire and brimstone wiped every vestige of the wicked cities from the area.

The thing to consider is, Jesus said it will be just like this when He next intervenes. People will be going about business as usual, yet the wickedness, the vileness, and violence will have reached God's tipping point. His cup of wrath will begin overflowing. Judgment will fall the very day the "Son of Man" — a reference to Jesus' humanity (fully man and at the same time fully God) — is revealed (His intervention known, worldwide).

The removal of Noah and Lot from the judgment-bound planet's surface was at an unknown time to Noah and Lot and to the people who were about to experience God's judgment. It came like a "thief in the night," as is written about the Rapture in other passages, for example in 1 Thessalonians 5:1–2.

Again, this unknown time to which Jesus referred, as given in Matthew 24:36, does not fit the Second Advent when Christ returns at Armageddon. People of that terrible era can know almost to the hour when Christ will return. The number of days, particularly from the midpoint to the end of the Tribulation era, is specified in Scripture. Those who have become believers during the Tribulation will be counting down the days until Jesus appears in the sky to rescue them.

How Near the Tipping Point?

Again, seminaries — even those who teach about the Rapture from a pre-Tribulational point of view — most always come against any notion that Jesus was talking about the Rapture of His Church when giving the prophecy about the days of Noah and of Lot. Most of these believe that Jesus was speaking almost exclusively to the Jews, because He had not yet died, resurrected, and ascended when He gave the prophecy during what has become known as the Olivet Discourse. Having a theological doctorate behind their names almost guarantees the seminary graduates don't see the days of Noah and days of Lot as having anything to do with the time of the Rapture.

Yet such marvelous Bible expositors as Dr. Adrian Rodgers and Dave Hunt spoke and wrote strongly for this prophecy. They saw it as being about

Christ taking His Church home to heaven, as given in John 14:1–3, when the Lord was sitting that day atop the Mount of Olives.

However, it is the Holy Spirit-given understanding, based upon what is taught in God's Word, not man's opinion, that we should depend upon in rightly dividing the word of truth (the Bible).

Keeping that in mind, without intending to take unto myself any glory — for it all belongs to the Lord — I believe that holding this view of Jesus' words about the days of Noah and days of Lot was confirmed to my spirit as absolute truth Good Friday, April 22, 2011, as the preface to this book explains.

And, I want to say here that I'm aware that many Bible students have their own views on the exact day Jesus was crucified and many don't agree that Friday was the day. However, the Christian world for the most part holds that it was Friday — thus, the term "Good Friday." I am absolutely certain that the experience taking place on that day is significant in validating that my trip to the periphery of the heavenly realm was a vision given by the Lord.

Fears That the End Is Near

Not long before that clinical death experience and vision of those jubilant, cheering young people who met me in that heavenly place, I completed a series of articles for our website, www.raptureready.com.

I began that series, which I gave the title "Scanning a Fearful Future," upon receiving many emails from those who expressed their anxieties over what some well-known people were saying about the immediate future. The predictions were dire, and our website's readers were obviously filled with fear that the nation and world would collapse around them within days. I was, I believe, prompted by the Holy Spirit to address their fears in the article series, which ultimately amounted to ten commentaries.

I have presented in-depth excerpts of those commentaries here to give a flavor of the anxiety spawned during that time by the fearful predictions of imminent national and worldwide collapse.

Commentators, secular and religious, weigh in incessantly on all aspects of the issues of greatest concern for these angst-ridden times. Those issues of most profound worry are collapsing economy, loss of personal liberty, and what is going to happen in the immediate and long-term future.

One can almost physically feel the fear in the emails I receive daily. Worries over what the future holds fill the articles and, more to the point for this commentary, dominate the personal missives that search for answers that might provide some degree of comfort.

One of the more mildly fearful emails I received this week says in part, "I watched the Hal Lindsey Report yesterday in which he said that he believes before the Rapture that Christians were going to be persecuted. After reading your nearing midnight article today I can see that Christians becoming more and more isolated for their support of Israel is just another sign that he is right. If Hal is right, with the Rapture being as close as it is, then persecution for Christians has to be very close. What is your take on this?"

I listened to what Hal Lindsey had to say in that particular program, and he did paint a bleak picture for the immediate future of planet earth. He correctly pointed to even more terrible times for the world a bit further out — during the Tribulation. I had so many urging me to watch Glenn Beck's program that I tuned in to that show on the several days he painted a frightening picture of what he says he believes George Soros and the New World Order minions have in mind for the world — particularly for the citizens of the United States.

Mr. Beck, like Hal Lindsey, gave as part of his view of things the prescription he thinks necessary to help with curing the sickness from which the United States and the world suffer. It is interesting that both Lindsey and Beck — one Christian, the other secular (in that he has been a Fox News pundit) — give faith turned toward God as a major part of any such remedy.[1]

Terrible times like no other in American history lurk somewhere in the future, according to former Fox News Channel's Glenn Beck. He is joined in his stated apprehension for what is coming by thousands of American citizens. Many of these are fear-filled Christians who look to Beck and others to inform them of the proposed terrors to come, and to tell them what to do about it. I continue to hear from some of these through email on a weekly, even daily, basis.

---

1. Terry James, "Scanning a Fearful Future: Part 1," www.raptureready.com, November 22, 2010.

I would like us to look briefly at developments across today's socioeconomic landscape, thus to examine as analytically and as fairly as possible the portentous matters that give Beck and others fodder for their doomsday scenarios.

Economics-minded forecasters great and small watched the stock market bubble build during the days preceding the Lehman Brothers collapse of 2008, speculating wildly what the bubble's burst might bring. That financial aneurysm, they determined, would certainly rupture — and, of course, it did. Governmental insanity created by ultra-liberal politicians saw to it that people with champagne tastes and beer drinkers' budgets for years received home loans they didn't have much more than a prayer of ever repaying.

We are now familiar with the terms "Freddie Mac" and "Fannie Mae." We are equally acquainted with names such as Barney Frank, Charles Schumer, and others, who — in the name of "fairness" to those who couldn't afford housing like the more affluent — demanded these be given the loans anyway, despite the fact the recipients didn't have the income or collateral to support that level of debt.

Rather than govern the housing industry responsibly, the elected officials invested with the responsibility to oversee things, in concert with their Wall Street cohorts, foolishly threw caution to the fiscal winds. A banking crisis of unprecedented magnitude was thus created, with the housing bubble rupture setting in motion bank failures and threats of even greater crises.

Calls for massive bailouts to avert what the president of the United States and others in government and media speciously screamed would otherwise be world-rending calamity brought about the most devastating crisis of all. Trillions of dollars were, in effect, created out of thin air by the Federal Reserve Bank to save entities "too big to fail."

The totally irresponsible sleight-of-hand accomplished only the creation of an exploding national debt that most likely can never be repaid. Decisions made by some of the same people who help create the problems strapped on the back of American citizens financial burdens with which generations far into the future will have to deal.

The resulting economic uncertainty deepened an abyss-like recession that more soundly thought-out measures would have surely lessened in severity. Jobs, as we know, are being lost; businesses are closing their doors; deflation or hyper-inflation — the experts can't figure which — might collapse the American economy within a near time frame (which the experts can't predict, either).

The stability of the global economy hangs in the balance, with the other nations and their monetary gurus wondering about the financial fate of the U.S. and its all-important dollar. And, make no mistake: under present world economic structures, the fate of the American dollar is absolutely critical.

Enter Glenn Beck at the tip of the gloom iceberg. And "iceberg" is a viable term here because the things he and others are forewarning are indeed chilling. Statements the TV and radio show host make almost daily send shivers down the spine of many of his viewers and listeners. He says things like (I paraphrase), "Change is coming, and when it happens, you won't recognize your country. You will wake up next day, and it will no longer be America as you've known it. And, it will happen just that fast. I can't tell you when that transformation is coming, but it's coming."[2]

The Federal Emergency Management Agency (FEMA) has internment compounds placed strategically around the United States. These will be used as concentration camps when anarchy reaches a critical point in America and the world. This sort of warning has been at the heart of fear-filled emails I've been receiving for the past seven years, at least.

Today, the trepidation concerning the likelihood of the collapse of America and the world issues daily from a populist mouthpiece. There are others, but Glenn Beck fills the role as chief forecaster of impending doom. He says frequently that we will awaken one morning and find that America has changed. We won't recognize the nation. It will happen just that swiftly, and the transformation will involve, among other things, probable hyper-inflation that will make money valueless for most people in America. This means that the entire world will follow suit. Global depression, we infer, will

2. Ibid., Part 2, November 29, 2010.

be the plight of all but the ultra rich of the world — the George Soroses, etc.

Based upon Beck's dire suppositions, we consider things to come. Just how far into the future all of this evil lurks, Beck doesn't know. However, based upon the rapid movement in economic uncertainties, it is likely, he implies, that it will happen sooner rather than later. That new dawning — or perhaps "nightfall" is the more apropos term — will be bleak, he predicts. The dollar will have fallen as the reserve currency for most of the world's economies. Entire bank accounts will be wiped out, in that their contents likely won't be sufficient to feed a family for a day, much less for longer. Governments will be forced to cut social programs of every sort — completely eliminating them in most cases. Rioting will explode while those on welfare roll and others used to government largess will turn violent. The big inner cities will be particularly hard hit.[3]

To this point, Hal Lindsey's view of Bible prophecy and Glenn Beck's analyses and forecast for America's destiny have run relatively parallel. Both Lindsey and Beck see a time coming in the near term when America will suffer financial collapse. It will be, they each predict, a time of national and worldwide societal darkness worse than the bleakest years of the Great Depression. Based upon the staggering debt of the U.S. and of most every other major nation on earth, theirs is the only conclusion that can reasonably be reached using informed rationale.

Lindsey and Beck also envision a singular moment when America and the world will change forever. It will be an instant so calamitous that it will, in effect, eventuate in a totally transformed global order for every facet of human interaction.

This, however, is where similarities in their view of the future end. Now the views diverge as dramatically as the difference between the eternal places called heaven and hell. . . .

Hal Lindsey, like me and those who believe that Bible prophecy clearly speaks of what conditions will be like at the very end of the age, also sees America and the world headed into an economic

---

3. Ibid., Part 3, December 6, 2010.

morass. Unlike Glenn Beck, however, we are of the conviction that if indeed we are at the end of this dispensation — the Age of Grace (Church Age) as we believe is the case — this nation is beyond anything human intervention can do to save it.[4]

We began looking into prospects for the near future by considering an email I received from one such concerned Christian. Again, he wrote the following, in part:

> I watched the Hal Lindsey Report yesterday in which he said that he believes before the Rapture that Christians were going to be persecuted. After reading your "Nearing Midnight" article today, I can see that Christians becoming more and more isolated for their support of Israel is just another sign that he is right. If Hal is right, with the Rapture being as close as it is, then persecution for Christians has to be very close. What is your take on this?

This writer's perspectives carry much weight. It is Dr. Lindsey's view of things that impressed the emailer to write. Since I am asked for my "take" on Hal's position regarding severe persecution for believers being imminent, I must be true to my study of prophecy and risk going somewhat counter to his stated belief that Christians in America are necessarily going to suffer such intensive, satanically engendered travail.

I mean no disrespect for this man, certainly a special servant chosen for the Lord's prophetic ministry for these closing hours of the age. However, my assessment differs from his forecast to an extent that I sense it needs to be presented here.

We have spent time thus far looking into the eerie, troubling changes taking place across the socioeconomic landscape of America and the world. Mostly, we have tried to get our brains around the apparent insanity of our leaders and why they have created crises and then printed trillions of dollars to throw at those crises — all of this sleight-of-hand chicanery done to stave off supposed national and world cataclysm those leaders warned would otherwise destroy civilization as it has been known. Their supposed attempts

---

4. Ibid., Part 4, December 13, 2010.

to preempt economic Armageddon now threaten to bring about the collapse of every economy on the planet.

The foundation had to be laid thusly in order to begin answering the question so many people want to know. Our emailer framed well the fears of many who worry what the near future might hold. Since world conditions are in configuration that includes issues and events much like those for the Tribulation given in Bible prophecy, will Christians in America face severe persecution before Christ returns to this desperately wicked planet?[5]

The emailer, after prefacing his question by saying that Lindsey stated persecution is coming for Christians, asked: "Persecution for Christians has to be very close. What is your take on this?"

First, I must rephrase his question to get to the heart of what he and so many others are asking. The question they mean to ask is: "Persecution for the Church in America has to be very close. What is your take on this?"

Believers in Jesus Christ — the born again (John 3:3) — are being persecuted around the globe at this very moment. Many are suffering torture and martyrdom. Members of the true Church of Jesus Christ have always suffered and died, and will do so right up until Christ's call, "Come up hither!" (Revelation 4:1). So, what American Christians are concerned about in regard to this question is whether Christians in the United States will suffer the level of persecution endured by believers like those in, for example, the Sudan. For that matter, the question implies asking whether American believers will suffer to a major extent in any way whatsoever. Hal Lindsey expressed in several of his TV programs that he believed Christians in America will suffer persecutions, and, I infer, he was speaking of persecutions of the fearful sort — those that might include loss of life in martyrdom. This fearful future, again I infer, will likely be part of a severe societal/cultural breakdown brought about by economic cataclysm. This, as pointed out previously, is much like Glenn Beck's forecast for Americans in general.

My answer to the emailer and others who continue to ask similar questions is that I don't believe Christians in America are

---

5. Ibid., Part 5, December 20, 2010.

prophetically scheduled for severe persecution like that being experienced by those in Sudan, China, and other such places around the globe.

Now I can almost hear the clicking of emails being typed. Some are already conjuring the questioning flames of retort. "Do you think American Christians are too good to suffer persecution?" "Do you think America is God's pet nation? — That the U.S. doesn't deserve judgment?!" Please . . . save your fingers the pain from the white-hot irritation shooting from your keyboard. I agree completely with you. American Christians are NOT too good to be persecuted. The U.S. does deserve judgment. There is no argument there. Now, please allow me to give my scripturally based reasoning in disagreeing with Dr. Lindsey on these matters.

I begin by inserting this caveat about my assertion that American Christians won't suffer persecution of the most heinous sort. My belief in this regard is predicated upon my prayerfully studied understanding that the world as we know it would have to first come tumbling down, then rearrange to be configured exactly as it is now in order to accommodate American Christians going into such persecution as feared by my emailer.

That world crash, then turn-around, just isn't going to happen. Everything is in place for Bible prophecy to unfold. Based upon this reality, my case follows in presenting why I'm so sure that what I believe about things to come in the very near future correctly diverges from what Dr. Lindsey and Mr. Beck say they believe is about to happen.

Each is certain that the United States is facing economic catastrophe that will bring about food and other shortages, thus will engender rioting that will bring anarchy and collapse. Lindsey's fears are less adamantly presented than Beck's, but the implication that such is in the very near future is there in Hal's TV program narratives. While Beck doesn't consider anything regarding true Bible prophecy at all, Hal Lindsey believes that severe persecution for Christians is also in that bleak future.

To briefly state my "take" in answer to my emailer, I believe that America will not suffer catastrophic collapse while Christians (true believers in Jesus Christ) remain on planet earth. You and

I — whether believer or nonbeliever — are, I'm firmly convinced, members of the most privileged generation in history. We are alive at the very end of this fascinating moment in human advancement. For believers, however, the privilege is magnified beyond imagination.

Believers in Jesus Christ are alive during this end of the Church Age for a divinely appointed purpose. We are witnesses to and participants in the very time the Lord Jesus Christ Himself prophesied would see Him revealed in spectacular fashion. The prospect for those who name the name of Christ is truly glorious.

While "Scanning a Fearful Future" is an accurate title for purposes of this examination of things to come, an equally appropriate title for those who are born again would have been "Scanning a Fabulous Future."[6]

Now, here's where things can get quite confusing, if careful attention isn't paid to the thoughts I'm trying to convey. I am of the conviction that America and the world will suffer Lindsey and Beck's predicted economic, thus societal, catastrophe. Persecution and martyrdom will coalesce to make life for believers even in the U.S. region hell on earth as a result of that immense calamity.

I am at the same time equally convinced that there will neither be national and worldwide economic and societal collapse nor severe persecution and martyrdom for American Christians. Lunacy? Not if one views things to come through Bible prophecy as it is truly given for us to understand.

God's ways are not our ways and His thoughts are not our thoughts (Isaiah 55:8). Believe it or not, like it or not, God's Word demonstrates that He deals with mankind in dispensations — distinctive eras that He alone determines. This generation is part of the dispensation of grace — the Church Age. This dispensation will morph into the Tribulation, a period of seven years of God's judgment and wrath also known as Daniel's 70th week.

My seemingly irrational claims, viewed in light of dispensational truth, are on sound biblical footing. Please consider slowly and carefully. Putting forth that I believe America and the world both

6. Ibid., Part 6, December 27, 2010.

will experience and will not experience apocalyptic socio-economic collapse makes sense from dispensational perspective. Holding that American believers in Jesus Christ will not go through such persecution that includes martyrdom, all the while proclaiming that believers living in this nation will suffer persecution and martyrdom, is a biblically correct dispensational pronouncement.

These paradoxical proclamations are made understandable by the words of the greatest of all prophets — the Lord Jesus Christ. His astonishing prophecy about the end of this dispensation in which you and I are living addresses the two questions for which we seek answers.

Bible prophecy's answers to these are as follows, I'm firmly convinced:

1) Neither America nor the world will suffer societal and monetary catastrophe that will bring about apocalyptic collapse due to man-made accidental bungling or contrived manipulation. However, there will be a crash of the world's socio-economic system, which will cause chaos of unfathomable scope, brought about by the God of heaven in an instant of time.

2) Christians in America today will not face persecution of the sort suffered by martyrs in past ages and by believers in parts of the world at present. But, following God's next catastrophic intervention into earth's history, believers in North America — as well as all other believers in Jesus Christ — will suffer persecution even worse than that inflicted upon believers of previous times.

Most Relevant Prophecy

When thinking on prophecies that are stage-setting for the windup of history, we most often point to prophecies involving Israel being back in the land of promise as most key to where we stand on God's end-of-the-age timeline. The peace process and Jerusalem being at the center of the world's spotlight show precisely the lateness of the hour.

That said, I believe no prophecy is more relevant for this moment in history than that given by Jesus Christ Himself, which encompasses not just the future of Israel and Jerusalem, but of the entire world:

And as it was in the days of Noe, so shall it be also in
the days of the Son of man. They did eat, they drank, they
married wives, they were given in marriage, until the day
that Noah entered into the ark, and the flood came, and
destroyed them all. Likewise also as it was in the days of
Lot; they did eat, they drank, they bought, they sold, they
planted, they builded; but the same day that Lot went out
of Sodom it rained fire and brimstone from heaven, and
destroyed them all. Even thus shall it be in the day when the
Son of man is revealed (Luke 17:26–30).

This prophetic declaration by the Creator of all things is about
the generation that will be alive at the dénouement of the age. Specifically, it refers to one catastrophic moment in the present dispensation when all of this world system will come crashing down.[7]

We will now try to answer the questions about world collapse,
whether persecution for American Christians is imminent, and how
it might all be tied together prophetically. We will do so by looking
in-depth at the details wrapped up in Jesus' forecast for earth's near
future.

Jesus gave what I am convinced is the premiere end-of-the-
Church-Age prophecy in Luke 17:26–30. He describes in considerable detail world conditions and activities at the moment He breaks
in on things of this present age.

He tells in His prophecy just the opposite of what Glenn Beck
says is on the brink of happening to the people of America and
the world. That is, the Lord's description of how the worldwide
catastrophe will happen differs greatly from the Fox host's prediction of the cause of the calamity he says is just around the corner.

Remember, Mr. Beck is predicting for the near future the direst
of socio-economic collapses. He recommends that we prepare for,
quite likely, hyper-inflated times to come, at the very least. He indicates that he fears that from the collapse will spin draconian governmental measures to quell the rioting that will occur when those
millions who are given government hand-outs no longer receive the

---

7. Ibid., Part 7, January 3, 2011.

largess. There is more than enough evidence of unchecked government today to prove Beck's fears are well founded. The phenomenal growth of federal intrusion into practically every facet of the citizen's life today portends grave consequences for liberty in the months and years just ahead. For example, bureaucratic regulation such as the move of the unelected FCC apparatchiks to invoke "net neutrality" — a Big Brother-like regulatory process that could eventuate in establishing dictatorial power over Internet usage — threatens anyone who would express opinions that run counter to state-approved language. The current administration intends to implement this despite the fact that a federal appeals court has ruled that the administration doesn't have the authority to do so.

Hal Lindsey sees the same cataclysm approaching, basically for the same reasons. He also recommends that we prepare for possible food shortages, and he says he believes Christians in this country will face severe persecution, which I infer to mean persecution of the sort suffered by martyrs for the cause of Christ. I must add here that I agree with both of these gentlemen — to some degree. And I disagree, also, with both — for differing reasons. But I reserve my thoughts in that regard for the biblically based logic I hope will make itself manifest as I analyze the words of the greatest of all prophets. . . .

Let's dissect carefully what Jesus predicts for the times just ahead. I say with confidence that Jesus tells the future from this moment forward, based upon what I'm convinced His words are speaking to this generation at this very hour. He prophesied in the Luke 17:26–30 passages that in the "days" He, the "Son of man," is about to break into earth's history, mankind will be doing certain things. It will be a time like the days of Noah before the Flood and the days of Lot while he was still in Sodom.

People, the Lord said, will be eating, drinking, marrying, building, buying, selling, and planting. Things will be going along pretty much as normal for the time. The Lord indicates no catastrophic, worldwide socio-economic breakdown of any sort in this time immediately before "the Son of man is revealed" (Luke 17:30) — the time He breaks into human history.

This time cannot be the Second Advent of Revelation 19:11. At the time the Lord of lords and King of kings breaks through the planetary darkness of death and destruction at Armageddon, perhaps as many as three-fourths of all people on earth will have died as a result of wars, pestilence, and geophysical disasters brought about by God's judgment and wrath upon an incorrigibly wicked, unrepentant world of earth-dwellers.

In other words, planet earth's living conditions at the time of Christ's return in power and glory at Armageddon will not be anything like living conditions at the time of His intervention into human affairs as He describes in the days of Noah, days of Lot prophecy. At the end of the seven-year Tribulation period, it will be anything but business as usual. It will truly be hell on earth when Jesus comes to destroy all human government and the soul-rending carnage it has produced.

So, Jesus, in the Luke 17 account, was foretelling the days leading up to the time when He calls His Church to Himself — "His Church" meaning all born-again believers who have lived and died during the Church Age (Age of Grace). This is known as the Rapture. To learn more about this stupendous event, read 1 Corinthians 15:51–55, 1 Thessalonians 4:13–18, John 14:1–3, and Revelation 4:1–2.

To repeat, Jesus was not describing His coming back to earth in the Luke 17:26–30 prophecy. He was telling about His coming to the planet to receive His people — Christians — to Himself. Christians — the Church — then will accompany Him back to the heavenly places He has prepared for them in the Father's house — heaven.[8]

Two statements are necessary at this point. First, it is God's staying hand that prevents the impending calamities outlined in this essay from collapsing America and the world into the worst times in history. Second, if things continue on their present course geopolitically and socio-economically — and if God takes His hand of control off developments — the collapse feared by Beck, Lindsey, and many others will certainly come at some point. The longer the rebellion-engendered crises build, the more devastating will be the crash when it comes.

8. Ibid., Part 8, January 10, 2011.

I begin my analysis of what lies just ahead in that fearful future about which Beck, Lindsey, and others have conjectured, and over which so many emailers have fretted. Again, I believe that the answers reside cocooned within Jesus' "days of Noah, days of Lot" prophecy. Now, we apply His analogy to the present generation.

Jesus foretold that human activity will be going along in a business-as-usual manner. God, in one day, will take His family — believers — out of harm's way. That very day, His judgment and wrath will begin falling on those not taken. To reiterate, because the point can't be overemphasized: if one accepts Christ's words as true and as literal, as I do, one must agree that things must be going along as normal for the time when the sudden intervention happens. Jesus plainly says that the generation alive at the time of that divine intervention will be removed to safety before the devastating events of judgment take place.

Both Beck and Lindsey say they believe a world-rending socio-economic collapse is imminent. Beck, at least, believes the crash and totally changed America and world will be brought about by the diabolical efforts of New World Order types like George Soros. Both Beck and Lindsey are recommending that we make preparations to survive that coming time of devastating collapse.

Yet Jesus tells us that it will be business as usual right up until the moment He removes believers from the planet. There is no man-made, worldwide catastrophe in Christ's prophecy. As a matter of fact, Jesus says all will be relatively normal, in terms of human activity, until that removal. Then He will be revealed by way of His cataclysmic judgment that begins to devastate planet earth. It is God who causes the cataclysm, not George Soros or any other human or other entity. Mankind's involvement in the whole matter is that of displaying total rebellion and refusing to repent of sin, thus bringing on God's righteous judgment. One era — the Church Age — comes to an end with the removal of believers. The next era then begins at some point with the confirming of the covenant with Israel, as given in Daniel 9:26–27. That period will be the seven years of Tribulation, the last three and one-half years about which Jesus said: "For then shall be great tribulation, such as was not since the beginning of the world to this time, no, nor ever shall be" (Matthew 24:21).[9]

Every signal across the geopolitical, socio-economic, and religious spectrum — even signals involving the geophysical and astrophysical — scream through the sirens of forewarning. We are at the very end of the Church Age — on the brink of the Tribulation. Yet most in America — including most believers in Jesus Christ — are going about business as usual. Except for the relatively few voices forewarning of the impending cataclysm, there is no recognition of or interest in the end-times storm warnings.

Jesus, as we have seen, said human activity will be like it is at present when He next breaks into earth's history like a thief in the night. Again, we look at the Lord's words in the book of Matthew:

> But of that day and hour knoweth no man, no, not the angels of heaven, but my Father only. But as the days of Noah were, so shall also the coming of the Son of man be. For as in the days that were before the flood they were eating and drinking, marrying and giving in marriage, until the day that Noe entered into the ark, and knew not until the flood came, and took them all away; so shall also the coming of the Son of man be. Then shall two be in the field; the one shall be taken, and the other left. Two women shall be grinding at the mill; the one shall be taken, and the other left. Watch therefore: for ye know not what hour your Lord doth come (Matthew 24:36–42).

As we have examined, this break-in upon mankind's history cannot be describing the Second Advent. It will not be business as usual at that time, when the planet is decimated by wars and God's judgment and wrath. Jesus is here speaking of the Rapture — His imminent, catastrophic break-in upon earth's history.

So we come to our present hour. America is the apex nation of the world. That is, it is the most materially blessed nation and one of the most spiritually blessed nations ever to exist. This, despite the fact that it has degenerated in many ways to become perhaps the

---

9. Ibid., Part 9, January 17, 2011.

most wicked in human history. The United States is so blessed with material wealth that every nation on earth is inextricably linked to its economy in one way or another.

It is true that its dominance is under threat and is eroding quickly. The economic meltdown and unavoidable implosion of America's monetary hegemony is imminent. But everything of global financial significance still hinges on the health and fate of the American dollar. This is to the great consternation of the people Glenn Beck rails against as wanting to bring the dollar down so that a new monetary regime can be brought to bear on the hapless citizens of what they envision as a Babel-like, one-world order.

Despite incessant assaults, the American economy hasn't collapsed. It should have by now, but it hasn't. It is, despite ominous signs ahead, business as usual — just as Jesus said it would be at the end of the age. If America's economy crashes — as Beck says it will very shortly — the entire world will collapse to rubble. The business-as-usual element of Christ's prophecy about it being like the days of Noah and Lot would be out the proverbial window.

If the U.S. economy collapsed, taking the world's buying and selling capability into the darkest times in history, it would take years — if ever — for everything to recover so that things would again come into business-as-usual configuration. Yet the devastating, world-rending collapse is coming. It cannot be stopped. I completely agree with Glenn Beck and Hal Lindsey in seeing that coming economic catastrophe in the immediate future. However, I disagree that the folly of man or the deliberate manipulations of human diabolists will bring the fearful disaster. And the disaster will not happen until God's prophetic timing allows. It will continue to be business as usual despite increasing harbingers of economic calamity. Perhaps conditions will even look like they are improving. But if so, it will be smoke and mirrors — a sham "recovery." The damage is done. Recovery is impossible.

This all means that Jesus Christ is poised to do exactly what He foretold. The prophetic signals and conditions prevalent in America and the world should have the attention of every believer. Jesus is about to fulfill His glorious promise as recorded in John 14:1–3.

The Rapture, I believe Jesus is telling us, will be the sword of judgment that pierces the building, festering boil of humanistic rebellion. When the Church is taken to heaven, the minds of those left behind who want to control will no longer have restraint on their thoughts and ambitions. There will cease to be a governor on man's conscience, according to 2 Thessalonians 2:7–8, because the Holy Spirit will allow the evil within mankind to do its dastardly work.

This will be the time — during the chaos of the days immediately after the Rapture — that all of Mr. Beck's fears will come to fruition. Neither patriots nor anyone else will be able to save America and the world.

Now to try to answer my emailer concerning whether Christians in America will suffer severe, even deadly, persecution, as I infer Hal Lindsey believes. Christians of America in this pre-Rapture time certainly are not immune from persecution — even from the persecution like that suffered by the Christian martyrs of history. However, it would take a horrendous catastrophe — such as the one Beck predicts — for American society to totally turn its back on Christianity, thus to begin physically attacking Christians in the way Lindsey fears might happen.

The Church, with the Restrainer resident within each believer, will continue to be salt and light — to exert influence over America's societal and cultural conditions. That influence, although observably becoming less and less effective, will be sufficient to prevent all-out, Nazi-like persecution against Christians in this nation.

When the Church Age saints go to Christ upon His call to them (1 Thessalonians 4:16–17; Revelation 4:1–2), America and the world will be devoid of the Church's buffering influence. Those who accept Christ during the Tribulation will undergo the most horrific persecution of human history.

Again, if a calamity like the one Beck forecasts were to befall this nation before Christ's foretold intervention into earth's history, such a collapse would take the U.S. and the world out of the time of "business as usual" that Jesus said will be in place when He pays the earth that surprise visit.

Jesus was telling us in Luke 17:26–30 and Matthew 24:36–42 specifically about His coming for the Church, and the general time frame of that event. With all that is in alignment precisely as Jesus and the prophets described, I am convicted in my spirit that now is that time.

Those who haven't become part of God's family — believing in Jesus Christ for their personal salvation — face a fearful future indeed. They will be left behind in an instantly changed world gone mad with chaos infinitely worse than even Glenn Beck predicts.

There is still opportunity in this Church Age for the person who hasn't accepted the Lord Jesus as personal Savior to do so. But time is fleeting. The Rapture could take place at any moment.

Here is what God's Holy Word, the Bible, has to say to you, if you want to escape from this world that is soon to suffer God's righteous judgment. Truly follow these instructions from the heart of the God who loves you and wants you to be safe with Him forever. You will then be assured not of a fearful future, but of a future that is fabulous beyond description.

> That if thou shalt confess with thy mouth the Lord Jesus, and shalt believe in thine heart that God hath raised him from the dead, thou shalt be saved. For with the heart man believeth unto righteousness; and with the mouth confession is made unto salvation (Romans 10:9–10).[10]

Heavenly Confirmation

I remain convinced in my spirit that the three times I visited that heavenly realm on suffering clinical death due to the widow-maker heart attack on Good Friday, April 22, 2011, validates that the cheering by the beautiful beings had much to do with this series of articles.

The many issues and events that have continued to unfold since the writing of those articles and the clinical dying and reviving are proof — to me, at least — that the end isn't just near . . . *the end is here!*

---

10. Ibid., Conclusion, January 24, 2011.

UFO SIGHTINGS AND OTHER STRANGE STUFF

Reason #2: The world is being spiritually and psychologically prepared to believe the deluding lie described in 2 Thessalonians chapter 2. This is a prime reason I'm convinced this is the generation that will be left behind when Christians go to be with Christ in the Rapture.

Planet earth is about to change in one electrifying second. If you are left behind when it happens, your world will be suddenly turned upside-down in ways that are almost beyond comprehension. Fear and panic will consume your every waking moment, and sleep will come grudgingly.

In America, this will be the one time when almost everyone will forget about shopping, entertainment, and all other forms of human interaction. Everyone will be tuned into NBC, ABC, CBS, CNN, Fox News, and all of the other forums of news reporting that are available. The ratings for news watching will achieve an all-time high immediately following the vanishing of millions of people throughout the world.

So many ramifications will result from the havoc created by the disappearances that it is impossible to contemplate them all. Just one example of the terror and anguish that will occur is the disappearance of every young child on the planet, including the disappearance of each and every baby in the wombs of their mothers.

We will look more closely at this and other ways the Rapture will affect those left behind in due course.

I must interject here that I am neither a prophet nor the son of a prophet in the sense that the God-inspired prophets of the Old and New Testaments were. My thoughts on things to come, however, are Holy Spirit-imparted to my own spirit (my spiritual senses) in that I am supposed to know the times and seasons of Christ's return, according to and based upon God's Word. Analyzing and reporting on these things to come is my life's work — my commission from the Lord for these times that are the closing of the Age of Grace. In that sense, I accept that I've been charged with conducting the gift of prophecy. I take my commission in that regard very seriously — with fear and trembling, that is, with the utmost respect and reverence for my Savior and Lord.

God's words about those with responsibility for discerning the prophetic times are most humbling and fearful:

> Surely the Lord GOD will do nothing, but he revealeth his secret unto his servants the prophets (Amos 3:7).

We also get some idea of His holy opinion on those who claim to be His prophets but are not. We learn of His displeasure from the prophet Jeremiah:

> I have not sent these prophets, yet they ran: I have not spoken to them, yet they prophesied. But if they had stood in my counsel, and had caused my people to hear my words, then they should have turned them from their evil way, and from the evil of their doings (Jeremiah 23:21–22).

The Lord states further:

> I have heard what the prophets said, that prophesy lies in my name, saying, I have dreamed, I have dreamed. How long shall this be in the heart of the prophets that prophesy lies? yea, they are prophets of the deceit of their own heart. . . .Behold, I am against them that prophesy false dreams, saith the LORD, and do tell them,

and cause my people to err by their lies, and by their lightness; yet I sent them not, nor commanded them: therefore they shall not profit this people at all, saith the Lord (Jeremiah 23:25–32).

My most profound hope for this book is that it be used to impress upon the spiritual dimension within each person who reads the exhortations written here that Jesus Christ is on the very brink of calling His Church home. When the Rapture takes place, the opportunity to avoid going through, literally, hell on earth, will be gone. Those left behind will face unfathomable hardships and even death.

I have made it my prayerful effort to "stand in God's counsel" before examining the issues and events that look to be signals of the end of days, as the secularists would call these end times. We are seeing forewarnings — precursors — of those horrible times to come even now.

Signs and Wonders

Some years ago, I was asked to be part of the History Channel's series called *The Nostradamus Effect*. Many readers will remember this series, I'm sure. It is still running on that channel on occasion.

The series was on prophecy in general, built around 16th-century French seer Michel de Nostradamus, who was credited with giving many prophecies that have since come to pass. He gave these prophecies through a series of quatrains — coded lines of poetic meanderings that were purported to tell the future. His fame arose when he was said to have predicted the death of a king during a joust, in which a shattered lance from the king's opponent entered the king's helmet eyehole and impaled the king through his eye socket. He died later from the injury.

Nostradamus is credited in modern times with having predicted the rise of a "second Antichrist," the first Antichrist he supposedly foretold having been Napoleon Bonaparte. A quatrain listed the name "Hister" as a person who would, Nostradamus said, be an evil man who would arise with Antichrist qualities. This was, those who give Nostradamus' veiled prophecies credence believe, about Adolf Hitler's rise to power.

Some might accuse me of having joined with those who promote a false prophet. The primary reason that other prophecy scholars, broadcasters, writers, and I agreed to participate in *The Nostradamas Effect* series was because we hoped to get truth from God's Word about the soon coming of

Christ to millions who otherwise wouldn't hear that truth. At least, that was my reason for joining the project.

Actually, despite all of the nonsense about Nostradamus in that series — and despite the erroneous viewpoints given by a number of liberal theologians who symbolized and allegorized or mocked a literal interpretation of Bible prophecy — we who teach the literal interpretation were for the most part given a voice in the series. Most of our answers survived the editors' cutting-room floor.

The Nostradamus Effect, like most documentaries produced today, was meant to emphasize the sensational in order to enhance entertainment value. In that regard, I would say that we who presented Bible prophecy from the literal, biblically correct point of view did much more to titillate the viewers than did our liberal counterparts. That's because the windup of human history as portrayed by John the Revelator, Ezekiel, Daniel, and other Old and New Testament prophets is indeed sensational within itself.

The chapters that follow will, I believe, validate that fact many times over. We don't have to enhance the truth in order to make the matters involved fascinating to the reader, listener, or viewer. As a matter of fact, these prophecies from God's Word are so strange and terrifyingly riveting that they are used — although often in ways that aren't accurate — in books and movies involving fictional accounts of apocalypse to bring huge revenue into the theater box offices (for example, the film *The Omen*).

Unfortunately, too many Christians in the pews of the churches just glimpse the prophetic Scriptures quickly and then turn their eyes and ears away. Sadly, many of the preachers in the pulpits also prefer to look in directions other than toward the end of the age.

Ministers who shy away from Bible prophecy in their preaching and teaching, I have found, (1) are afraid it is too frightening to their flocks, (2) fear that bringing messages on prophecy will drive down attendance numbers, (3) are too lazy to delve into the study of prophecy, or (4) believe prophecy is not to be considered as literal, thus not worthy of bringing before their congregations.

It is amazing how any true Bible student can read through the Word of God and believe that prophecy is irrelevant. Somewhere between 25 and 30 percent of the Bible, it is estimated, consists of prophecy. About half has come to pass, and about half is on the cusp of fulfillment.

Those who earnestly desire that Jesus Christ come back to earth are promised a specific reward.

The Apostle Paul said:

> Henceforth there is laid up for me a crown of righteousness, which the Lord, the righteous judge, shall give me at that day: and not to me only, but unto all them also that love his appearing (2 Timothy 4:8).

The phrase "loving Christ's appearing" means the Christian Paul is talking about will be looking for and longing for the Lord's return. He or she will be observing the times as described for the prophesied days of His coming again given in the Bible.

Paul certainly did his utmost to bring prophetic truth to the people who would follow down through history. He prophesied extensively on the very topic of this book — the Rapture. He revealed the mystery of that event, which Jesus first gave as recorded in John 14:1–3:

> Let not your heart be troubled: ye believe in God, believe also in me. In my Father's house are many mansions: if it were not so, I would have told you. I go to prepare a place for you. And if I go and prepare a place for you, I will come again, and receive you unto myself; that where I am, there ye may be also.

Paul, be assured, earned the crown of righteousness, and said as much before becoming a martyr under the oppressive hand of the ancient Roman Empire.

Jesus made sure that those who would love His appearing down through the centuries would have signposts to tell when His return is near. God's prophets, too, prophesied many signs and wonders for the end of the age and beyond.

Strange Stuff

I believe that it is much more than significant that Jesus gave the prophetic indicators in the order He gave them while overlooking the Temple that day just before His crucifixion. The very first forewarning of things that would be present on the scene at the end of the age should be on the scene today if, indeed, this generation is near the time of Christ's return.

Jesus' first forewarning was very clear:

> And Jesus answered and said unto them, Take heed that no man deceive you. For many shall come in my name, saying, I am Christ; and shall deceive many (Matthew 24:4–5).

Two things are cautioned in this prophecy:

1) At the very end of the age, there will be those who falsely claim they are Jesus Christ, Himself. The warning includes that there will be those who come naming the name of Christ in their teachings, but they are none of His.
2) The very first caution in this prophetic warning is that there will be deception that is of a very virulent or highly dangerous sort.

I believe we see this deceptiveness to come reflected in Paul's later prophecy:

> But evil men and seducers shall wax worse and worse, deceiving, and being deceived (2 Timothy 3:13).

Jesus again emphasized the nature of the deception that is coming upon the world at the end of the age as His return nears:

> For there shall arise false Christs, and false prophets, and shall shew great signs and wonders; insomuch that, if it were possible, they shall deceive the very elect (Matthew 24:24).

I don't know what more adamant warning could have been given us than that given here by the Lord. There is frightful deception scheduled for the very end of the age. We are to be watching for this deception and for these deceivers.

There's no doubt that we have been victims time after time of politicians who promised us transparency. Every generation has experienced leaders making such deceptive promises of honesty and integrity, with nothing hidden from us. This has been the case both nationally and globally. Promising transparency is perhaps the grandest of all deceptions, politically speaking.

However, the deception Jesus and the Apostle Paul warned about that will come at the very end of the Age of Grace is something of a truly profound nature. It will be of a nature that is stranger than fiction, yet it will be of the sort that will literally, eventually, delude the whole world, with the exception of those who are God's children.

That end-times deception will truly be made of strange stuff. We get a flavor of what it will entail in Paul's prophecy that involves the coming of the Beast of Revelation 13 — the man who will be Antichrist.

> Even him, whose coming is after the working of Satan with all power and signs and lying wonders, and with all deceivableness of unrighteousness in them that perish; because they received not the love of the truth, that they might be saved. And for this cause God

shall send them strong delusion, that they should believe a lie: That they all might be damned who believed not the truth, but had pleasure in unrighteousness (2 Thessalonians 2:9–12).

We will look much more closely a bit later at what might be wrapped up in this biblically prophesied "lie" and global delusion.

Foundation for Fooling the World

Satan continues to be the subtle, smooth-tongued serpent, like in his time spent in the Garden of Eden with Eve. He seeks to lead mankind further and further away from the Creator. He is doing a very thorough job in this regard.

In every case, he whispers, "Yea, hath God said?" This anti-God question is at the heart of deception as he deals subtly although in deadly treachery with men, women, and children, individually and collectively.

As stated above, Satan has infused the political process with his deadly venom of deceptiveness. He deludes with the promise of transparency. But those who would be our masters — the leaders of the humanistic sort — use the term "transparency" like a matador uses a cape to divert attention until the *coup de grâce* can be delivered and the people brought under governance, be it republic, democracy, or dictatorship. The evil one has worked his deception in every facet of the human condition. He now masterfully controls geopolitics, socio-economics, and religion. He rules societies, cultures, and world media forums.

Deception in those areas, however, is but the more visible manifestation of Satan's preparation for building the anti-God, Antichrist world he desires. His ground laying goes much, much deeper, and is made of much darker realities beneath the surface of the tangible world. These are some of the strange things cocooned within the supernatural dimension we will examine for the moment. The purpose of the exploration is meant to achieve understanding of just how preparation is being made by the grand deceiver for the most terrible time of human history that awaits those left behind when Christ calls His Church to Himself.

Again, as great as is the deception we can more easily detect on the surface of world human interaction today, Jesus' words of prophecy given in the Olivet Discourse imply a profoundly more significant deception scheduled for the end of the age. It will be steeped in supernatural powers of the dark side, which will eventuate in victimizing the entire world with an immense lie. It will be the satanic lie that will lead most into an eternity apart from the Creator who loves them and gave His Son to die in their place for sin that separates lost mankind from Himself.

Satan, in order to lay a foundation for establishment of his own kingdom on planet earth, has always first attacked the trustworthiness of God's Word. The serpent questioned the first woman, Eve, with the sly raise of a snakelike eyebrow, and asked whether God had actually said that she and her husband would die if they ate of the fruit of the forbidden tree of the knowledge of good and evil. He then told her, "Ye shall not surely die." He next made the Creator out to be a liar who wanted to be the only being that had the knowledge that the tree guaranteed for the person who partook of its fruit (Genesis 3:1–5).

Since this is his method of doing things, it doesn't surprise that Satan has spent millennia working his nefarious subterfuge and all other evil within the ranks of the people who profess to be Christians. He has been successful to a large degree in perverting the concept of Christianity in order that the world accepts the perversions as being part of genuine Christianity. It is a deception that continues today and grows dramatically, it seems, with every day that passes in this late hour of the Church Age.

Here, I must give my definition of Christendom versus Christianity. Christendom, in my view of religiosity, includes all people who, like those Jesus mentions in the Olivet Discourse, say they are of Christ, but are not. These simply consider themselves under the religious cover that purports to be Christianity. These are all who fit the Apostle Paul's "perilous times prophecy," in that they have "a form of godliness," but deny "the power thereof" (2 Timothy 3:5).

The "power" of being truly godly is in the supernatural, saving quality of the shed blood of Christ for the remission of sin. Belief in this salvation process — in Christ's death, burial, and Resurrection, alone — is what makes a person a Christian, not simply belonging to any religious organization.

Such belief makes one a Christian. All other belief systems are anti-God systems. Like it or not, believe it or not, the following heavenly prescription is God's definition of what it takes to be His born-again child — a Christian. We have seen this before in this book, and we will see it again, because it is gospel truth.

> That if thou shalt confess with thy mouth the Lord Jesus, and shalt believe in thine heart that God hath raised him from the dead, thou shalt be saved. For with the heart man believeth unto righteousness; and with the mouth confession is made unto salvation (Romans 10:9–10).

That said, Satan has worked without ceasing to pervert this truth within the spirits of all of humanity. Christendom (false Christianity) has trapped within its religious system millions who believe they are headed for heaven, but are not.

The great deception that was born of this system and that is perpetuated by this satanic lie is the sort of end-times deception about which the Lord forewarned that day while He and the disciples overlooked the doomed Temple. It is at the heart of the coming delusion of 2 Thessalonians chapter 2 that Paul prophesied will cause people of the Tribulation to believe the lie. (More about that shortly.)

Christendom's Weird Wickedness

The Babylonian system of religiosity has festered at the heart of the Babylonian system of humanistic government throughout the ages. That system of wickedness is fodder for another book at another time. Suffice it to say that everything within those systems of religion and government that have moved down the corridors of time has brought out the very worst in the worshipers of the false gods harbored therein.

From sexual perversions of every sort, conducted in the very temples of that worship system, to the bloody sacrificial murders of men, women, and children upon the altars of their idols, mankind has by far chosen this satanic system rather than the true worship of the true and living God of heaven — the Creator of all that is.

Even those forms of Christendom that don't today go to those extremes of evil nonetheless exhibit their rebellion and adherence to that ancient Babylonian system. They usurp Jesus' place in the salvation process and in His role as the only mediator between the Father and mankind (1 Timothy 2:5). Their history has in many instances been as bloody in dealing with the people entrapped within their evil mother-son worship as other of the Babylonian idolatrous bodies.

The modern incarnations of the strangeness are sometimes amusingly unbelievable, although sad for the millions mesmerized by the deception. The following are some indicators of the ways the world is in preparation for the great lie to come, according to the 2 Thessalonians 2 prophecy. This first account will probably be familiar.

HOLLYWOOD, Fla. — A woman who said her 10-year-old grilled cheese sandwich bore the image of the Virgin Mary will be getting a lot more bread after the item sold for $28,000 on eBay.

GoldenPalace.com, an online casino, confirmed that it placed the winning bid, and company executives said they were willing to spend "as much as it took" to own the 10-year-old half-sandwich with a bite out of it.

"It's a part of pop culture that's immediately and widely recognizable," spokesman Monty Kerr told *The Miami Herald*. "We knew right away we wanted to have it."

"I would like all people to know that I do believe that this is the Virgin Mary Mother of God," Duyser, a work-from-home jewelry designer, said in the casino's statement.

Duyser said she took a bite after making the sandwich 10 years ago and saw a face staring back at her. She put the sandwich in a clear plastic box with cotton balls and kept it on her nightstand. She said the sandwich has never sprouted a spore of mold.[1]

*****

Dragicevic is one of six who claim the Virgin Mary appeared and spoke to him in 1981 in Medjugorje, a town situated in the Herzegovina region of Bosnia.

Vicka Ivankovic, Mirjana Dragicevic, Marija Pavlovic, Ivanka Ivankovic, and Jakov Colo are said to have been with Dragicevic on that day. Most were teenagers at the time. After the apparition, they are said to have run down a hill at lightning speed, bursting through the doors of the parish church.

They told the priest there that they had seen a woman with a long, flowing dress and veil who had identified herself as the Virgin Mary.

The six say the Virgin Mary has continued to reappear to them ever since. For three of the seers, the visions are daily. She shows up only once a year for the other three. Typically, she makes an appearance at 6:40 p.m. The central message is one of peace. Since 1981, millions of faithful have flocked to Medjugorje, or what's known as the "village of miracles."[2]

1. Associated Press, " 'Blessed' Cheese Sandwich Sells for $28,000," FoxNews.com, http://www.foxnews.com/story/2004/11/23/blessed-cheese-sandwich-sells-for-28000/, November 23, 2004, accessed May 7, 2015.
2. Lilly Fowler, "St. Louis Archdiocese Cancels Speech by Visionary Who Saw the Virgin Mary at Medjugrorje," *National Catholic Reporter, St. Louis Post-Dispatch, Religion News Service,* http://ncronline.org/news/faith-parish/st-louis-archdiocese-cancels-speech-visionary-who-saw-virgin-mary-medjugrorje, March 18, 2015, accessed May 7, 2016.

*****

SACRAMENTO (AP) — Carrying rosary beads and cameras, the faithful have been coming in a steady stream to a church on the outskirts of Sacramento for a glimpse of what some are calling a miracle: a statue of the Virgin Mary they say has begun crying a substance that looks like blood.

It was first noticed more than a week ago, when a priest at the Vietnamese Catholic Martyrs Church spotted a stain on the statue's face and wiped it away. Before Mass on Nov. 20, people again noticed a reddish substance near the eyes of the white concrete statue outside the small church, said Ky Truong, 56, a parishioner.

Since then, Truong said he has been at the church day and night, so emotional he can't even work. He believes the tears are a sign.

"There's a big event in the future — earthquake, flood, a disease," Truong said. "We're very sad."[3]

*****

A young Italian man, Giorgio Bongiovanni, says that in 1989 he had many miraculous contacts with the Virgin Mary and, since that time, with Jesus. Both Mary and Jesus have given him information regarding the secrets of Fatima, as well as the Second Coming of Christ, contact with UFOs, and other topics. In addition, Bongiovanni daily experiences stigmata — unexplained bleeding from his hands, feet, forehead, and chest, mirroring the wounds on the crucified body of Jesus. Giorgio travels the globe presenting his message. He has met with Queen Sophia of Spain, Mikhail Gorbachev and other top officials in Russia, and has spoken at the United Nations. His goal is to "sensitize the consciousness of humanity to the great changes about to occur in the world."

Share International's U.S. editor Monte Leach interviewed Bongiovanni.[4] The man claims that while walking down the street in Sicily, in April 1989, he saw a vision of a blond-haired woman in a white dress with a rose on her chest who told him she was Miriam,

---

3. *USA Today* — Religion, "Believers Flock to Virgin Mary Statue 'Crying' Red Tears," November 27, 2005, accessed May 7, 2015.

4. Monte Leach, Share International, "The Second Coming, UFOs, and the Future of Humanity — Interview with Giorgio Bongiovanni," http://www.share-international.org/archives/appearances/ap_ml2ndcoming.htm, accessed May 7, 2015.

who he recognized as the Virgin Mary. She was made of light. Her main message to him was the third secret of the Fatima (the first two are already known to the Catholic Church).

*****

His stigmata initially appearing at a friendly get together, 31-year-old Croatian priest Zlatko Sudac's wounds have been declared by the Vatican to be "not of human origin." The first wound, an indentation approximately an inch long, appeared on his forehead in 1999. A year later, markings appeared on his hands, feet, and side. He describes the stigmata as filling him with "a tremendous fear of the Lord." Sudac says that the wounds cause him no pain except when he is praying, at which time he feels them pulsing.

Along with the stigmatization, Sudac claims to have received the divine gifts of levitation, prophecy, and bilocation — the ability to be in two places at one time.[5]

The question will be asked: What is wrong with these accounts of visions? As weird as they might be, might they not be genuinely from God? Could they be true, heavenly visions?

No is the answer.

Such visions or whatsoever they are run counter to what God's Word, the Bible, says. They are like the delusions conjured up from the ancient Babylonian religious cults.

Here is what the Apostle Paul said about such lies from the dark side.

> But though we, or an angel from heaven, preach any other gospel unto you than that which we have preached unto you, let him be accursed. As we said before, so say I now again, if any man preach any other gospel unto you than that ye have received, let him be accursed (Galatians 1:8–9).

He wrote further:

> And no marvel; for Satan himself is transformed into an angel of light. Therefore it is no great thing if his ministers also be transformed as the ministers of righteousness; whose end shall be according to their works (2 Corinthians 11:14–15).

---

5. Mark Jacobson, "Sudac the Mysterious," *New York* — News and Politics, http://nymag.com/nymetro/news/trends/columns/cityside/5990/, accessed May 7, 2015.

The Apostle John wrote:

> Beloved, believe not every spirit, but try the spirits whether they are of God: because many false prophets are gone out into the world (1 John 4:1).

God says in the first chapter of Romans that He is revealed through the creation. He is revealed through His Word, the Bible. His salvation plan is revealed through His Son, Jesus Christ.

Jesus said:

> I am the way, the truth, and the life; no man cometh to the Father but by me (John 14:6).

Strange manifestations such as those given here that are reported almost daily point to another power of the supernatural sort. They are designed to get people to think on the supernatural and not on the deep things of God, which can be accessed only through Holy Spirit impartation when one seeks the Lord with all his or her spiritual heart.

The supernatural must always be looked at with probing discernment and skepticism. The ancient Babylonian system of this sort is alive and well, especially in these days so near the time of Christ's return.

I must admit that the artifact known as the Shroud of Turin is one such article that seems to pass that discernment and skepticism test. It rates being given credence, in my view, because it points in stunning, scientifically examined ways to the death, burial, and Resurrection of the Lord Jesus Christ. This, despite the fact that worldly skeptics have done all they can to prove it is a fraud. The more it is examined, the more genuine it appears.

The bottom line on the weird things that are proliferating in these strange times is that humanity is being prepared for the time when there will be a lie of supernatural proportion presented by the father of lies. Satan has laid the foundation for the structure that will be his neo-Babylonian order, ruled over by that *son of perdition* who will be said to be the ultimately evolved man.

We will next look at what I am convinced in the deepest reaches of my spirit is the core of preparation for the great, satanic lie to come once the Rapture of the Church occurs.

Even Stranger Stuff

Jesus, the greatest of all prophets, gave a primary prediction about astrophysical manifestations that would herald His Second Coming:

And there shall be signs in the sun, and in the moon, and in the stars (Luke 21:25).

Although He gave this prophecy for the time following the Rapture in particular, He also indicated that such signals would begin at an earlier time in a way that would alert those who will be looking for His appearing (Luke 21:28).

People no doubt still smile or even snicker at such things as claims that there are apparitions of iconic religious beings appearing on half-eaten toasted cheese sandwiches. However, there are, in these strange times, fewer grins of mocking disbelief directed at reports of weird goings-on in the skies above the earth.

Earlier generations would have considered men walking on the moon and floating around in space as absolutely flabbergasting. Man-made machinery crawling across the surface of Mars and other planets and sending back pictures, and even photos of the big, blue marble taken from the surface of the moon would have astonished anyone prior to the 1960s. But even these technological achievements by man pale in comparison to the sort of stunning things I believe Christ was prophesying.

Numerous documentaries present nonfiction accounts of UFO sightings and encounters that lend believability to the fiction the moviemakers produce about visitors from other worlds. Accounts by presidents, governors, senators, and others of personally seeing strange things in the skies have brought credibility to the postulation that we are not alone. Let's look at these reports of UFOs that continue to accumulate.

> **The Roswell Incident** — Without a doubt, this is the most famous UFO encounter in history. Roswell, New Mexico, mid-1947, a crash of a military Air Force surveillance balloon at a ranch near Roswell, New Mexico, gave rise to claims alleging the crash was of an extraterrestrial spaceship.
>
> After an initial spike of interest, the military reported that the crash was merely of a conventional weather balloon. Interest subsequently waned until the late 1970s when ufologists began promulgating a variety of increasingly elaborate conspiracy theories claiming that one or more alien spacecraft had crash-landed and that the extraterrestrial occupants had been recovered by the military who then engaged in a cover-up.

The Kenneth Arnold Sighting — This is often said to be the first-ever UFO sighting. While this could not be further from the truth, it can be considered the first UFO sighting of the modern era. In 1947, private pilot Kenneth Arnold spotted a fleet of nine UFOs while flying in the vicinity of Mount Rainier, Washington. He described the craft as being crescent-shaped, but also noted that they "flew like a saucer would if you skipped it across the water," spawning the term "flying saucer."

Washington UFO Flap — 1952 saw the largest number of UFO sightings ever recorded over the East Coast of America. The largest concentration of UFOs occurred in July that year, with literally dozens spotted in the skies over Washington, D.C. While a large number of these sightings were made by members of the public, an alarming number of reports came from commercial pilots, air traffic controllers, and even from within the Air Force itself.

On the evening of July 19, the Washington UFO flap exploded into an all-out invasion of the capital. At midnight, the radar tower at Washington National Airport picked up eight unknown objects traveling at 120 mph and heading straight for the White House. Staff at the nearby Andrews AFB witnessed a glowing ball of orange flame in the sky. It had a revolving tail that zoomed around with unbelievable speed. At the same time, a Capital Airlines pilot spotted seven more UFOs. By 2:00 a.m., flaming objects were seen all over Washington, and it was clear to all observers that something was seriously amiss.

Some have suggested that the night of July 19, 1952, was when the U.S President met alien officials for the first time in the White House. Others blame bizarre weather conditions for false radar blips and optical illusions. As always, the truth remains a mystery.

The Kecksburg UFO Crash — This is Roswell's less famous, often overlooked younger brother. Witnessed by thousands in both the United States and Canada as it streaked across the skies of the Great Lakes area in 1965, the Kecksburg UFO was widely presumed to be a meteor. It caused sonic booms in western Pennsylvania and dropped hot metal debris, starting grass fires in Michigan and Ohio. The object crashed down about 30 miles southeast of Pittsburgh, near the small village of Kecksburg. Villagers saw wisps of blue smoke coming from the woods, and the local volunteer fire department was dispatched to investigate. What they found was no meteor. The object was about the size of a Volkswagen Beetle, shaped like an acorn, and adorned with hieroglyphics.

The Shag Harbor Incident — Canada had its own "mini-Roswell" event in 1967 when an unidentified object crashed into the waters of Shag Harbor, Nova Scotia. At least 11 people saw a low-flying object heading toward the harbor and several more saw it hit the water as they heard a whistling sound and a loud crash. A search and rescue operation was launched, but no debris was found. Only an orange foam was visible on the surface. The Canadian military was baffled, and the object was officially classified as a UFO. An anonymous witness claiming to be one of the U.S divers involved in the search has since given a detailed account of what happened at Shelburne. In his version of events, there were two alien craft in the waters near Shelburne, and one seemed to be repairing the other.

The Cash-Landrum Case (USA) — This is famous in ufology circles, largely because of the extreme physical symptoms suffered as a result of the sighting.

On the evening of December 29, 1980, Betty Cash, Vickie Landrum, and seven-year-old Colby Landrum were driving toward Huffman, Texas, when they saw a diamond-shaped UFO hovering at tree level. The object expelled bursts of flame from its underside, apparently to keep itself airborne, and the three reported that they could feel intense waves of heat. The dashboard of the car became so hot that when Landrum touched it, she left a handprint in the softened vinyl. After hovering for a while, the UFO moved to a higher altitude, where, according to Cash and Landrum, it was met by a number of Chinook helicopters. A police officer from Dayton also saw several Chinook helicopters moving toward the vicinity of the sighting, but did not witness the UFO itself.

Following the encounter, all three witnesses suffered the effects of radiation sickness, experiencing a burning sensation in their eyes, nausea, vomiting, and diarrhea.

The Phoenix Lights (USA) — Witnessed by thousands of people across the U.S states of Nevada and Arizona, and the Mexican state of Sonora, the Phoenix lights are the United States' largest "mass sighting."

Five lights in a triangle formation (usually presumed to be one large craft) were first seen above Henderson, Nevada, at 7:55 p.m.

on March 13, 1997. Subsequent sightings have the object moving over Prescott, Arizona, heading southeast. From this trajectory, it is safe to assume that it traveled from the vicinity of the Groom Lake Facility in Area 51 and went unnoticed in the skies over Las Vegas (hardly surprising).

By 8:30 p.m., the lights had reached the city of Phoenix, Arizona, where thousands of people witnessed the phenomenon. Among them was state governor Fife Symington, a former Air Force pilot, who has publicly stated that the lights did not resemble any man-made object he'd ever seen.

Guadalajara, Mexico — Guadalajara is Mexico's second-largest city and also holds the record for the highest number of reported UFO sightings in the country. In June 2004, it was also host to the largest concentration of UFOs ever sighted. A swarm of bright lights gathered over the city and hung around for several hours.

In 2004, the Mexican Air Force released a video of a fleet of UFOs declaring it a mystery. The video was shot using infrared cameras and shows 11 spherical heat sources above Campeche, Southern Mexico. The spheres were not visible to the naked eye.[6]

Continuing reports pour in each month of UFO sightings and even personal encounters with supposed visitors from other planets. We all know about the recounting of abductions during the night by small, gray creatures with big, bug-like eyes who take victims to spaceships where they perform experiments on abductees.

There are so many such reports that psychologists and others who study and analyze the things involved conclude that either the abductions are possibly really happening or they are part of mass hysteria of some sort. My contention is that these abduction experiences are indeed along the lines of supernatural mass hypnosis taking place. The hypnotist is none other than Lucifer, the fallen one, preparing the way for the Antichrist regime to come.

For example, the entertainment industry — a primary tool of the prince of the power of the air (Ephesians 2:2) — continually turns out movies for television and theaters that pave the way for the great delusion of 2

6. Paranormal Haze, "Amazing UFO Sightings from around the World: North America," http://www.paranormalhaze.com/amazing-ufo-sightings-from-around-the-world-north-america/, accessed May 7, 2015.

Thessalonians 2:11. This has been the case, particularly, since the time of the sightings over Washington, D.C., in 1952, as reported earlier.

The film *The Day the Earth Stood Still* laid the groundwork for the mass hypnosis to come, as did H.G. Wells' radio drama *War of the Worlds* broadcast in 1938. Many productions, such as *ET the Extra-Terrestrial, Independence Day, 2001: A Space Odyssey*, and myriad others have influenced the minds of much of mankind in such a way that when the *lie* is told in the post-Rapture world, it will be almost totally accepted as truth.

Explaining the Disappearance

Believe it or not, accept it or not, like it or not, the Creator of all things is about to again catastrophically intervene into the rebellious, sin-filled, human sphere like He did in the antediluvian days of Noah (Matthew 24:37). Jesus will step out on the clouds of glory and shout, "Come up here!" (Revelation 4:1). In less than the blink of an eye, millions of people will vanish from the planet's surface to be with the Lord.

We will consider the many consequences of that sudden catastrophe while we progress through the following chapters. For example, we will think on how the inhabitants left behind will react to the disappearance of every young child and those yet unborn in the wombs of their mothers. We will ponder the ramifications of the effects that event will have on the societies, cultures, and governments of mankind.

For now, however, we will look into this preparation for foisting the great delusion of 2 Thessalonians 2:11 upon those left behind who will be caught in the wake of the Rapture.

The first minute or so following that instant of Rapture will have most every person on earth who is aware during that moment asking one question: "What just happened?!"

Extreme fear will grip those who are awake. Those asleep at the time will awaken to a world gone mad with confusion and terror. All will soon search frantically for answers to why people have vanished, many having watched those they knew and loved disappear from their presence.

Like a person about to drown who is thrown a lifeline or life preserver, those caught in the panic aftermath of this earth-shattering event will clutch desperately to any vestige of hope.

There will, possibly within hours, come forth that lifeline of explanation. While it might not at first be overly comforting, it will be, I think, grasped by almost everyone who hears the explanation. That explanation will have been demonically programmed into the minds of the masses for decades, if not centuries. Its essence will be, "We are not alone."

Those who embrace the New Age, divinity-of-man belief system have held that all human beings are potentially gods. There exist ascended masters who look upon humankind from their other-dimensional perches of superior wisdom. These are scheduled one day to bring harmonious convergence to planet earth. This will result in establishment of the "Age of Aquarius," a state of spirituality in which peace and love will reign supreme. Those unable or unwilling to fit within this new paradigm must be removed from the earth.

The following presents the all-inclusive, Babylonish constituency cocooned within this Satan-inspired system.

> The New Age movement includes elements of older spiritual and religious traditions ranging from monotheism through pantheism, pandeism, panentheism, and polytheism combined with science and Gaia philosophy; particularly archaeoastronomy, astrology, ecology, environmentalism, the Gaia hypothesis, psychology, and physics. New Age practices and philosophies sometimes draw inspiration from major world religions: Buddhism, Taoism, Chinese folk religion, Christianity, Hinduism, Sufism (Islam), Judaism (especially Kabbalah), Sikhism; with strong influences from East Asian religions, Esotericism, Gnosticism, Hermeticism, Idealism, Neopaganism, New Thought, Spiritualism, Theosophy, Universalism, and Wisdom tradition.[7]

The answer to what the disappearance is about sought by all of the terrified people who are left behind at the Rapture will likely include at least some elements of the New Age explanation.

Likely, too, the answer will include in large part an explanation of how *Space Brothers*, or other beings of a benevolent sort from other star systems, have decided to intervene in the affairs of mankind to prevent all-out nuclear destruction.

One theory that is gaining credence is the "seed theory," which postulates that extraterrestrial beings "seeded" the planet with human beings in some way.

---

7. "New Age," Wikipedia, en.wikipedia.org/wiki/New_Age.

Again, people of earth have been programmed to accept such explanation for years within modern times.

A recent report explains:

> Scientists in the U.K. have examined a tiny metal circular object, and are suggesting it might be a micro-organism deliberately sent by extraterrestrials to create life on Earth.
>
> The University of Buckingham reports that the minuscule metal globe was discovered by astrobiologist Milton Wainwright and a team of researchers who examined dust and minute matter gathered by a high-flying balloon in Earth's stratosphere.
>
> "It is a ball about the width of a human hair, which has filamentous life on the outside and a gooey biological material oozing from its centre," Wainwright said, according to Express.co.uk.
>
> "One theory is it was sent to Earth by some unknown civilization in order to continue seeding the planet with life," Wainwright hypothesizes.
>
> Panspermia is a theory that suggests life spreads across the known physical universe, hitchhiking on comets or meteorites.[8]

The Great Delusion

When screams of agony caused by fear-engendered panic calm to sobs of realization that the world has been forever changed for the worse, the search for the answer to the vanishing of millions of people will become all consuming. The well-known words of one political hack — "Never let a crisis go to waste" — will take on a whole new dimension of application.

Those who have longed to take advantage of crisis in order to bring about control of monumental proportion will have just been presented with opportunity to fulfill their greatest dream. The Rapture will create a vacuum into which will rush every evil entity imaginable — of both the human and the supernatural sort.

Again, we consider the words of Paul the Apostle and the prophecy most pointedly directed at this unprecedented occurrence in human history:

> For the mystery of iniquity doth already work: only he who now letteth will let, until he be taken out of the way. And then

---

8. Lee Speigel, "UK Scientists: Aliens May Have Sent Space Seeds to Create Life on Earth," HuffingtonPost.com, February 13, 2015, accessed May 7, 2015.

shall that wicked be revealed, whom the Lord shall consume with the spirit of his mouth, and shall destroy with the brightness of his coming: Even him, whose coming is after the working of Satan with all power and signs and lying wonders, and with all deceivableness of unrighteousness in them that perish; because they received not the love of the truth, that they might be saved. And for this cause God shall send them strong delusion, that they should believe a lie: that they all might be damned who believed not the truth, but had pleasure in unrighteousness (2 Thessalonians 2:7–12).

This foretelling by Paul speaks directly to the time immediately following the Rapture of the Church into heaven. It then goes on to explain the way things will play out, and why.

The prophecy tells us that a mysterious iniquity (supernaturally evil force) has been in effect throughout time and is going strong at the time this great event — the Rapture — takes place. This satanic evil, however, has been restrained (kept from its full power to afflict mankind) until this moment of the Church (Christians) being removed from earth. The prophecy includes the gospel fact that the Church — each believer — is indwelt by God, the Holy Spirit, the third Person of the Trinity.

It is the Holy Spirit — God in His omnipresence (always being everywhere at the same time) — who is restraining evil to this point of Rapture. The prophecy here tells that the Holy Spirit will no longer restrain evil when the Church departs, or is raptured.

God the Holy Spirit will still be on earth, because He is omnipresent, but He will now manifest God's presence in ways different than before the taking of the Church into heaven. When the Holy Spirit no longer restrains evil, that malevolent force will rush in to fill the vacuum created. The desperately wicked minions — both of the human and superhuman varieties — will move among mankind, whose own consciences, individually and collectively, will no longer be governed by God's influence.

Mankind will no longer be able to easily discern truth from lie. And this is where the lie, the great delusion of this prophecy, will come in.

The one who will be the most prolific and proficient liar of all time will be the "man of sin" or "son of perdition" — the Antichrist. This "beast," as he is called in Revelation 13, will garner the adoration and, eventually, the worship of the whole world of those left behind in the wake of the Rapture.

So what will be the nature of that lie, that delusion prophesied in this passage? The answer might be a letdown, after this buildup of the magnitude of its threat.

No one knows for sure what it will involve, exactly. However, I am more than ready to offer a very strong suggestion to at least part of what will be involved in this great deception. All of the stage-setting for this lie, I am convinced, has been put in place for this moment when Satan will provide the lie that will delude the minds of humanity, now unrestrained by God's precautionary discernment.

The lie will include the announcement that those who disappeared were taken away for retraining, because they were not ready for the New Age harmonic convergence that has now come to the planet for the initiation of the Age of Aquarius. This new paradigm cannot include those who hold intolerantly to such theology as that presented by fundamentalist Christianity. Those left behind are the ones who have shown the willingness to accept a belief system that includes all forms of religious thought.

Now for a speculation sidebar I promised regarding this disappearance phenomenon the world will experience: I believe that every child on planet earth will disappear at the moment of that great event. That is, every child below the age of accountability will vanish in that twinkling of an eye.

Children who are too young to make a decision to accept or reject Jesus Christ as Savior are written in the Lamb's Book of Life until they are old enough to decide. When the Holy Spirit convicts their spiritual minds to accept Christ, and if they reject God's offer, that child then has his or her name removed from that book. This is what is meant when Jesus talks about a name being blotted out of the book of life (Revelation 3:5).

When they then receive Christ at some point, their name is written in that volume. So a child below the age of accountability is counted as being in relationship with Christ. Such children will go to be with Him when He calls (Revelation 4:1). Every child in this age category will be raptured. This includes every child in the womb, from the moment of conception.

In that instant, the Lord is going to make a profound statement about His opinion of abortion and the definition of human life and when it begins. Every womb of pregnant women left behind will become empty. There will be terrified wonderment on what has happened to all the children — to all the babies in the now-empty wombs.

I believe the answer that will come as part of the "lie" of 2 Thessalonians 2 will be that these children were taken to be properly inculcated into the new paradigm into which the planet had just shifted. The children will be returned once this has been accomplished.

The Rapture is an inseparable part of salvation itself, as indicated in 1 Thessalonians 5:9. The children won't be coming back. They will be forever with their Savior and Lord in the safety of their heavenly home.

Included in the lie as prophesied in 2 Thessalonians 2 will be the introduction to the star beings — the supposed extraterrestrial beings who have long been watching the earth's inhabitants. They will now, it will be promised, help bring peace to a planet on the verge of destroying itself through nuclear war.

I believe that Antichrist might be put forth as the ultimately evolved man, the one who has the answers. Maybe he will even be said, himself, to be a space brother.

Now, I can understand where my thinking as given might be considered more out there in space than the postulated space brothers. Everything that has truth at its center must have a biblically scriptural basis. This seemingly way-out supposition is no exception.

Here is the scriptural basis upon which I set my thinking. John the Apostle and prophet was given the following as part of Revelation:

> And there was war in heaven: Michael and his angels fought against the dragon; and the dragon fought and his angels, and prevailed not; neither was their place found any more in heaven. And the great dragon was cast out, that old serpent, called the Devil, and Satan, which deceiveth the whole world: he was cast out into the earth, and his angels were cast out with him. And I heard a loud voice saying in heaven, Now is come salvation, and strength, and the kingdom of our God, and the power of his Christ: for the accuser of our brethren is cast down, which accused them before our God day and night. . . . Therefore rejoice, ye heavens, and ye that dwell in them. Woe to the inhabiters of the earth and of the sea! for the devil is come down unto you, having great wrath, because he knoweth that he hath but a short time (Revelation 12:7–12).

This prophecy does not refer to Satan and his angels being cast out in their original rebellion in heaven. We know this, because the Scriptures tell us that Satan stands before God today, accusing believers. This casting out of the devil and his angels, then, is yet future — during the era known as the Tribulation.

When this second great battle in the heavenlies takes place, Satan is thrown to earth and can never again move in the heavenly regions. He will at this time begin to work his evil on this planet as never before. Part of that will be to foist the lie of 2 Thessalonians 2:11 on those left behind after the Rapture.

This casting down of Satan to earth will be used by that most evil being to put forth the lie that will delude those left behind. The lie will include, no doubt, that these who are coming to earth are the star beings who originally planted human seed on this planet. Satan's coming to earth will be viewed as explanation for the many UFO sightings and other phenomena over the centuries.

As the fallen angels descend into earth's atmosphere, they will likely give the deluding appearance of light orbs or possibly interstellar spacecraft invading earth.

Yes, I have further scriptural evidence that this scenario is plausible according to Bible prophecy.

We next pick up the prophecy from Revelation in the following chapter.

> And I beheld another beast coming up out of the earth; and he had two horns like a lamb, and he spake as a dragon. And he exerciseth all the power of the first beast before him, and causeth the earth and them which dwell therein to worship the first beast, whose deadly wound was healed. And he doeth great wonders, so that he maketh fire come down from heaven on the earth in the sight of men, and deceiveth them that dwell on the earth by the means of those miracles which he had power to do in the sight of the beast; saying to them that dwell on the earth, that they should make an image to the beast, which had the wound by a sword, and did live (Revelation 13:11–14).

Two "beasts," as the prophecy calls them, will supposedly be two humans — the False Prophet and Antichrist, the last and most violent dictator of history. I say "supposedly" because I have some questions about these "beasts" being truly human, since neither will stand before God's Great White Throne for judgment. They are the only people who will go directly into the "Lake of Fire" for eternal punishment, following Christ's Second Coming.

Every other person will be brought before that Great White Throne for final judgment and sentencing.

As you see from the prophecy, we again witness fiery entities descending from above the planet. The False Prophet invites these down in the sight of men and the image of Antichrist. All on earth are deceived, the prophecy foretells.

I believe this is one of the signs and wonders this religious charlatan will use to help Antichrist and, of course, their master, Satan, deceive the whole world. Again, it will likely be claimed that these are the space brothers come to earth to prevent nuclear war and the end of life on earth. From this moment, Lucifer the fallen one and his minions will turn the planet into hell on earth.

CHAPTER 3

PLANET EARTH
NEEDS A SHRINK

Reason #3: Today, the nations and peoples are in ever-increasing distress, with great perplexity. This is a significant reason to believe that this is the generation that will be left behind in the wake of Rapture.

News reports assault the senses hourly in this age of instant communications. Most of it, by far, is of the sort that causes us to joke: "No news is good news." Or maybe we aren't always joking. The cumulative effect of such reports can be depressing. Some can be downright distressing.

Considering the many signals we are examining in this book, it shouldn't come as a surprise that such upsetting news is given as a major prophetic indicator of the sort that will be prevalent at the very end of the Church Age.

As we have confirmed, according to Bible prophecy, no sign is given that is to specifically announce that the Rapture of the Church is about to take place. It is an event that will come as a complete surprise to the entire world, except for those who are anticipating Jesus Christ's imminent (any-moment) calling of believers to Himself (Revelation 4:1). The disappearance of millions of Christians around the world in that microsecond of Rapture, however, will not occur without due forewarning.

The following perhaps overused analogy is the best to use in describing the relationship of the timing of the Rapture to the moment at Armageddon when Christ returns victoriously to the planet.

When He comes back at the end of the Tribulation (the last seven years of human history described in the Book of Revelation), most of earth's inhabitants will have died in the judgment and wrath predicted for that era. The Bible promises that all believers of the era immediately preceding that seven years of horror will leave the planet for safety in heaven with Christ.

In this analogy, we use Christmas Day as Christ's Second Coming and Thanksgiving Day as the Rapture of the Church.

These days, when promotion for Christmas begins to bombard us earlier and earlier each year, you can know Thanksgiving is at hand when you begin to see all of the Christmas advertisements. The analogy has it that Jesus and the prophets gave signals for the Second Coming or Second Advent of Christ's return at the time of Armageddon, but gave no signs of His coming for the Church in the Rapture. Since we are being bombarded by every signal that the time of Christ's Second Advent is drawing near, we know that the Rapture, which will occur at least seven years earlier, is about to take place.

These many signals or signs of Christ's Second Coming are literally exploding upon the world scene. They are in every direction on the prophetic landscape. These are prime indicators forewarning that this appears to be the generation that will be left behind.

We are exploring those many indicators, and there is none more prominent in our hourly headlines than one in particular the Lord warned about while prophesying near the top of the Mount of Olives in Jerusalem nearly two thousand years ago. That particular sign that shows His Second Coming must be very near is found within the following Scripture:

> And there shall be signs in the sun, and in the moon, and in the stars; and upon the earth distress of nations, with perplexity; the sea and the waves roaring (Luke 21:25).

This chapter involves exploration of the second and third indicators within this prophecy. They are parts of the same forewarning, I believe. Nations will be "in distress," with "the sea and the waves roaring." The entire world scene at the time Christ's Second Coming approaches will be one of perplexity.

The seas and waves that will be roaring are, in this prophetic instance, the billions of peoples of earth.

Worldwide Distress

It's a Mad, Mad, Mad, Mad World! was the title of a wild madcap movie made in the early 1960s. It described a hilarious set of circumstances the characters went through in their lives and how they ultimately interacted in a frantic effort to find the treasure that had been hidden. Today, we often hear the words — or say them ourselves — "This world has gone insane." But this is no hilarious comedy we now go through on a daily basis.

News coming out of every nation on earth proves just how crazy life on earth has become. Threats of every sort lurk in far distant places, and more and more often directly assault much nearer to where we live.

The problems here in America are usually far less threatening in the sense of immediacy than those faced by people in such places as Sudan, Ethiopia, and certain regions of the Middle East. Some of the distresses in those faraway places do, however, sometimes reach into our lives here.

For example, the Islamist terrorists who for centuries have made those distant lands places of extreme distress for the inhabitants came to the United States with the attacks in New York City and Washington, D.C., with assaults against the World Trade Towers and the Pentagon in 2001. They came to Boston, Massachusetts, in 2014 with the murderous attacks during the Boston Marathon. They came to San Bernardino, California, with the murder of 14 and the wounding of 21 at the center for the disabled in December of 2015. They likely have come to America since with terror attacks since this writing.

Distress of a biological sort has made its way to America with disease threats such as HIV and Ebola virus. Other virulent biological dangers like the return of the Bubonic Plague are rumored to be on the way even to America.

All of the aforementioned has caused increasing anxieties for life in this part of the planet that previously remained relatively tranquil. Even the wars that have taken hundreds of thousands of American lives have been fought in faraway places, with the exception of the American Civil War of almost a century and a half ago. Now, technology has shrunk the globe to the point that even places like the Middle East seem near our backyard.

Daniel the prophet foretold just such a time as I believe we have entered:

> But thou, O Daniel, shut up the words, and seal the book, even
> to the time of the end: many shall run to and fro, and knowledge
> shall be increased (Daniel 12:4).

Can there be much doubt that Daniel was herein describing a time like the present?

Like Jesus' prophecies given in the Olivet Discourse, Daniel's prophecy doesn't simply imply a casual reference to how the prophecy will play out when fulfilled. The "knowledge" foretold and the "running to and fro" (travel) will be stunning, with exponential increase.

This prophecy, in process of fulfillment, is obviously part of the great perplexity and distress of these closing days of the Church Age. We have been told since the 1960s that the world is but 30 minutes away from total nuclear annihilation. The intercontinental ballistic missiles (ICBMs) are poised to destroy the world. The very term for the nuclear standoff has been "MAD" ("Mutually Assured Destruction"). In that sense, it is indeed a *mad* world, as the moviemakers would have it.

We have witnessed just how shrunken the world is by the speed of travel — and, for that matter, how great the increase in knowledge is.

The 19 Islamist hijackers trained in the technology of how to fly jumbo jets boarded those aircraft that were laden with tons of fuel with the specific goal of flying into buildings in New York and Washington, D.C. More than three thousand lives were taken that day. Such tremendous fear was generated by the attacks that people have been willing to have large parts of their liberty taken away with the creation of "Homeland Security" — a term that, to me, smacks of pre-Nazi Germany.

Yet we consider such diminishing of our personal freedoms to be acceptable as sacrifice for gaining safety here in America.

The "distress" the terrorists have created has caused and continues to create untold "perplexity" in this nation and around the world. Perplexity is a state of mind in which people don't know what to do about situations that confront them. The national leaderships of much of the countries of the world seem as if they have reached this point, just as prophesied by Jesus nearly two thousand years ago.

It is as if the majority of those leaders are making decisions from thinking that demonstrates dangerously flawed reasoning. Because the world has reached a point of trying to withdraw from anything to do with the God of heaven, the Apostle Paul's words are becoming ever-more applicable to this generation of earth dwellers.

> And even as they did not like to retain God in their knowledge, God gave them over to a reprobate mind, to do those things which are not convenient; being filled with all unrighteousness, fornication, wickedness, covetousness, maliciousness; full of envy, murder, debate, deceit, malignity; whisperers, backbiters, haters of God, despiteful, proud, boasters, inventors of evil things, disobedient to parents, without understanding, covenant breakers, without natural affection, implacable, unmerciful: who knowing the judgment of God, that they which commit such things are worthy of death, not only do the same, but have pleasure in them that do them (Romans 1:28–32).

Reprobate thinking is thinking that is upside-down. It is thinking that demonstrates it is greatly perplexed. This certainly seems to be the condition of the decision-makers in high places these days.

Sinful lawlessness such as is wrapped up in this list by the Apostle Paul closely mirrors his "perilous times" prophecy found in 2 Timothy 3. These are characteristics of mankind that will be prevalent at the very end of the age, and they are here in abundance, as our daily news reports verify upon scrutiny by observers of our present times.

The distress spawned by the lawlessness represented in particular by the Islamist terrorists known as ISIS (or ISIL) present perplexity beyond dealing with possible attacks on the homeland. Liberty is again at stake, and not necessarily because ISIS and other of Islam's militant radicals want to replace all other laws with sharia law. The first and foremost danger of loss of liberty in the United States might come from the very military and civilian law enforcement agencies charged with keeping the nation free of outside threats. Dealing with the attempts of militant Islam to establish a worldwide caliphate is more perplexing in America than perhaps in any other nation. The balancing act of maintaining as much personal liberty as possible, while pursuing actions that protect the nation from terror attacks, is delicate to the point of being almost impossible to perform.

Anyone who flies commercially today will attest to the ways increased rules and regulations have forever changed things. From full-body x-ray scans to physical pat-downs by airport security personnel, our privacy has suffered, and the invasive procedures are likely to get worse with each succeeding terrorist threat.

The reality that such threats are on the increase, thus the security measures scheduled to get much more invasive, comes from such reports as the following:

> US counterterrorism intelligence officials have told *Homeland Security Today* they "have every reason to believe" small cells of Islamist jihadists — all Muslims or individuals who recently converted to the Muslim faith who've been radicalized by online jihadist propaganda — or recruiters at the Mosques they attend — are believed to be planning "far more spectacular attacks in the US" than the attempted attack in Texas a week ago, at which time officials acknowledged there may be hundreds, if not thousands of radicalized individuals in the US — some undoubtedly in direct contact with jihadists overseas.
>
> "I think there's been an uptick in the threat streams out there. The level of chatter, Internet calls to arms, if you will, to light up potential ISIS followers in the United States and attack military installations," House Committee on Homeland Security Chairman Rep. Michael McCaul (R-Texas) told *Fox News Sunday*. "We're seeing these directives almost like on a daily basis. It's very concerning."[1]

The perplexity noted in Representative McCaul's expression of concern shouldn't be taken lightly. He is, as noted, chairman of the House committee on Homeland Security, and knows of what he speaks. Our government officials don't know which way to turn in striking the balance between security and liberty.

The article gives further evidence of the perplexity those charged with U.S. security face.

> This chatter, officials told *Homeland Security Today*, comes from intercepted, near-real time communications in recent weeks that's been "pinpointed taking place between ISIS and allied jihadi groups

1. Anthony Kimery, "Exclusive: Directed Attacks in US Believed Planned by ISIS Followers," *Homeland Security Today*, HSToday.com, May 12, 2015, http://www.hstoday.us/industry-news/general/single-article/exclusive-directed-attacks-in-us-believed-planned-by-isis-followers/a70c4da7f43b90ea39efe591f3adc20d.html, accessed May 16, 2015.

and Western recruits under these organizations' direction residing in the US."

FBI Director James Comey noted that jihadist propaganda has shifted in recent weeks from a message of urging jihadists to join ISIS in its jihad in Syria and Iraq, to telling followers to kill infidels wherever they live.

One seasoned counterterrorism intelligence analyst *Homeland Security Today* interviewed on background said he fears the "new message to stay in place and carry out attacks here could, in my estimation, mean Americans — and other Westerners — we don't know about who already have been trained and fought overseas may be being sent back to the states with specific directions to hook up with specific jihadi-inclined persons ISIS — or even Al Qaeda recruiters — have been communicating with in order to surreptitiously form cells whose members can be trained here, then sent on pre-planned targets in the US."[2]

Economic Distress

There exist no more problematic issues around which distress and perplexity revolve than those involving economy. The Bible warns about the central troublemaking element that rules the ambitions of much of mankind today:

> For the love of money is the root of all evil: which while some coveted after, they have erred from the faith, and pierced themselves through with many sorrows (1 Timothy 6:10).

Paul seems in this letter to Timothy to be referring particularly to those who claim religious faith, but who have acted to do other than stay within true faith. These who "err" from the faith given in the Scriptures lust after riches, is his charge. Money is the primary instrumentality that inhabits their thinking, and is at the root of all kinds of evil.

When thinking on the tremendous wealth accumulated by the Vatican, keeping in mind the many evil things that religious system perpetrated during past ages, we might think Paul's words were prophetic. Certainly, even Catholic Church historians themselves admit to such evil influences in certain periods such as in medieval times.

---

2. Ibid.

But, Jesus Himself, in His resurrected and ascended form, gave John prophecy of profound evil that will appear on the scene at the close of the Church Age (Age of Grace). And it obviously will involve the whole sphere of end-times Christendom.

> And unto the angel of the church of the Laodiceans write; These things saith the Amen, the faithful and true witness, the beginning of the creation of God; I know thy works, that thou art neither cold nor hot: I would thou wert cold or hot. So then because thou art lukewarm, and neither cold nor hot, I will spue thee out of my mouth. Because thou sayest, I am rich, and increased with goods, and have need of nothing; and knowest not that thou art wretched, and miserable, and poor, and blind, and naked: I counsel thee to buy of me gold tried in the fire, that thou mayest be rich; and white raiment, that thou mayest be clothed, and that the shame of thy nakedness do not appear; and anoint thine eyes with eyesalve, that thou mayest see (Revelation 3:14–18).

Jesus, walking among the candlesticks and addressing the seven churches in John's Revelation vision, had His harshest words for this church system. Yet He still indicated He loves those — particularly believers — caught up in this terrible system that preaches prosperity as its main focus rather than true faith that is wrapped up in the gospel of Jesus Christ and the true doctrines given by the Holy Spirit. The Lord exhorts and admonishes believers within this system that teaches and preaches such error. Jesus follows up His condemnation of the Laodicean system of worshiping money (riches) by saying the following:

> As many as I love, I rebuke and chasten: be zealous therefore, and repent (Revelation 3:19).

The ascended Lord here, I believe, clarifies the heavenly system of rewards for the way the true believer (the born again, John 3:3) conducts his or her life. He exhorts believers to repent of seeking earthly treasure, which makes them paupers in God's view of things. Believers must instead seek the "gold" that is the reward for godly living under Holy Spirit guidance while here on earth.

Jesus indicates that believers should invest in the white robes of righteousness, rather than earthly pursuits — riches that moths eat and rust corrupts. This further makes clear a Rapture Scripture that has often been confused as indicating believers must be living a life of nearly perfect right-eousness in order to go to Christ when He calls the church (Revelation 4:1).

Jesus here says the following:

> I counsel thee to buy of me gold tried in the fire, that thou mayest be rich; and white raiment, that thou mayest be clothed, and that the shame of thy nakedness do not appear (Revelation 3:18).

Jesus, just before His crucifixion, said the following while giving the disci-ples prophecy about His coming again at the end of Armageddon:

> Watch ye therefore, and pray always, that ye may be accounted worthy to escape all these things that shall come to pass, and to stand before the Son of man (Luke 21:36).

Jesus is saying here, as well as He said in His ascended form, giving the Rev-elation to John, that the believer, in order not to be ashamed when he or she appears before Christ at the bema (judgment seat of Christ), should seek to send heavenly treasure on ahead, while living life here on earth. This should be done so as to not be "ashamed" and to be "worthy" to stand before their Lord.

This exhortation by Jesus Christ has nothing to do with the loss of salva-tion, and does not mean any Christian will miss the Rapture for those who have truly been saved. It refers to "worthiness" for heavenly rewards, once in heaven for the life lived while on earth.

This is dealt with more in depth later in this book.

So earthly riches and the pursuit thereof is a major cause of the distress and perplexity that Bible prophecy says will signal Christ's Second Coming. If the Rapture of the Church, which will take place at least seven years before the Second Coming, is upon the near end-times horizon, there should be major indication of economic chaos.

Monetary Madness

A strange, deliberately induced economic unawareness has the world in its grip. While experts in monetary matters who know intimately how eco-nomic dynamics work are predicting absolute disaster for national and international economies, the major broadcast networks and cable TV net-works are acting as though everything is fine.

Meanwhile, the United States, to whose dollar most all of the world is intricately tied, is $19 trillion-plus in debt, and is printing money, without anything to back it, while preventing interest rates from changing as should be the natural course of adjustments. This kind of stress upon any other economic system in history would — say most experts truly in the know — long ago have collapsed into a depression of enormous magnitude.

Despite every signal that any number of crises could burst the economic bubble that grows by the minute, an artificial calm pervades the monetary markets for the most part, and Wall Street and other financial centers conduct business as usual. The stock market continues to see gains — sometimes spectacular gains. But the symptoms are undeniable. Europe, in particular, is experiencing the fiscal sickness that the experts say is the beginning of the end of financial stability for the world:

> WASHINGTON — The world's financial leaders see a number of threats facing a global economy still on an uneven road to recovery with U.S. and European officials worrying that Greece will default on its debt.
>
> The finance ministers and central bank governors ended three days of meetings in Washington determined to work toward "a more robust, balanced and job-rich economy" while admitting there are risks in reaching that objective, the steering committee of the International Monetary Fund said in its communique Saturday.
>
> Seeking to resolve Athens' debt crisis, Greek Finance Minister Yanis Varoufakis held a series of talks with other finance officials on the sidelines of the meetings . . . focus now shifts to Riga, Latvia, where European Union finance ministers meet next week.
>
> The head of the European Central Bank, Mario Draghi, said it was "urgent" to resolve the current dispute between Greece and its creditors. He said that while the international finance system had been strengthened since the 2008 crisis, a Greek default would still put the global economy into "unchartered waters" with its effect hard to estimate.[3]

3. Harry Dunphy, Associated Press, "Finance Officials See Risks in World Economy Rebound." CTV News, April 18, 2015, http://www.ctvnews.ca/business/finance-officials-see-risks-in-world-economy-rebound-1.2333914, accessed May 17, 2015.

Remedy Brings Crises

Regardless of the eventual outcome of this ongoing economic turmoil in the short term, it is this distress and perplexity that will, ultimately, bring fulfillment of the Revelation 13:16–18 prophecy. Greece is looked at by many economic analysts as presenting the prototype problem within the dilemma that faces every Western nation that in the future plans to bring debt under control. That ancient nation is at the very heart of the EU, with the fiscal sickness spreading like metastasizing cancer. When socialistic largesse is cut off — as happened in Greece — riotous behavior and governmental response will bring chaos. Italy has contracted the disease:

> MILAN, Italy — (Reuters) Police fired tear gas at demonstrators on Friday as violent protests marred the start of the Milan Expo, a global fair the government had hoped would help to put a new face on Italy after years of economic decline.
>
> Thick clouds of smoke from burning cars filled parts of central Milan, where groups of protesters, their faces masked against the fumes, threw stones and petrol bombs and faced off against lines of police in riot gear. The fair mobilised a range of left-wing protesters, from anti-globalisation and environmentalist activists to students and anti-austerity campaigners, who see it as a symbol of waste and corruption. Thousands of police had been deployed to counter the threat of violence.[4]

The economic disease that seems to be part of the distress and perplexity that Jesus prophesied for the time immediately preceding His Second Advent is not confined to the Western world by any means:

> ISTANBUL, Turkey, May 1 (UPI) — The celebration of May Day, the labor holiday, took place around the world Friday, with demonstrations, protests and violence in some cities.
>
> Friday's biggest clash with police occurred in Istanbul, Turkey, where defiance of a ban on organizing in the city's Taksim Square led

---

4. Sara Rossi, "Italian Police Battle Rioters as Violent Protests Kick off Milan Expo," *The Globe and Mail,* May 1, 2015, http://www.theglobeandmail.com/news/world/italian-police-battle-rioters-as-violent-protests-kick-off-milan-expo/article24217353/, accessed May 16, 2015.

to the firing of tear gas, use of water cannon to disperse of tens of thousands and at least 136 arrests.[5]

*****

Despite some hopeful signs for its economy, spiraling inflation has hit Russian consumers hard, leading to skyrocketing prices of food and other basic commodities. Russia's consumer price inflation hit a thirteen-year high of 16.9 percent in March.[6]

*****

China's downshift is already unmasking Asia's underlying cracks. After a decade of stellar performance the region is expanding no faster than in the early 2000s. . . .

"Asia has had an easy ride for many years, initially enjoying the fruits of reforms implemented much earlier and then seeing its run extended by an extraordinary monetary stimulus," warns HSBC economist Frederic Neumann. "This, however, led to a neglect of further reforms, with easy gains dispelling any sense of urgency to sustain progress with politically painful policy decisions."

It's hard to exaggerate how devastating a Chinese crash would be for Asia. Even an orderly deceleration of China's economy will likely prove a crisis.[7]

*****

Ukraine is on the verge of economic collapse and subsequent social upheaval, French daily *L'Humanite* reported. With the average salaries at 2,000 hryvnias ($94), and pensions for senior citizens at 1,200 hryvnias ($55), Ukrainians can no longer cope with ever-rising prices and inflation.

---

5. Ed Adamczyk, "May Day Brings Labor Demonstrations around the World, Some Violent," UPI.com, May 1, 2015. http://www.upi.com/Top_News/World-News/2015/05/01/May-Day-brings-labor-demonstrations-around-the-world-some-violent/3041430496711/, accessed May 16, 2015.

6. Aditya Tejas, "Putin Says Sanctions Amid Falling Oil Prices Cost Russia $160B, But Economy Will Recover," *International Business Times*, April 28, 2015, http://www.ibtimes.com/putin-says-sanctions-amid-falling-oil-prices-cost-russia-160b-economy-will-recover-1899194, accessed May 17, 2015.

7. William Pesek, "Asia's Growing China Problem," BloombergView, April 20, 2015, http://www.bloombergview.com/articles/2015-04-20/asia-s-growing-china-problem, accessed May 17, 2015.

To pay back a $17.5 billion loan approved by the Troika of creditors (the European Central Bank, the EU and the IMF) in March, Ukrainians literally risk losing it all.

In exchange for the money received, Ukraine was put under strict conditions, similar to those in Greece and Spain: the government's budget was to be severely cut, salaries of public servants were reduced and gas prices increased threefold.

"These measures could eliminate up to 90% of the purchasing power in households. We're heading towards a social upheaval," said Yevgeny Tsarkov, Ukraine's Communist Party deputy leader, as cited by *L'Humanite*.[8]

*****

Global institutions, constrained by competing national priorities, have now largely become complacent to the four-year-old Libyan imbroglio. Apart from bringing about one of the worst humanitarian and refugee crises, Libya's enduring fighting since the eight-month bloody civil war that broke out in February 2011 has driven the country to the brink of an inevitable financial collapse.[9]

*****

A senior South Sudanese religious leader, the Assistant Archbishop of Juba, on Wednesday (April 15) called the two rival leaders to take bold decisions to end the ongoing conflict and avert a looming economic collapse. Archbishop Santo Laku said it was time to act to avoid "this house collapsing on us."[10]

Monetary madness, to the observer of these chaotic times from the pre-Trib biblical prophecy perspective, is a key indicator of the end of the age. Economic tumult signifies that this generation has entered the time of "distress with perplexity" given by Jesus in the Olivet Discourse.

8. French Media, "Ukraine On Verge Of Economic Collapse," InSerbia Network Foundation, May 2, 2015, http://inserbia.info/today/2015/05/ukraine-on-verge-of-economic-collapse-french-media/, accessed May 17, 2015.

9. "Economic Collapse of Libya Looms as Forex Reserves Drain Gulf Times," May 5, 2015, http://www.gulf-times.com/opinion/189/details/438008/economic-collapse-of-libya-looms-as-forex-reserves-drain, accessed May 17, 2015.

10. "South Sudan Bishop Calls on Rival Leaders to Avert Economic Collapse and Make Peace," AllAfrica, April 16, 2015, http://allafrica.com/stories/201504200923.html, accessed May 17, 2015.

This belief is further validated by the societal insanity that moves in tandem with economic madness toward that stupefying moment of Rapture of all believers in Jesus Christ.

Seas and Waves Roaring

Jesus, the greatest of all prophets — and, this is so because He is God — pointed to the fact that at the time signs of His coming back to earth approach, the "seas and waves" will be "roaring." The implication is that this will be due to the distress and perplexity that will afflict all peoples of the world.

The sea, in this apocalyptic reference, is representative of the billions of people that populate the earth. The waves, I believe, are the surges of human unrest and chaos the great economic tumult and societal insanity produce. Thus, there is "distress of nations with perplexity."

We in America and most of the Western world can easily see the tremendous upheaval taking place across the rest of the world. Even those almost oblivious to upheaval in their own neighborhoods in the so-called civilized world at least recognize the starvation, genocide, and murderous activities carried on by the tyrannical governments of other parts of the world.

Americans, however, are for the most part so busy going about their daily lives that they are willfully uncomprehending of the assaults that will, perhaps sooner rather than later, bring this nation — previously insulated against such hardship — to a state of distress with perplexity.

Although there are socio-economic odors in the air that warn of such times to come, most Americans can't smell them. The populace as a whole has become desensitized to the incremental assaults on sensitivity to the threats.

There are many things going on in America that should alert any thinking person to the societal sickness we face and to the reality of the threats to our liberty. Some of these include:

- the debauching of our society and culture by the entertainment industry

- the Judeo-Christian values regarding traditions and institutions being attacked by the homosexual minority (only 2 percent within America are homosexual, yet their perverse demands reign supreme because of media propaganda and governmental and church acquiescence)

- the murderous practice of abortion that has taken the lives of more than 55 million children still in the womb since *Roe v. Wade* in 1973

- the welfare system that has long ago destroyed any chance of future economic stability in an America that is free (more than $22 trillion has been thrown at the system since 1964 and the "war on poverty," and people on welfare are worse off than ever)

We will look in some depth only at one recent assault on the nation. It is conducted by communist-like ideological forces that want to sow discord by creating racial divide. This, in itself, seems to represent a prophecy given by Jesus as part of the Olivet Discourse.

Then said he unto them, Nation shall rise against nation, and kingdom against kingdom (Luke 21:10).

The word "nation" in this prophecy is given in Greek as *ethnos.* This is the word from which we derive in English the word "ethnic." This, of course, denotes race or racial constituency. Jesus is telling us here that there will come great racial or ethnic division and strife of unprecedented magnitude just before He returns to earth.

Although the Lord was foretelling that this future racial trouble will be occurring during Daniel's 70th week (the Tribulation), we know that, like all other prophetic signs Jesus gave, they will *begin* to happen *before* that seven-year period. We should be watching for the earliest appearances of these signals so we will know the time of His approaching return.

What I say unto you I say unto all, watch (Mark 13: 37).

Race-Baiters Set America Ablaze

Recent and glaring examples of the deliberate attempts at spawning racial upheaval are the riots in Ferguson, Missouri, and Baltimore, Maryland. While these cities were looted and burned, self-serving politicians and pundits — including our president, his U.S. attorney general, local politicians, and the leftists in the media — were quick to stereotype law enforcement as a bunch of racist thugs, responsible for the immoral conduct of the masses unfolding before our eyes.

During night after night of looting and burning, the people in government — local, state and federal — did little to support re-establishing law and order; rather, they laid phony charges at the feet of law enforcement. Underlying this seemingly insane disconnect between concocted fable and truth-based reality was the ludicrous charge that white (Caucasian) police want to murder young, black men — thus, it is meant to be inferred, carrying out the wishes of most white people in America.

All one has to do to understand the satanically spawned delusion within this roaring of the seas of people in these burning cities is to understand that almost all African Americans not only in the cities affected, but across America, believe the lie that white cops want to murder young, black men.

Captain William E. Simpson, writing for *Western Journalism,* had this to say:

> Attacking the police for lawless behavior caused by other social conditions in an inner city or elsewhere is morally repugnant. This unethical and immoral behavior only serves to foment disorder, confusion, and encourage further lawlessness, thereby placing law-enforcement personnel and innocent citizens into more potentially hazardous situations. When police begin to feel that political leaders no longer support them in their mission to protect and serve their citizenry, and when there is a sense that they are being unduly judged, excoriated, or discarded unfairly by politicians or pundits with unsavory personal or political agendas, police officers tend to be more tentative in the discharge of their duties because they have no expectation that law enforcement actions or use of force applications will be supported, even when totally justified.[11]

We begin to understand just how mad the world is becoming. Insanity or reprobate thinking (Romans 1:28) has infected the nation and world, because mankind has determined to exclude the God of heaven from all human activity.

These constitute a sure signal that Christ's any-moment call to summon *born-again* believers into heaven might be very near indeed.

---

11. William E. Simpson, "Is 'Wrong' Replacing What Was 'Right' in America?" *Western Journalism,* May 14, 2015, http://www.westernjournalism.com/is-wrong-replacing-what-was-right-in-america/, accessed May 21, 2015.

CHAPTER 4

BIG BROTHER FOR A NOT–SO–BRAVE NEW WORLD

Reason #4: Greatly advanced technologies and control instrumentalities that have developed for the coming 666 beast-state system of Revelation 13, I believe, is a reason to say this is the generation about to be left behind when the Rapture occurs.

Every dictatorship throughout history has made its foremost priority controlling the masses of people in its ever-tightening grip. The dictator always begins regime-building with promises directed at the individual citizen, assuring life better than before — usually declaring that prestige and powerful influence will be restored to the homeland. Safety and security will remove all fear from daily life, and peace will prevail under the leadership of the yet-to-be-unveiled tyrant's absolute rule.

Despots vault to their position of power when vigilance against such evil diminishes during times of deepening, seemingly unsolvable economic hardship. There is coming upon the world such a time of hardship, the depths of which humanity has never experienced. We can say this with certainty because Jesus Christ foretells the following about that future time:

> For then shall be great tribulation, such as was not since the beginning of the world to this time, no, nor ever shall be (Matthew 24:21).

Just as the times will be the worst in human history, so will a tyrant of unprecedented evil come forth, wielding the most dictatorial power ever. We will learn more in chapter 12 about this "prince that shall come," as the prophet Daniel calls him.

As mentioned, human government has always sought ever-increasing authority — more and more power that is held by a circle of as few elite oligarchs as possible. These construct ever-more-restrictive rules and regulations and increasingly draconian methods of keeping their victims under control.

The United States has enjoyed more than two centuries of relative freedom from such government as has afflicted the nations and empires down through history. Still, there has been a growing trend toward that type of government in America. Humanistic governmental infection has now set in, and this greatest experiment in liberty that has ever been attempted is in the throes of decline.

There are forces that desire to bring this once-great republic down so that the way will be clear for those who desire such change to reshape the entire world in the evil ways they imagine. These forces are constituted by both human and supernatural entities. We again look to Scripture from God's Word to understand the threat:

> For we wrestle not against flesh and blood, but against principalities, against powers, against the rulers of the darkness of this world, against spiritual wickedness in high places (Ephesians 6:12).

Satan's supernatural minions rule the minds of fallen mankind — people of the mindset to establish worldwide control over everyone else.

We can see this malevolent force at work through witnessing the rise of militant Islam. Particularly, the force known as ISIS or ISIL is led by human agents who are directed by entities that Paul, in writing to the Ephesians, calls "powers" and "principalities" in "high places."

As deadly and threatening as is this horde of hate-filled Islamists, we are being assaulted in America and the Western world by an even more sinister force, one much more powerful and more deadly in its potential. This is because it is clandestine and covert — a cabal that seeks to remove every vestige of the God of heaven so that pure evil can fill the vacuum created when the goal is accomplished.

Conspiracy kookdem? If so, I'm in good company, because God's Word foretells just such an effort for the days immediately preceding the time when He again takes control of this fallen world.

> Why do the heathen rage, and the people imagine a vain thing? The kings of the earth set themselves, and the rulers take counsel together, against the Lord, and against his anointed, saying, Let us break their bands asunder, and cast away their cords from us. He that sitteth in the heavens shall laugh: the Lord shall have them in derision. Then shall he speak unto them in his wrath, and vex them in his sore displeasure (Psalm 2:1–5).

We learn from this prophecy that this attempt to forever remove God from dealing with His creation called "man" will ultimately fail. However, prophecy foretells that there is coming a man — a dictator — and a system of control that is made up of Paul's prophesied powers and principalities.

John the Revelator was given the prophecy. There is coming a second beast, as the prophecy calls him. He is a religious False Prophet who will make everyone worship a man the Bible calls the beast. This man to be worshiped by everyone on earth at the time is also called the "son of perdition," the "man of sin," the "king of fierce countenance," and Antichrist.

> And he causeth all, both small and great, rich and poor, free and bond, to receive a mark in their right hand, or in their foreheads: And that no man might buy or sell, save he that had the mark, or the name of the beast, or the number of his name. Here is wisdom. Let him that hath understanding count the number of the beast: for it is the number of a man; and his number is six hundred threescore and six (Revelation 13:16–18).

This is the system of control that is even now being prepared through many manipulations by the powers and principalities in high places of Ephesians 6:12. In order for this system to have a chance to be installed on a global scale, America will have to be removed as the apex nation — earth's lone super power at present. This is because all nations of the world who do commerce are linked to greater or smaller extent by the U.S. currency unit, the dollar.

The coming world economic system is where Satan and his chosen end-times dictator, the Antichrist, will derive power to exert control. Money is power: the ability to control who eats and who doesn't. When Satan and his minions control buying and selling, they will have power over the ability to buy the most basic necessity for life: food. It is a maddeningly clever plan, and these evil ones are working it to perfection, even today while the groundwork is being laid for this final regime's power structure.

From Fiction to Fact

Thinkers and writers have cogitated on this Revelation 13:16–18 prophecy down through the centuries. Two writers in particular have used this prophetic passage from the Bible in thinking on their fictional works, which have been lauded as masterpieces by the literary powers that be.

Aldous Huxley wrote *Brave New World* and George Orwell wrote *Nineteen Eighty-Four* near the mid-20th century. The following tells a bit about the books and authors:

> *Brave New World* is a novel written in 1931 by Aldous Huxley and published in 1932. Set in London of A.D. 2540 (632 A.F. — "After Ford" — in the book), the novel anticipates developments in reproductive technology, sleep-learning, psychological manipulation, and classical conditioning that combine profoundly to change society.[1]

*****

> *Nineteen Eighty-Four*, sometimes published as *1984*, is a dystopian novel by English author George Orwell published in 1949. The novel is set in Airstrip One (formerly known as Great Britain), a province of the superstate Oceania in a world of perpetual war, omnipresent government surveillance and public manipulation, dictated by a political system euphemistically named English Socialism (or Ingsoc in the government's invented language, Newspeak) under the control of a privileged Inner Party elite, that persecutes individualism and independent thinking as "thought crimes."
>
> The tyranny is epitomised by Big Brother, the quasi-divine Party leader who enjoys an intense cult of personality but who may

---

1. "Brave New World," en.wikipedia.org/wiki/Brave_new_world.

not even exist. The Party "seeks power entirely for its own sake. We are not interested in the good of others; we are interested solely in power."[2]

Although both novels depict life that is miserable in most every way imaginable, the warnings about such a despotically controlled world apparently haven't registered with today's would-be new world leaders. These are reputed to be among the brightest and best thinkers on the planet, so surely they have read these highly acclaimed classics.

Perhaps, more likely, the warning passes through their alert sensors without registering because all that really matters is exactly what mattered to Orwell's fictional leaders. Those oligarchs said that their party "seeks power entirely for its own sake. We are not interested in the good of others; we are interested solely in power."

America, the land of the level of liberty enjoyed by no other people in history, now has in place the making of tyrannical government to rival the fictional worlds of Huxley and Orwell. According to some researchers, there are instruments for instituting such a despotic regime, just awaiting a crisis that will require their implementation.

Certainly, reviewing these crisis-management measures makes clear just how very tentative our liberties are. According to the researchers, these are a list of executive orders that have been transferred to the Federal Register, and now legitimately may be employed by any president — as a given crisis, according to that president, might require.

Executive orders date back as far as Franklin Delano Roosevelt. President Carter signed No. 12148 delegating the power to run the entire country to FEMA (Federal Emergency Management Association), then on June 3, 1994, Clinton signed a new executive order transferring control of the country in an emergency from FEMA to the National Security Council and the national security advisor. Some of the executive orders that subsequently have made their way into the Federal Register (and are now laws) are reported by McAlvany as follows:

10995 — All communications media seized by the federal government.

---

2. "Nineteen Eighty-Four," en.wikipedia.org/wiki/Nineteen_Eighty-Four.

10997 — Seizure of all electrical power, fuels, including gasoline and minerals.

10998 — Seizure of all food resources, farms, and farm equipment.

10999 — Seizure of all kinds of transportation, including your personal car, and control of all highways and seaports.

11000 — Seizure of all civilians for work under federal supervision.

11001 — Federal takeover of all health, education, and welfare.

11002 — Postmaster General empowered to register every man, woman, and child in the USA.

11003 — Seizure of all aircraft and airports by the federal government.

11004 — Housing and Finance Authority may shift population from one locality to another. Complete integration.

11005 — Seizure of railroads, inland waterways, and storage facilities.

11051 — The director of the Office of Emergency Planning authorized to put Executive Orders into effect in "times of increased international tension or crisis." He is also to perform such additional functions as the president may direct.

In short, if there should be nationwide riots (*a la* Los Angeles in '92) for any reason; a national crisis; massive social upheaval (i.e., a huge quantum jump in crime); major resistance to national gun confiscation or to the installation of the New World Order or other socialist/police state measures; etc., *[the president] ... and his "comrades" have the power and machinery to instantly suspend the Constitution and declare a total dictatorship.*[3] (emphasis added)

Authority to implement governmental controls, then, as well as specific things to be included in that control, are in place. Today, technical equipment needed to do the actual controlling exceeds, in capability, the fictional instrumentalities and machinery of Orwell's *Nineteen Eighty-Four.*

Such subjugation of victim-citizens as presented in that novel would not have been possible prior to the development of satellite technologies.

---

3. Tom Horn and Terry Cook, *BeastTech* (Crane, MO: Defender, 2013), p. 55–56.

Television was in its infancy when Orwell's book first reached the eyes of the public. Man didn't reach space in a utilitarian way until well after Sputnik was launched by the Soviets in 1957.

Likewise, computer science struggled out of its primitive stages during the 1940s to link with the space technologies in the late 1950s and forward. The race for space and all of the burgeoning technologies came forth to ignite an exponential leap forward, finally putting man on the moon.

Daniel's prophecy, foretelling when the end of the age would be at hand, came alive before our eyes, and continues at an ever-accelerating pace:

> But thou, O Daniel, shut up the words, and seal the book, even to the time of the end: many shall run to and fro, and knowledge shall be increased (Daniel 12:4).

Antichrist's Subjugation Technology

Huxley and Orwell were unwittingly complicit in fulfilling Daniel's 12:4 prophecy. In the matter of knowledge increasing explosively in the realm of communications and collateral instrumentalities, progress has been truly phenomenal. Accordingly, this all proves, along with so many other signals flashing at this generation, that we are bumping up against the very end of the age.

During the height of the Nazi regime, Adolf Hitler, Hermann Wilhelm Göring Himmler, Joseph Goebbels, and all other of the masters of the Third Reich had some, by today's standards, primitive technologies at their disposal. Some electronic-type things, like the telephone and some encryptographic machinery and listening devices were employed to control.

The Soviet Union and other despotic regimes later used ever-advancing technologies to become much more invasive to citizens and to visitors to their dark realms.

There were constant efforts of the Soviets to eavesdrop on any visiting diplomat in hotels or in the embassies. And, to be honest, America employed the same devices and strove to produce more and more sophisticated such technologies. That effort is going on today, more intensively than ever, as we've just seen.

The invasive technologies and procedures are claimed by the American clandestine activities industry to be for assuring that U.S. security is preserved. The Russians, especially under its latest dictator, Vladimir Putin, don't bother to try to justify the use of ever-more-restrictive efforts.

The old KGB is back, if under a different name, and it is more equipped than ever to carry out its mission of subjugating its citizenry.

Like in so many cases in which the Soviets copied from the U.S. laboratories and technology developments, the USSR got much of its eavesdropping/snooping know-how directly from spying and through espionage against this nation.

America's history of developing technologies in these areas is without peer. The history is fascinating, if troubling, with regard to what might be the ultimate outcome of the intelligence that continues to tighten the noose around the neck of personal liberty.

History of Last-Days Technology

Herbert O. Yardley, November 16, 1912 — this is the first entry on the National Security Agencies website outlining their pre-1952 historical timeline of the United States cryptologic history.[4]

During World War I, Herbert Yardley ran the eighth section of military intelligence, MI-8, the War Department's code-breaking organization. MI-8 was tasked with intercepting and decrypting international telegrams for the purpose of protecting national security. To accomplish this task, MI-8 had to persuade American cable companies, including Western Union Telegraph Company and Postal Telegraph Company, to illegally supply them with those communications. The cable companies eagerly — but secretly — agreed to do so, in violation of the 1912 Radio Communications Act.

After World War I, Yardley convinced the U.S. Army and Department of State to continue funding his tremendously effective surveillance operation. They appointed him chief of a group named the Black Chamber, also known as the Cipher Bureau. This was the United States' first peace-time intelligence agency, a precursor to the National Security Agency (NSA). The Black Chamber was a covert surveillance agency located in a private brownstone in New York City. It successfully deciphered diplomatic codes of a number of nations, including Japan, and did so by illegally obtaining communications of foreigners as well as American citizens. Yardley's signature achievement was breaking Japanese military and diplomatic codes prior to

---

4. "Pre-1952 Historical Timeline," National Security Agency/Central Security Service, https://www.nsa.gov/about/cryptologic_heritage/center_crypt_history/pre_1952_timeline/, accessed May 25, 2015.

the 1921 naval disarmament conference in Washington, D.C. This conference was held between five major naval powers—the United States, France, Italy, Great Britain, and Japan — the purpose of which was to stabilize the ratio of warships held by these countries in the Pacific Ocean during a time of peace.

The Japanese government was aggressively pursuing 21 battleships. However, the decrypted messages provided by the Black Chamber to the American delegation gave them crucial knowledge about the Japanese government's willingness to settle for less. Prior to negotiations, the Americans were aware that Tokyo had privately acknowledged political realities and were willing to concede to a reduced ratio of battleships. This gave the United States a negotiating advantage, which it used with confidence. Japan ultimately settled for 18 warships while the United States and Great Britain negotiated for 30 each.

Although the Black Chamber was extraordinarily successful, President Hoover's Secretary of State, Henry L. Stimson, had a philosophical objection to its activities, and when learning of the program in 1929, he promptly shut it down with his now-famous comment, "Gentlemen do not read other gentlemen's mail."[5]

Broke, unemployed, and desperate for money after the stock market crash that same year, Yardley published his first book, *The American Black Chamber*, revealing the extent of the United States' cryptographic capabilities, while also becoming the first American intelligence whistleblower. The book was an international bestseller, especially in Japan. The Japanese Foreign Ministry was outraged to learn that the United States had intercepted and decrypted their codes. They promptly responded to these revelations by changing their cipher systems, which some say cost America greatly in the war with Japan eight years later.

During World War II, the Army had legal access to all communications from Western Union International, RCA Global, and ITT World Communications, but when the war ended in 1945, access to those telegraphs became illegal under section 605 of the Communications Act of 1934 as well as the Fourth Amendment of the Constitution.

However, those illegal activities continued under a covert program — Operation SHAMROCK. Operation SHAMROCK began as a military

5. Ibid., "Pearl Harbor Review," https://www.nsa.gov/about/cryptologic_heritage/center_crypt_history/pearl_harbor_review/black_chamber.shtml, accessed May 26, 2015.

intelligence-gathering program under the Army Signal Security Agency in 1945 and was tasked with tapping international cables and eavesdropping on foreign coded communications. The program, however, expanded, and eventually began intercepting civilian and military wire communications. Under this expansion, SHAMROCK was tasked with attempting to identify domestic spies and communist sympathizers, becoming a covert, illegal, domestic spy program as well.

The NSA was secretly formed by President Harry S. Truman under executive order in 1952. The NSA immediately took control of Operation SHAMROCK. A spinoff program of SHAMROCK, named Project MINARET, was also operated by the NSA between 1967 and 1973. MINARET was developed during the Vietnam War to spy on American citizens who were targeted as activists and war protestors. Those identified were put on watch lists disseminated to the Federal Bureau of Investigation, the Central Intelligence Agency, the Secret Service, the Department of Defense, and the Bureau of Narcotics and Dangerous Drugs. Some 1,650 American citizens found themselves on the watch list including Jane Fonda, Joan Baez, and Dr. Martin Luther King, Jr.[6]

Operation SHAMROCK continued in secrecy for about 30 years, until it was exposed by L. Britt Snider, a congressional investigator in the mid-1970s. At that time, it was estimated that SHAMROCK was intercepting some 150,000 domestic communications each month.

In the midst of the Watergate scandal in 1975, and allegations of domestic spying by the United States government, the Senate voted to establish an 11-member investigative body to probe the misdeeds of the American intelligence community and to hopefully restore the public's trust in government. That body was chaired by Senator Frank Church.

The Church committee hearings "exposed how under the guise of national security, agencies spied on American citizens for political purposes during the Kennedy, Johnson and Nixon administrations."[7] Senator Church also said Operation SHAMROCK was "probably the largest government interception program affecting Americans ever undertaken."[8] As

---

6. "Project MINARET," http://en.wikipedia.org/wiki/Project_MINARET, accessed May 26, 2015.
7. Katelyn Epsley-Jones and Christina Frenzel, "Spying on the Home Front: The Church Committee Hearings and the FISA Court," PBS.org, http://www.pbs.org/wgbh/pages/frontline/homefront/preemption/churchfisa.html, accessed May 26, 2015.
8. Peter Fenn, "Throwing America's Privacy Under the Bus," *US News & World Report*, June

the committee's revelations came to light, NSA director Lew Allen, seeing the writing on the wall, shut it down on his own authority.

As a result of these hearings, Congress passed the Foreign Intelligence Surveillance Act in 1978 (FISA), establishing a secret court responsible for issuing warrants for the purpose of domestic spying. This secret court remains controversial. The *New York Times* published an article in December 2005 alleging that then President George W. Bush, in 2002, had "secretly authorized the National Security Agency to eavesdrop on Americans and others inside the United States to search for evidence of terrorist activity without the court-approved warrants ordinarily required for domestic spying."[9]

This illegal practice continued under the Obama administration. In June 2013, Edward Snowden, an infrastructure analyst inside the NSA, rocked the intelligence community when he leaked thousands of classified documents that showed the NSA was spying on American citizens. He presented documents that showed the NSA was sweeping the phone records of U.S. citizens from essentially every phone company in America. In addition to collecting phone records, the NSA was collecting about two hundred million text messages daily through its program Dishfire. Snowden was immediately on the run, knowing the consequences of his actions, and today, as of this writing, is reportedly receiving refuge in Russia.

The Snowden leaks revealed that the spying was not limited to domestic targets. His leaks also showed that the NSA collects phone data from the Bahamas, Mexico, Kenya, the Philippines, and Afghanistan, and has spied on at least 122 world leaders, including German Chancellor Angela Merkel, Mexico's former President Felipe Calderon, Brazil's President Dilma Roussef, and G8 and G20 summit leaders while in Toronto in 2010.

Snowden's information brought to light the program known as PRISM — the NSA's intelligence-gathering system designed to secretly obtain user data from companies such as Google, Facebook, Microsoft, Apple, and others — data including audio, video, photos, emails, and Internet searches. In addition, the XKeyscore program was uncovered, a tool that allows the

6, 2013, http://www.usnews.com/opinion/blogs/peter-fenn/2013/06/06/nsa-phone-records-collection-signals-the-end-of-privacy, accessed May 26, 2015.

9. James Risen and Eric Lichtblau, "Bush Lets US Spy on Callers Without Courts," *New York Times*, December 16, 2005, http://www.nytimes.com/2005/12/16/politics/16program.html?ex=1292389200&en=e32070e08c623ac1&ei=5089&_r=0, accessed May 26, 2015.

NSA to search virtually everything an individual does while on the Internet through international data intercepts.

PRISM is not the first spyware of its kind. ECHELON, dating back to 1971, exploded in its capabilities under President Bill Clinton and was made known to the public in the late 1990s. ECHELON is a global satellite intercept and relay system operated by the United States NSA, and four of its allies, the United Kingdom, Canada, Australia, and New Zealand. Sometimes called Five Eyes, it is run under a multilateral UKUSA agreement between these five countries, a cooperative agreement in signals intelligence. ECHELON captures all types of electronic communications and then uses super computers to analyze that data by keywords.

A similar program, CARNIVORE, developed by the Federal Bureau of Investigation in 1997 under President Bill Clinton, was a device that when physically attached to an Internet service provider with a specific target, could record all Internet sending and receiving traffic, including emails, at that target point. It was abandoned in 2001, only to be replaced by more sophisticated software programs such as NarusInsight.

In May 2015, a New York federal appeals court ruled that NSA's collection of millions of Americans' phone records is unlawful. Circuit Judge Gerard Lynch wrote, "Such expansive development of government repositories of formerly private records would be an unprecedented contraction of the privacy expectations of all Americans. . . . We would expect such a momentous decision to be preceded by substantial debate, and expressed in unmistakable language. There is no evidence of such a debate."

About two weeks later, top executives from Google, Apple, and Vodafone, a British multinational telecommunications company based in London, secretly met with spy chiefs from seven different countries at the Ditchley Foundation's countryside mansion in England. Attendees included "the CIA, President Obama's Intelligence Advisory Board, the British surveillance agency Government Communications Headquarters (GCHQ), the National Crime Agency, the German federal intelligence service the BND, Sweden's surveillance agency the FRA, the Canadian Security Intelligence Service, and the Australian Security Intelligence Organisation."[10]

---

10. Stephen Tweedie, "Apple and Google Met with Spy Chiefs at an 18th-Century Mansion in England to Secretly Discuss Government Surveillance," *Business Insider*, May 23, 2015, http://www.businessinsider.com/apple-and-google-attend-spy-summit-to-discuss-government-surveillance-2015-5, accessed May 31, 2015.

The leaked itinerary revealed that topics to be discussed included, "Are we being misled by the term 'mass surveillance'?" "How much should the press disclose about intelligence activity?" and "Is spying on allies/friends/potential adversaries inevitable if there is a perceived national security interest?"[11]

The British spy agency, Government Communications Headquarters (GCHQ), was also caught in Edward Snowden's snare when he exposed the UK for secretly, but apparently legally, tapping into transatlantic undersea fiber optic cables carrying worldwide communications, including phone calls, emails, Internet search histories, and Facebook postings. Snowden said this was "the largest programme of suspicionless surveillance in human history. . . . It's not just a US problem. The UK has a huge dog in this fight. . . . They [GCHQ] are worse than the US."[12]

Germany found itself in hot water recently when documents were leaked by the German media alleging that the German intelligence agency Bundesnachrichtendienst (BND) has been secretly cooperating with the NSA since 2002 in covert spy operations — political and economic espionage — targeted at institutions of the European Union and European neighbors. The governments of Belgium and the Netherlands are furious about these findings and have opened an investigation into the claims, stating up front that they will be demanding an explanation from Germany, should any nefarious activity be found. The German government has also launched two parliamentary investigations into these allegations, with German Chancellor Angela Merkel reassuring the world that she will fully cooperate with the inquiries.

Crossing the Atlantic, in May 2015 the United States charged six Chinese citizens with conspiracy to commit economic espionage for stealing wireless technology trade secrets from American companies in Silicon Valley. According to special agent David Johnson of the FBI, this was a "methodical and relentless effort by foreign interests to obtain and exploit sensitive and valuable US technology through the use of individuals operating within the United States."

China has a long history of suspected economic espionage against the United States and many other countries. In fact, the 2013 published findings

11. Ibid.
12. Ewen MacAskill, Julian Borger, Nick Hopkins, Nick Davies, and James Ball, "GCHQ Taps Fibre-Optic Cables for Secret Access to World's Communications," *The Guardian*, June 21, 2013, http://www.theguardian.com/uk/2013/jun/21/gchq-cables-secret-world-communications-nsa, accessed May 31, 2015.

of *The Commission on the Theft of American Intellectual Property* (IP) found that "of the counterfeit or pirated goods seized by U.S. Customs and Border Protection in 2012, 72 percent were Chinese in origin. Seven of the eleven cases brought under the Economic Espionage Act since 2010 concern stolen IP destined for Chinese entities. For almost all categories of IP theft, currently available evidence and studies suggest that between 50 percent and 80 percent of the problem, both globally and in the United States, can be traced back to China."[13]

NSA Super Snooping System

While the human-rights-oppressor nations like Russia and China steal American snooping technologies — with China, in particular, demonstrating a high level of creativity in such technology thievery and copying — American efforts forge ahead with cutting-edge eavesdropping breakthroughs.

The Utah NSA Data Center is the latest and greatest effort at gathering intelligence on governments, commercial entities . . . and individuals under one roof, so to speak.

> As Americans demand answers about the government's wholesale electronic snooping on its citizens, the primary snooper — the National Security Agency (NSA) — is building a monstrous digital data center in Utah capable of sorting through and storing every email, voicemail, and social media communication it can get its hands on.
>
> This top-secret data warehouse could hold as many as 1.25 million 4-terabyte hard drives, built into some 5,000 servers to store the trillions upon trillions of ones and zeroes that make up your digital fingerprint. . . .
>
> Some reports have suggested the data center could hold as much as 5 zetabytes, an astronomical sum equivalent to 62 billion stacked iPhone 5s. [Charles] King [principal analyst at data center consulting firm Pund-IT], called that number "difficult, if not impossible to conceive." Located just outside of Bluffdale, the NSA center is powered by 65 megawatts of electricity and has a series of back-up battery sites, according to U.S. Army Corp of Engineers documentation. . . .

---

13. "The Report of the Commission of Theft of American Intellectual Property," The IP Commission Report (chapter 1, page 15), May 2013, http://www.ipcommission.org/report/ip_commission_report_052213.pdf, accessed May 31, 2015.

> Is the NSA planning to use the Utah facility for spying? Experts say no.
>
> "The National Security Agency is not spying on our U.S. citizens — and the thought is not only illegal, it's ludicrous," said James C. Foster, CEO and Founder of Riskive.
>
> [Vanee] Vines [a public information officer for the NSA] told FoxNews.com a similar story, reiterating a statement about how the facility will be used: "One of the biggest misconceptions about NSA is that we are unlawfully listening in on, or reading e-mails of, U.S. citizens. This is simply not the case."
>
> "NSA is unwavering in its respect for U.S. laws and Americans' civil liberties."[14]

We must consider the veracity of the statement by NSA's spokesman. Not long after the statement, another piece of news reached the American public's eyes and ears.

> For the last two months, we've been bombarded with stories about the information-collection practices of the NSA thanks to documents leaked by the agency's most regretted contract employee, Edward Snowden. The degree of forced exposure has gotten to the point that once secret information gathered for the agency — whose acronym is jokingly said to stand for "No Such Agency" and "Never Say Anything" — was the subject of a press release on Friday; the Office of National Intelligence announced that it got the legal sign-off for a fresh batch of "telephony metadata in bulk" from companies such as Verizon and AT&T — despite continuing controversy over that including the call records of millions of Americans who are non-terrorists and non-criminal suspects.[15]

The proverbial cat is out of the proverbial bag with regard to this massive undertaking on behalf of the most advanced data-collection apparatus of history to this point. The foreign press, too, whose UK region spawned Aldous Huxley and George Orwell, took particular notice.

---

14. John Brandon, "Inside the NSA's Secret Utah Data Center," Fox News, http://www.foxnews.com/tech/2013/06/11/inside-nsas-secret-utah-data-center/.

15. "Blueprints Of NSA's Ridiculously Expensive Data Center In Utah Suggest It Holds Less Info Than Thought," *Forbes*, http://www.forbes.com/sites/kashmirhill/2013/07/24/blueprints-of-nsa-data-center-in-utah-suggest-its-storage-capacity-is-less-impressive-than-thought/.

Deep in Mormon country between the Wasatch and Oquirrh mountains, nestled on the outskirts of Bluffdale (population 7,598), it was designed to be largely anonymous. Instead, after Guardian disclosures of data-mining programs involving millions of Americans, the Utah Data Center provokes an urgent question: what exactly will it do?

NSA says it will not illegally eavesdrop on Americans but is otherwise vague. Its scale is not in doubt. Since January 2011, a reported 10,000 labourers have built four 25,000-square-foot halls filled with servers and cables, plus an additional 900,000 square feet of space for technical support and administration. Generators and huge fuel and water tanks will make the site self-sustaining in an emergency.

Outside experts disagreed on the centre's potential. Some said it will just store data. Others envisaged a capacity to not just store but analyse and break codes, enabling technicians here to potentially snoop on the entire population for decades to come.[16]

Concerns among members of congress about NSA's data gathering on citizens caused some attempts at lessening the power such agencies have had. The IRS was found to have collected information on private citizens and others, aided by NSA and other snooping agencies. This information was said to have been used to influence political outcomes in U.S. and some state election processes.

Much turmoil resulted in 2015, with NSA snooping on private citizenry and others at the center of the controversy. This resulted in the Patriot Act, enacted after the attacks of September 11, 2001, in New York City and Washington, D.C., being allowed to expire. Senator Rand Paul, a Libertarian, invoked a rare Senate procedure to bring about the Patriot Act's demise, in that it was not extended.

While the Patriot Act is to be discontinued, the Freedom Act is intended to maintain and implement new security measures deemed necessary.

What is changing? The expiry of the Patriot Act brings to an end bulk collection of Americans' phone metadata — who called who, when and for how long, but not the content of calls — by the U.S. Under its successor, records must be held by telecommunications

---

16. "Welcome to Utah, the NSA's Desert Home for Eavesdropping on America," The Guardian, http://www.theguardian.com/world/2013/jun/14/nsa-utah-data-facility.

companies and investigators need a court order to access specific information. Technology companies will be given greater leeway to reveal data requests. The measures are intended to balance concerns on privacy with providing the authorities the tools they need to prevent attacks.

What stays the same? Key parts of the Patriot Act are retained in the Freedom Act. They include the provision allowing the monitoring of "lone wolf" suspects — potential attackers not linked to foreign terror groups, despite the U.S. authorities admitting the powers have never been used. The Freedom Act also maintains a provision allowing investigators to monitor travel and business records of individuals, something law officers says is more effective than bulk collection.

On Sunday [Paul] said: "This is what we fought the revolution over, are we going to so blithely give up our freedom?"

After the deadline passed, he added: "Tonight begins the process of ending bulk collection. The bill will ultimately pass but we always look for silver linings. I think the bill may be replacing one form of bulk collection with another but the government after this bill passes will no longer collect your phone records."[17]

If Senator Paul's prediction is correct, it will be the first time such a temporary, stop-gap measure has worked to impede, much less to stop, such agencies from constantly and consistently expanding their reach.

Tracking Intelligence in Place

Capability of governments to keep track of people isn't something new. The technology has been in place for decades now and has grown in networking and sophistication. Should the longed-for-by-the-globalists new world order suddenly spring to life, the technology in place at present would need little tweaking in order to keep track of most every person on the planet.

With regard to the prophecy that all will be required to buy and sell through a distinctive mark on their hands or in their foreheads (Revelation 13:16–18), the Universal Product Code (UPC), in conjunction with some of the computer-chip instrumentalities available at this very moment, could,

---

17. "Surveillance Powers Expire as Senate Deal Fails," BBC News, June 1, 2015.

with minimum technological manipulation, bring the control necessary to implement the 666 regime of Antichrist.

The intricate linkages from continent to continent, country to country, state to state, and city to city through satellite technology, computers, television, and other communications methods are progressing geometrically. The Internet, for example, is already spreading to some of the most remote places on earth.

Global Positioning Satellite (GPS) technology makes tracking products implanted with computer microchips traceable at every step along their journeys from one position on the globe to the next. Many people have already been chipped for security purposes so that they may be instantaneously located in case of accident, kidnapping, or other unforeseen problems with their whereabouts. The following excerpt further enlightens.

> Most readers are undoubtedly familiar with the development of radio-frequency identification (RFID) technology that, under certain applications, is forecast to be connected to future human-enhancement technologies, especially neurosciences, brain-machine interfacing, and cybernetics.
>
> These RFID chips employ tiny integrated circuits for storing and processing information using an antenna for receiving and transmitting the related data. . . .
>
> The company who developed the technology informs that . . . the implantable transceiver "sends and receives data and can be continuously tracked by GPS (Global Positioning Satellite) technology." The transceiver's power supply and actuation system are unlike anything ever created. When implanted within a body, the device is powered electromechanically through the movement of muscles and can be activated either by the "wearer" or by the monitoring facility. In the wake of the terrorist attacks in New York City and Washington, D.C., an information technology report highlighted the company's additional plans to study implantable chips as a method of tracking terrorists. "We've changed our thinking since September 11 [2001]," a company spokesman said. "Now there's more of a need to monitor evil activities."[18] As a result, PositiveID has been offering the company's

---

18. "Will You Grin for the RFID Mark of the Beast?" Before It's News, October 26, 2010, http://beforeitsnews.com/alternative/2010/10/will-you-grin-for-the-rfid-mark-of-the-beast-236019.html.

current incarnation of implantable RFID as "a tamper-proof means of identification for enhanced e-business security . . . tracking, locating lost or missing individuals, tracking the location of valuable property [this includes humans], and monitoring the medical conditions of at-risk patients." While PositiveID offers testimony that safeguards have been implemented to ensure privacy in connection with its implantable microchips, some believe privacy is the last thing internal radio transmitters will protect — that, in fact, the plan to microchip humanity smacks of the biblical Mark of the Beast. Has an end-times spirit indeed been pushing for adoption of this technology this generation?[19]

The 666 marks-and-numbering system is on the cusp of becoming reality. Big Brother can't be too deeply within the shadowy future for planet earth. Christians will be removed to be with their Lord before this system is fully implemented and before Antichrist can step onto the world stage. The stunning moment of Rapture of all who believe in Jesus Christ for salvation must be near indeed!

19. Horn and Cook, *BeastTeach*, p. 113–114.

CHAPTER 5

VAMPIRES, ZOMBIES, TRANSHUMANS, AND OTHER FIENDS

Reason #5: Today, like in the days of Noah, thoughts of mankind are only on evil almost continually. This is a major reason this looks like the generation that will be left behind for God's judgment.

One particular thing made God regret that He created man, according to His own Word.

> And God saw . . . that every imagination of the thoughts of [man's] heart was only evil continually (Genesis 6:5).

This is what the collective mindset had come to by the time the Flood of Noah's day was sent to kill all life on earth that breathed air — with the exception of Noah and his seven family members. Every form of evil had saturated the earth to the point that even the genetics of life forms were corrupted.

At the forefront of the evil that led to the corruption of life on earth were a number of the angels who fell with Lucifer in the rebellion against God.

They seduced human women and thus began corruptive mutation of human DNA. Genesis, the book of Moses, tells that the results of these sexual unions were giant offspring. From those giant, half-human creatures came the legends of such fictional characters as Hercules, Atlas, and myriad others.

These were not just horror stories, however. The Bible records distant relatives of these pre-Flood beings in scriptural accounts. The most prominent giant, of course, was Goliath of Gath, the Philistine warrior whom David killed with a stone thrown from his slingshot. The Bible reports that Goliath had four brothers who were also giants. Joshua and his scouting party likewise reported "giants" in the land they were ordered by God to take on behalf of the future nation of Israel.

Fairy Tales and Mind Melds

Jack and the Beanstalk entered the minds of the children of my generation at a very early age. The fairy tale set the imaginations of youth on a course of fascination with the scary evil that was wrapped up in that cannibalistic giant who bedeviled Jack's family and the entire countryside. The fascination was intensified at every stage of life, as the monsters grew more bloody and voracious. It was all nothing short of transfixing — this love/hate relationship with evil. That relationship has obviously continued the intensifying process through subsequent generations, until now, the evil imaginings have saturated our culture.

History of Horror Entertainment

Exploration into the evil realm as entertainment is as old as mankind. From the dark ballads and poems of antiquity to modern-day horror films, a willing audience has never been difficult to find. There is something in human nature that causes fascination with the dark and evil side of this world.

The first great modern horror classic was written by Mary Shelley in 1818 — *Frankenstein.* By the middle of the 19th century, writers on both sides of the Atlantic were producing horror fiction with elements of the supernatural, such as Charles Dickens' use of ghosts in *A Christmas Carol* and Herman Melville's use of prophetic characters and a whale with supernatural powers in *Moby Dick.* Later in the century, Edgar Allen Poe was writing short stories and poetry in the horror genre such as *The Raven,* a story in which a young man is grieving the death of his beloved mistress Lenore when he is visited by a talking raven who speaks only one word —

"nevermore." The man asks him a series of questions, knowing each time he will get the same response — "nevermore," a response he does not want to hear. By the end of the poem, the man is driven to insanity by his own self-torture of the questioning when the raven tells him that his lost love Lenore will return — "nevermore."

By the end of the 19th century, with the works of Sigmund Freud becoming well known, and building on the earlier works of Poe, many writers began producing stories with a mind-bending focus in their horror fiction, allowing the reader to determine if the descent into madness was supernatural or psychological in etiology. The 1898 Henry James' novella *The Turn of the Screw* psychologically torments a governess by use of supernatural apparitions who are haunting her young charges. Bram Stoker's 1897 *Dracula* heated up the psychological horror by adding sexual seduction to this classic vampire tale.

The 20th century brought the horror genre to the silver screen. In the 1920s film *Dr. Jekyll and Mr. Hyde*, Dr. Jekyll recognized that dwelling within every human being is a good side and an evil side. He develops a potion to separate those opposing forces, only to become addicted to his dark side — the viciously violent Mr. Hyde. By the time Dr. Jekyll realizes the true depravity of Mr. Hyde, who has increasingly taken over his life, it is too late. In utter despair, Dr. Jekyll commits suicide.

In the 1930s and 1940s, while Hitler's evil regime was ravaging Europe, the most popular monsters in horror movies were man-beast characters such as in *The Wolfman,* who stalks and kills local villagers. Interestingly, "Adolf" means "noble wolf" in German,[1] and Hitler nicknamed himself "Herr Wolf," a name used only by his closest confidants.[2]

World War II, the deadliest of all wars in human history, ended in the summer of 1945 with the surrender of Japan. A war-weary world that had witnessed the dropping of the atom bomb and Nazi death camps influenced the horror genre to shift from man-beast monsters to those who through science and technology were modified for survival. Ironically, in 1954, the Japanese science-fiction film *Godzilla* was produced. This prehistoric monster is revived through nuclear tests in the Pacific and proceeds to terrorize Tokyo during its rampage through the city.

---

1. "Behind the Name: Adolf," http://www.behindthename.com/name/adolf, accessed June 10, 2015.
2. "Adolf Hitler: Facts and Factoids," http://ahitler.greyfalcon.us/, accessed June 10, 2015.

The famous Roswell incident in 1947, combined with numerous reports of UFOs in the '40s and '50s, in addition to the advancement of movie technology, spawned a number of UFO-influenced horror films such as the 1951 movie, *The Day the Earth Stood Still*, in which the alien Klaatu travels by spaceship to earth with his robot Gort. Earthlings had been observed by aliens in the nuclear arms race of the Cold War. The purpose of the visitation was to warn the earth's inhabitants that they must live in peace else they be destroyed by inhabitants of other planets who saw them as a danger to the galaxy. In the 1956 film, *Invasion of the Body Snatchers*, aliens occupy the bodies of humans who then become emotionless versions of their former selves — and chaos ensues.

The 1960s' counterculture and sexual revolution pushed the boundaries of what was acceptable to show onscreen in horror films. This was the decade of the Manson murders, Vietnam, illicit drug use, the moon landing, and John F. Kennedy. Alfred Hitchcock directed *Psycho* in 1960, starring a cross-dressing peeping Tom, Norman Bates, who stabs to death his unsuspecting victim while she is naked in the shower. Hitchcock followed that up with his 1963 film *The Birds*, in which a young woman comes to town, following a man who has caught her eye. Upon her arrival, birds begin to attack the residents with increasing viciousness, the purpose of which is never revealed. In 1968, Roman Polanski's *Rosemary's Baby* terrified audiences as they followed Rosemary through her discovery of the occult being who was victimizing her, and her resulting pregnancy, which concludes in the birth of the progeny of Satan.

Perhaps it was the 1960s' culture of sexual liberation, the birth control pill, and acceptance of divorce that caused the 1970s' horror films to turn toward children as the representation of evil. *The Exorcist*, released in 1973, is about the demonic possession and exorcism of a 12-year-old girl from a divorced family. *The Omen*, released in 1976, has as its main character a demonic little boy with supernatural powers that he uses to overpower adults, even to the point of death. It includes scenes of a decapitation of a journalist and the standing impalement of a priest by a lightning rod that falls from the top of his church during a rainstorm.

The 1980s brought with it rapid advances in the technology of special effects. This decade was known for materialism, greed, and a booming economy. Audiences demanded big productions with elaborate special effects. This brought us blockbuster horror flicks such as *Alien* (released mid-1979), a science fiction film set in outer space, where a female astronaut battles an enormous space alien while her entire team is picked off, one by one, in an uninhabited space station. *A Nightmare on Elm Street*, released in 1984, terrified American teenagers with the evil character Freddy Krueger, who stalks and kills them in their dreams with his knife-like fingers. Krueger's motive is to seek revenge on the children of his peers, who had burned him alive in his youth when they discovered he was a child killer. This was one of the films that came to be known as the "slasher-movie" genre, and it went on to become an enormously successful franchise, with its ninth sequel released in 2010. Other slasher films include the *Friday the 13th* franchise, which began in 1978 and produced its 12th sequel in 2009, and *Halloween*, which also produced its first film in 1978 and its 10th in 2009.

Perhaps the oversaturation of the slasher genre caused the audiences of the 1990s to demand something more sophisticated and sometimes even subtle. The answer was a variety of lone psychopathic serial killer movies, such as *Silence of the Lambs*, in which an FBI agent is chasing a murderer who hunts down women, murders them, and then skins them. The FBI agent, played by Jodie Foster, conducts multiple interviews with Hannibal Lecter, a cannibalistic serial killer and brilliant psychiatrist played by Anthony Hopkins. Lecter has agreed to assist her in her pursuit of the killer, while also psychologically tormenting her during the interviews. *Natural Born Killers* was Oliver Stone's 1994 movie in which a serial-killing couple cross the country on Route 66 and murder everyone in their path, just for the fun of it.

Supernatural horror has always been popular. Toward the end of the 1990s, a first-of-its-kind film, *The Blair Witch Project*, was released. This was a low-budget film that had tremendous box office success grossing nearly $250 million worldwide. The movie is about three student filmmakers who travel into the forest to make a documentary on the legend of the Blair Witch. They never return. Their film footage is all that is found, and it is terrifying!

The perception of fear was drastically changed with the terrorist attacks on America on September 11, 2001. That so shook the core of the nation that horror films were few and far between for several years, but they eventually made a comeback.

The first zombie movie that had a major cultural impact unleashed a cult-like sub-society in America. *The Night of the Living Dead* first aired in

Pittsburgh on October 31, 1968, and moved the horror, zombie genre from presenting placid, bug-eyed corpses walking around doing nothing particularly frightening to portraying a vicious horde of the living dead bent on devouring human flesh at every opportunity.

Even though that film was considered poorly done by the critics within the film industry, it was a hit among the moviegoers, moving it out of the mundane zombie films of earlier times that began with *White Zombie,* made in 1932. *The Night of the Living Dead* made millions of dollars after a budget that was around $60,000 at the outset of the filming. It is now acclaimed as a cult classic.

Psychologists and sociologists have offered that the reason this movie became so popular with the American public movie-going class was the bloody scenes, made more palatable because of the nightly news reports of the death and carnage watched on newscasts. Gore was made less shocking through the likes of Walter Cronkite and the nightly news reporting — often with the family gathered around the dinner table. The culture morphed into one of a sort of bloodthirsty entertainment cult in some sort of convoluted way that drained the bloodletting from the forefront of reality and made it all fictional.

Reflecting the mood of the culture, "zombie apocalypse" movies evolved dramatically, taking on a new dimension of horror. These continue to increase in popularity, with scenes of war, mass chaos, and rioting a common backdrop, as well as movies about the paranormal and supernatural, perhaps as a reflection of the vulnerability of the nation and some realizing the source of evil may not be from this world. One of the top-grossing horror films of all time was 2013's *World War Z,* with Brad Pitt portraying a United Nations employee tasked with the duty of stopping a zombie pandemic that was conquering worldwide governments and military forces, and threatening to destroy humanity itself. Another top-grossing film of that same year was *The Conjuring.* This film is about paranormal investigators trying to help a family who is being terrorized by evil forces in their farmhouse.

Earning more than $75 million at the box office in 2005 was *The Exorcism of Emily Rose* that won audiences over in its story about the prosecution of a priest for the wrongful death of a girl who was demonically possessed. A remake of *The Omen* was released in 2006, with box office sales of more than $119 million worldwide.

I believe the current insatiable appetite for horror of the most vile sort reflects that the imagination of the thoughts of man's heart is only on evil continually. It is yet another sure signal that this generation is nearing the point when the Creator again will say, as He did in Noah's day, "Enough is enough." Christ will call His Church to Himself, and judgment will fall that very day as Jesus Himself prophesied.

> And as it was in the days of Noe, so shall it be also in the days of the Son of man. They did eat, they drank, they married wives, they were given in marriage, until the day that Noah entered into the ark, and the flood came, and destroyed them all. Likewise also as it was in the days of Lot; they did eat, they drank, they bought, they sold, they planted, they builded; but the same day that Lot went out of Sodom it rained fire and brimstone from heaven, and destroyed them all (Luke 17:26–29).

It seems to me that Satan, the most diabolical agent of evil to ever exist, is personally putting his fingertips to the temples of America's entertainment-mad viewers today, and — like Mr. Spock of *Star Trek* — melding as one with their thoughts. Hollywood is quick to pick up on this mind meld and more than willing to turn it into a marketing bonanza. The love of money, again, is the root of all kinds of evil.

No collection of evidence more dramatically demonstrates the mixture of love for money with evil than do facts and figures about the holiday expressly celebrating evil that has exploded in growth in recent years.

The Halloween Phenomenon

According to the National Retail Federation, Halloween is the most rapidly growing consumer holiday in the United States. Americans were projected to spend more than $7.4 billion on Halloween in 2014. That includes amounts spent on decorations, candy, and costumes. Adult costumes were projected to reach $1.4 billion, more than the $1.1 billion spent on children's costumes, and another $350 million for pet costumes.[3]

Let me say at this point in our examination of Halloween that as a child in the late 1940s to the middle 1950s, I never thought once about

---

3. Jennifer Harper, "Americans Spent $350 Million on Halloween Costumes — For their Pet," *The Washington Times*, October 30, 2014, http://www.washingtontimes.com/news/2014/oct/30/americans-spent-230-million-halloween-costumes-the/, accessed June 10, 2015.

there being an "evil" aspect to the fun we had at the time we celebrated the holiday. I was raised in a Christian home that saw to it we were in church every time the lights came on in the building of worship. It was the most fundamentalist, Christian upbringing that could be found in America — a time, sadly, that is long past.

But, I never once heard that we shouldn't trick-or-treat because it was evil, or a bad influence or witness. I'm sure there were pastors in the pulpits preaching about those evils, but I never once remember hearing it. So it is easy to understand that today, with the culture totally saturated with the Halloween "spirit," children of today are immersed in the holiday called Halloween.

Today, the churches do preach and teach against it to some extent, and they create alternative celebrations so the kids aren't left out — or, don't feel left out — of this most aggrandized time in October. "Fall Festival," "Harvest Festival," and other names are given these alternative celebrations, often with costumes being geared toward Bible characters or other ostensibly benign characters.

However, I'm sorry to have to say, my beloved parents, who were indeed loving, and as "Christian" as any who have ever lived, were wrong. My wife and I were wrong. We celebrated vicariously through the cute little costumes our own children wore. It all seemed so innocent. It was done through blissful ignorance. Christians then and now had and have no business celebrating the occult, regardless of the ignorance of the matter that was and is a part of their thinking.

Like with so much of Satan's brilliant, although demented, strategy, the old serpent, through Halloween, worked and continues to work his black magic in attempting to establish his kingdom and replace God's plan for humanity. Halloween is truly the devil's holiday. There's no other way to put it in being honest in appraising the things associated with its celebration.

With that admission-caveat, we proceed to look at what has become as central a holiday theme as the celebration of the birth of Jesus Christ at Christmas.

Halloween's origins come from a mixture of old Celtic rituals and superstitions as well as early Catholic Church traditions. For the Celts who resided in Ireland, Scotland, Wales, and Brittany, it began with a pagan festival known as Samhain (pronounced *sow-wen* and literally translated as "summer's end"). This festival was held on the evening of October 31 to mark the momentous celebration of the end of the harvest season and the beginning of winter on November 1. The Celts believed that on the eve of the Samhain festival, the spirits of the dead could mingle with those of the living. The people would parade around in costumes, making a lot of noise and building bonfires to ward off these evil spirits.

Later, around the fifth century, the Catholic Church had missionaries who moved into these areas and took over the holiday. The Church's position regarding pagan rituals and festivals was to adopt the pagan practices and convert them to Christian festivals and celebrations. By the seventh century, Pope Boniface IV had designated October 31 as "All Hallows Eve," November 1 as "All Saints Day," and, eventually, November 2 as "All Souls Day," a day to honor the dead. These Catholic holidays were celebrated with parades, bonfires, and dressing up in costumes such as devils, saints, and angels. A custom was developed in which the celebrants would go door to door requesting sweets in exchange for prayers for their dearly departed. This may have been where the modern custom of handing out candy began. The Catholics believed that the dead were in a state of limbo and that the prayers of the living could influence the outcome of their eternal destiny.

Scottish and Irish immigrants carried the Halloween traditions to North America in the 19th century and, by the 20th century, other Western countries had embraced the holiday, including Australia, New Zealand, and the United Kingdom. As I've related in my personal family dealings with the "holiday," for some it is an innocent and fun holiday for children to dress up as superheroes and princesses going door to door in their neighborhoods while collecting candy. For others, it has a much more sinister consequence.

Aleister Crowley was an English occultist, magician, mystic, and drug addict. He joined the Ordo Templi Orientis (OTO) in 1910 and was appointed Grand Master to Britain and Ireland in 1912. The OTO is an international religious and fraternal organization originally based on the principles of freemasonry. However, under the leadership of Crowley, the OTO was reorganized under his written Law of Thelema (Greek for "will" or "intention"). The law is expressed as "do what thou wilt shall be the whole of the law," and "love is the law, love under will."[4] The OTO is a secret society popular with celebrities, who join the organization through a series of initiations. It is known for its occult practices, such as magic and warped sexual rituals,

---

4. "What Is Thelema?" Thelema 101, http://www.thelema101.com/intro, accessed June 11, 2015.

including a gnostic mass in which a robed priest presides over a naked woman on the altar and bodily fluids are used in their version of communion.

Crowley arrived in America on the evening of Halloween, 1914,[5] bringing with him the OTO. According to Major General J.F.C. Fuller, Crowley, who reveled when the popular press called him "the wickedest man in the world" and referred to himself as "the Great Beast 666"[6] was apparently a big fan of Halloween, which was an important ritual day to him and his followers.[7]

Anton LaVey, founder of the Church of Satan, claims that, after one's own birthday, Halloween and *Walpurgisnacht* (German for "Witches' Night") are the most important holidays of the year. A Satanist celebrates his own birthday as the highest holiday of the year due to the belief that he is god and should celebrate himself above all others. Walpurgisnacht falls on the evening of April 30. It is believed that on this night, witches, warlocks, and evil ghosts gather at the Brocken, the highest mountain peak in northern Germany, where they assemble with the devil. The festivals in Germany are much like Halloween in the United States, where people dress up in ghoulish costumes, light bonfires, and make loud noises to keep evil at bay. Sweet treats are left outside for ghoulish hounds that roam the night.

For Wiccans, Halloween, considered their spiritual New Year, is the highest holiday, a time to commune with the dead. Wiccans believe that on Halloween night, the separation of the physical and spiritual worlds is at its thinnest, allowing for those with necromantic gifts to speak with the dead. Wiccans celebrate by purifying themselves with a bath before gathering together with members of their coven. Once gathered, they create a sacred circle, bordered with four lit candles, and perform rituals to predict the future and contact the dead. This may include the use of tarot cards, runes, I Ching, and scrying — all forms of divination.

Does any of this seem to be the sort of activity the Christian would want to be engaged in at the stunning moment when Christ calls all believers to

---

5. Liberty and Aleister Crowley, "End Times Events as Viewed through the Lens of Scripture," *The Prophetic Explorer*, http://www.propheticexplorer.com/liberty_and_aleister_crowley.aspx#.VXmbTvlViko, accessed June 11, 2015.

6. Richard Price, "Forget Scientology, Celebs Are Now falling for an Even More Sinister 'Religion': Introducing the Satanic Sex Cult That's Snaring Stars Such as Peaches Geldof," *The Daily Mail*, April 21, 2013, http://www.dailymail.co.uk/femail/article-2312632/Introducing-Satanic-sex-cult-thats-snaring-stars-Peaches-Geldof.html, accessed June 11, 2015.

7. David L. Brown, "What Witches, Satanist, and Other Occultists Say About Halloween," Logos Resource Pages, Logos Communication Consortium, Inc., http://logosresourcepages.org/HalloweenBook/occult.htm, accessed June 11, 2015.

Himself in the Rapture? Too many believers, it must be said, are engaged in such thoughts as are conjured by the kind of activities that are a part of this pagan celebration.

This Present Darkness

A popular novel among a reading audience of Christian readers was *This Present Darkness* by author Frank Perreti. The story dramatized the evil, spiritual battle going on for the control of the lives and souls of people of contemporary times. The title of the novel couldn't be more appropriate for the battle going on at this very moment in human history.

We have looked at how people have been engrossed in the dark side of spirituality for decades — even centuries. The entertainment industry has burgeoned into a satanically inspired film production factory that continues to mesmerize the increasing numbers of those hungering for horror of the vilest kind.

I believe that the almost hypnotic effect these luciferian-spawned films and other forms of entertainment offerings has a direct correlation to the real-life evil that is pandemic in the world today. Let's explore this statement, which, I realize, will garner significant pushback. Like I've expressed, Halloween, for me, even as an adult with young children, has been difficult to associate with the pure evil that is now full blown in America and the world.

Good Neighbor Lucifer

Satan, called "the prince of the power of the air" (Ephesians 2:2), certainly has lived up to his reputation. He has worked diligently for many years to control the minds of men, women, and children through the airwaves — broadcast and cable entertainment venues.

Again, his brilliant although demented strategy has worked almost to perfection — so much so that he now has managed to get his own show . . . under his own name. He has managed to make himself appear to be just another of our good friends and neighbors. It is one more glaring proof that this generation stands as the one that has reached a reprobate mindset, as the Apostle Paul warns about in the first chapter of Romans.

All we have to do to prove just how effective the wicked one has been in turning the minds of humanity to himself is to consider the reprobate thinking that has resulted from his influence on the American political, governmental, and social structures.

We've all heard that one definition of insanity is to keep doing the same thing again and again expecting a different outcome, even though it fails every time. Nothing more aptly describes the liberal mindset in American politics and government than does the policy begun by the Lyndon B. Johnson administration in 1964.

Johnson's "War on Poverty" to create his "Great Society" was to eliminate poverty and assure that every citizen became more equal in achieving a prosperous life. A noble thought, right? Well, yes. I'll concede that many — including the president, himself — most likely really wanted that to happen. With liberals — they want to be called "progressives" — it's always the good intentions that count. But it didn't happen. It still has not happened.

Our government has now spent more than $22 trillion in exactly the same manner since 1964 — over and over again. Poverty is worse, and the welfare state has created and perpetuated a class of totally dependent people, people who for the most part are healthy, able-bodied, and would be capable of doing for themselves if not for the slothful element that government has encouraged and exacerbated.

I mention this economic fact only to show the insanity of the liberal — excuse me, I mean the "progressive" — thinking to which we are subjected every hour of every day. This mindset goes far, far beyond economic madness, as we will see.

Such thinking is prophetic. Paul foretold just such a mindset and where it would lead as the end of the age and the return of Jesus Christ nears:

> For the wrath of God is revealed from heaven against all ungodliness and unrighteousness of men, who hold the truth in unrighteousness; because that which may be known of God is manifest in them; for God hath shewed it unto them. For the invisible things of him from the creation of the world are clearly seen, being understood by the things that are made, even his eternal power and Godhead; so that they are without excuse: because that, when they knew God, they glorified him not as God, neither were thankful; but became vain in their imaginations, and their foolish heart was darkened. . . . And even as they did not like to retain God in their knowledge, God gave them over to a reprobate mind, to do those things which are not convenient (Romans 1:18–28).

Reprobate thinking, as we have seen before, is upside-down thinking. It is thinking that can neither see a problem in a clear-headed way nor formulate a reasonably effective solution to a problem. Thinking that excludes God produces a reprobate mind — one that will, for example, keep throwing trillions of dollars that don't exist (because we are broke) at a problem that money only makes worse, not better.

The progressive mindset demonstrates time after time, again and again, over and over, that it wants to carry on with life apart from governance from the God of heaven. Humanistic government on an ever-increasing grasp for power and control is at the core of the liberal — the progressive — way of thinking.

The Creator has said that marriage is for one man and one woman for life. The progressive says that this is a new time and place, and biblical thinking is old-fashioned, outmoded. We must progress. . . . But, nature itself— the way male and females of all species capable of reproducing are constructed — shows plainly that it is male-female, not male-male or female-female, that constitutes the sexual union God (or, if you prefer, *nature*) intended.

Paul the Apostle, in his letter to the Romans, again puts a scriptural finger on the rebellion that festers within the progressive mindset:

> For this cause God gave them up unto vile affections: for even their women did change the natural use into that which is against nature: and likewise also the men, leaving the natural use of the woman, burned in their lust one toward another; men with men working that which is unseemly, and receiving in themselves that recompense of their error which was [fitting] (Romans 1:26–27).

God says plainly in His Word what He thinks about the killing of babies in the womb. He speaks clearly about shedding blood of those who are a threat to no one, because they are, in human terms, "innocent":

> These six things doth the LORD hate: yea, seven are an abomination unto him: a proud look, a lying tongue, and hands that shed innocent blood (Proverbs 6:16–17).

We have come to a time of absolute fiendishness, butchering even the most innocent among us.

The progressive says that, in effect, God — if there is in fact a God — doesn't know what He is saying in His Word. Life in the womb isn't life — at least, not yet human life. The progressives have the right to choose whether the child in the womb is to live or not. They have the right to choose what is convenient for their own life, and this includes the right to choose to execute a defenseless baby before he takes his first breath for expediency's sake.

Entertainment media is the incubator for the progressive mind. In these last days, every thought of the heart is only on evil continually, as in Noah's day. The entertainment calls good evil and evil good, and the progressive mind becomes more reprobate by the hour. One such example of the entertainment world incubating this reprobate mindset is a soon-to-be-released television production. The announcement follows:

> The more subtle side of Satanism in Hollywood entertainment is now a thing of the past, as primetime television airs blatantly evil shows like the upcoming Fox drama *Lucifer*, which glorifies the goings about of the "lord of hell" after he fictitiously leaves the lake of fire and retires to Los Angeles. The premise behind the absurd drama, which is set to release in 2016, centers around so-called "Lucifer Morningstar" and his new life as the owner of Lux, an upscale nightclub located in the City of Angels.

Based on the show's trailer, the Lucifer character will be offered up to the masses who watch Fox as a likable character with moral and ethical convictions, fulfilling the biblical account of this insidious demonic entity. Described as the wisest creature that God ever created, Lucifer is said to be "full of wisdom, and perfect in beauty," that is, before he was cut down and destroyed by his Creator for elevating himself in place of God.[8]

Now, let me say as a caveat that political conservatism deserves little more praise than does progressivism. (Fox is claimed to be "conservative.") Humanism rules at the heart of all political and governmental entities upon this fallen and soon-to-be-judged planet. The greatest desire of all who name the name of Christ should be to wage a campaign to win the hearts and minds of mankind for the Lord we serve.

> But the natural man receiveth not the things of the Spirit of God: for they are foolishness unto him: neither can he know them, because they are spiritually discerned. But he that is spiritual judgeth all things, yet he himself is judged of no man. For who hath known

---

8. NaturalNews, http://beforeitsnews.com.

the mind of the Lord, that he may instruct him? But we have the mind of Christ (1 Corinthians 2:14–16).

Demonic Possession and the Occult

Amid growing interest in occult practices such as black magic, satanic rites, and pagan rituals, the Catholic Church has increased the number of priests and lay people such as doctors, psychologists, teachers, and pastoral workers to be trained as exorcists. The Vatican has held these courses annually for ten years. In April 2015 at the European University of Rome, 170 students began their training, an increase from 50 trainees in prior years.

The rise in occult practices has been attributed to a spike in websites offering everything from training in devil worship to black magic and the occult, as well as Hollywood's glamorization of the occult in movies, books, and television shows. According to Professor Giuseppe Ferrari, who is the head of the Group on Research and Socio-Religious Information, an Italian occult watchdog group:

> There are those who try to turn people into vampires and make them drink other people's blood, or encourage them to have special sexual relations to obtain special powers. . . . These groups are attracted by the so-called beautiful young vampires that we've seen so much of in recent years.[9]

> "I know of bars that serve drinks mixed with blood. This is very dangerous," he added.[10]

The children's book and movie franchise *Harry Potter*, which deals in witchcraft, wizardry, and magic, is valued at over $15 billion. The fantasy and romance franchise *Twilight*, with an estimated value of nearly $6 billion, largely targets adolescents and young adults. The story romanticizes vampires using young, attractive, and seductive characters. HBO's hit television series *True Blood*, which was a racy take on vampires for adults, was a ratings smash for HBO, earning the program a seven-season run.

9. Michael Day, "Exorcists Warn Vatican over 'Beautiful Young Vampires' and Satanic Yoga," *The Independent*, April 13, 2015, http://www.independent.co.uk/news/world/europe/exorcists-warn-vatican-over-beautiful-young-vampires-and-satanic-yoga-10174001.html, accessed June 13, 2015.

10. Claudio Lavanga, "Vatican Exorcism Course Aims Comes Amid Growing Interest in Occult," NBC News, April 17, 2015, http://www.nbcnews.com/news/world/vatican-exorcism-course-aims-educate-both-priests-doctors-n343516, accessed June 13, 2015.

An exorcism hotline, established in 2012 in the largest Catholic diocese in Europe, located in Milan, is reported to have received more than two thousand calls in 2014 from those seeking help for demon possession. Father Francesco Bamonte, president of the International Association for Exorcists, based in Italy, had this to say:

> Diabolical possessions are on the increase as a result of people subscribing to occultism. The few exorcists that we have in the dioceses are often not able to handle the enormous number of requests for help.[11]

Spanish exorcist Jose Antonio Fortea sent out a dire warning to parents over a game called the Charlie Challenge, a game to invoke the Mexican spirit Charlie that went viral over YouTube in multiple languages during the spring of 2015. He further warned that game players won't necessarily be possessed, but the invocation of spirits may cause that spirit to "stay around for a while."[12] Some are even warning that the game can cause "severe psychiatric disorders or suicide."[13]

Unrelated to the Charlie Challenge, one such story of demon possession hit international headlines early in 2012, when single mother Latoya Ammons and her three children, two sons aged 7 and 9, and her 12-year-old daughter moved into a modest, three-bedroom rental home in Gary, Indiana. Ammons claims that the house was inhabited by demons who possessed her and her children, causing them to be violent toward each other and to have deep voices, bulging eyes, and evil smiles. There were stories of levitations and a child walking backward up a wall witnessed by a social worker and healthcare provider.

Eventually, police officers, the Department of Child Services (DCS), psychiatrists, and healthcare workers became involved, and it is reported that the situation was only resolved after a series of exorcisms were performed.

---

11. Nick Squires, "Rise of the Exorcists in Catholic Church," *The Telegraph*, January 4, 2015, http://www.telegraph.co.uk/news/worldnews/europe/vaticancityandholysee/10550800/Rise-of-the-exorcists-in-Catholic-Church.html, accessed June 13, 2015.

12. Thomas D. Williams, "Exorcist Warns that 'The Charlie Challenge' Invites Demonic Activity," Breitbart, May 28, 2015, http://www.breitbart.com/national-security/2015/05/28/exorcist-warns-that-the-charlie-challenge-invites-demonic-activity/, accessed June 13, 2015.

13. "Hell Is Real and Lasts Forever," http://catolicosalvatualma.blogspot.it/2015/05/alerta-juego-satanico-charlie-charlie.html, accessed June 13, 2015.

Gary police captain Charles Austin, a 36-year police department veteran, said that after a series of interviews and visits to the house, "I am a believer." Valerie Washington, the DCS caseworker who led the investigation and witnessed the 9-year-old walking backward up the wall, reported that "he glided backward on the floor, wall, and ceiling," and that she believed it was possible that an "evil influence" was involved. Willie Lee Walker, a registered nurse who was with Washington during that incident, said:

> He walked up the wall, flipped over her, and stood there. . . . There's no way he could've done that. . . .
> We didn't know what was going on. . . . That was crazy. I was like, "Everybody gotta go." . . . This kid was not himself when he did that.

Walker also said that he believed there was "some demonic spirit to it." Ammons was examined by a psychiatrist and was determined to be of "sound mind."[14]

Soon thereafter, a hospital chaplain contacted a local priest, Reverend Michael Maginot, requesting that he perform an exorcism for the family. After several interviews with the family and multiple visits to the home, Maginot said, "He was convinced the family was being tormented by demons" and that "there were ghosts in the house."[15] He proceeded to perform a series of exorcisms on Ammons between April and June of 2012. The family moved to Indianapolis during that time, but Ammons would return for the exorcisms. After the final exorcism in June, she said that she and her family now live in peace without any demonic influences.

Rapture Ready Reasoning

We have looked yet again in this chapter at how our time on planet earth fits the description of the time Jesus prophesied for the very end of the Church Age (the Age of Grace). The Rapture will bring this dispensation, the Church Age, to an end. Millions of those who have been born again (John 3:3) into the family of God through belief in Jesus Christ for salvation of their souls will instantaneously go to be with Christ when He says, "Come up here!" (Revelation 4:1). These will spend eternity in the glory

---

14. Marisa Kwiatkowski, "The Exorcisms of Latoya Ammons," *Indy Star*, October 31, 2014, http://www.indystar.com/story/news/2014/01/25/the-disposession-of-latoya-ammons/4892553/, accessed June 14, 2015.
15. Ibid.

of heaven, living life that is ever-increasing with wonders beyond present human imagination. This is a promise from God's Word:

> But as it is written, Eye hath not seen, nor ear heard, neither have entered into the heart of man, the things which God hath prepared for them that love him (1 Corinthians 2:9).

The Rapture will also bring about judgment on planet earth the very day it occurs. We have Jesus' Word on it:

> But the same day that Lot went out of Sodom it rained fire and brimstone from heaven, and destroyed them all. Even thus shall it be in the day when the Son of man is revealed (Luke 17:29–30).

Judgment will begin to fall that very day. Billions of earth's inhabitants will be left behind to face God's judgment and Antichrist's beastly reign of terror, the time about which Jesus said the following:

> For then shall be great tribulation, such as was not since the beginning of the world to this time, no, nor ever shall be (Matthew 24:21).

The subtitle of this section is "Rapture Ready Reasoning." Here is what I mean. To begin, ask yourself: Is this world getting better, as the Utopian dreamers wish and predict? Or is it as the Apostle Paul prophesied?

> But evil men and seducers shall [become] worse and worse, deceiving, and being deceived (2 Timothy 3:13).

That's a *no-brainer,* as they say. Just remember how the politicians of our time promise all that "transparency" in their dealings with us. Do the Apostle Paul's words ring true for these times in which we find ourselves — or not?

Jesus promised He will break in on a generation of people who, for the most part, aren't expecting Him. As a matter of fact, most mock the very thought that such a thing could possibly happen. The Apostle Peter stated that this would be the very mindset of earth's inhabitants at the end of the age:

> Knowing this first, that there shall come in the last days scoffers, walking after their own lusts, and saying, Where is the promise of

his coming? for since the fathers fell asleep, all things continue as they were from the beginning of the creation (2 Peter 3:3–4).

Like in the days of Noah, we have come near the point that every imagination of the heart is only on evil continually. It is sad to say that, today, this is the mindset of the majority of those within the Body of Christ, those who have been born again. They will, nonetheless, go to be with Jesus when He calls them. They will then realize the lost opportunities they had to live in anticipation of His coming for them, as He promised.

> Let not your heart be troubled: ye believe in God, believe also in me. In my Father's house are many mansions: if it were not so, I would have told you. I go to prepare a place for you. And if I go and prepare a place for you, I will come again, and receive you unto myself; that where I am, there ye may be also (John 14:1–3).

The very Creator of all that is appeals to believers and unbelievers alike. His is the ultimate call to *reason* — to think not on the evil things of this world, but on things above. This is the mindset that is "Rapture Ready": prepared to meet the Lord, who doesn't want you to face judgment and wrath, but to bask in the eternal joy that awaits those who will but heed God's Word.

> Come now, and let us reason together, saith the LORD: though your sins be as scarlet, they shall be as white as snow; though they be red like crimson, they shall be as wool (Isaiah 1:18).

Here is the mindset that pleases the Heavenly Father:

> Finally, brethren, whatsoever things are true, whatsoever things are honest, whatsoever things are just, whatsoever things are pure, whatsoever things are lovely, whatsoever things are of good report; if there be any virtue, and if there be any praise, think on these things. Those things, which ye have both learned, and received, and heard, and seen in me, do: and the God of peace shall be with you (Philippians 4:8–9).

CHAPTER 6

THE RAVENOUS BEAR AND OTHER PROPHESIED WILD BEASTS

Reason #6: All nations in alignment for the wind-up

of human history in accordance with Bible prophecy

is a primary reason to understand that this will be the

generation that will be left behind when the Rapture occurs.

Bible prophecy describes the great empires of human history in terms of being likened to beasts of the animal world. Prophets Daniel in the Old Testament and John in the New Testament vividly portray the kingdom-representing animals, both as they are in real life, and as they are in ghastly configuration within the visions of the most terrible time to come, the Tribulation (the last seven years of this present world system of human government).

The following is an example of such prophetic descriptions in the Bible:

Daniel spake and said, I saw in my vision by night, and, behold, the four winds of the heaven strove upon the great sea. And four great beasts came up from the sea, diverse one from another. The first was like a lion, and had eagle's wings: I beheld till the wings thereof were plucked, and it was lifted up from the earth, and made stand upon the feet as a man, and a man's heart was given to it.

And behold another beast, a second, like to a bear, and it raised up itself on one side, and it had three ribs in the mouth of it between the teeth of it: and they said thus unto it, Arise, devour much flesh.

After this I beheld, and lo another, like a leopard, which had upon the back of it four wings of a fowl; the beast had also four heads; and dominion was given to it.

After this I saw in the night visions, and behold a fourth beast, dreadful and terrible, and strong exceedingly; and it had great iron teeth: it devoured and brake in pieces, and stamped the residue with the feet of it: and it was diverse from all the beasts that were before it; and it had ten horns (Daniel 7:2–7).

Daniel was here giving the great empires that would be manifest down through history. It was a mirror reflection of the vision of the man-image Babylonian King Nebuchadnezzar dreamed about in a night vision. This is recorded in Daniel, chapter 2.

The huge, metallic statue represented the kingdoms of history, and Daniel was given the interpretation of the dream to give the king, who was angry because his soothsayers or wise men couldn't tell him either what his dream was or what it meant. Nebuchadnezzar was going to have them all put to death. God gave Daniel the answers to give the king, and he and the phony fortune-tellers were spared.

The metallic image represented the kingdoms that began with Nebuchadnezzar as the head of gold. The statue-vision was composed of silver, bronze, iron, and clay in descending quality of metallic composition, to indicate that each succeeding empire would be inferior in power and glory to the previous. The empires of history will, according to the prophecy, conclude with the metallic image's toes made of iron mixed with clay as the world's final kingdom that will exist at the time when God will bring the earth's humanistic system of governments to a catastrophic end.

The later vision Daniel received and reported, involving the animal images, represented the same world kingdoms. They were properly characterized as beastly, because that is exactly what each worldly, humanistic empire has been — beastly.

I must inform the reader at this point that the final world kingdom of the metallic monster, and of the beastly images, is now coming into view. The arrangement of nations at this moment constitutes one of the most profound signals of all the indicators now on the world scene. This nations-in-alignment indicator, like the many other indicators, is flashing in bulletin-like fashion. *The Rapture is imminent!*

John's Mediterranean Nightmare

John, the Apostle, was the disciple whom the Scripture pointed out as one "who Jesus loved" (John 20:2, 21:7, 21:20). We get a sense that this caused a bit of irritation for Peter, another of Jesus' closest disciples. Peter once asked Jesus what would become of John, after Jesus had talked about His immediate disciples' futures. Jesus, in effect, indicated it wasn't Peter's business to know what John's future would entail.

The Scriptures — and history, of course — have provided the answer to Peter's inquiry about the much-beloved John. He was persecuted horribly, like the others, even to the point of being boiled in oil. He was exiled by the Roman Empire to the Aegean Island of Patmos in his very late years for faithfully presenting the gospel of Christ.

It was during that exile where this aged Apostle became the great revelator. He was given the most spectacular vision of the wrap-up of earth's history of any of the prophets. The Revelation is the one book that promises a special blessing for anyone who reads or hears the words of the prophecy.

John, like Daniel before him, was given a vision of the great, beastly kingdoms of humanistic government. His vision was of a jaw-dropping sort.

> And I stood upon the sand of the sea, and saw a beast rise up out of the sea, having seven heads and ten horns, and upon his horns ten crowns, and upon his heads the name of blasphemy.
>
> And the beast which I saw was like unto a leopard, and his feet were as the feet of a bear, and his mouth as the mouth of a lion: and the dragon gave him his power, and his seat, and great authority (Revelation 13:1–2).

The vision was almost identical to that given Daniel, as we saw earlier. This time, the vision-beast had seven heads and ten horns. Most scholars in the arena of eschatology agree that the ten horns John reported represent the same prophetic symbols as the ten toes that Daniel saw on Nebuchadnezzar's nightmarish, metallic man-image.

These seven heads are, I'm in agreement, representative of the seven governmental entities that will head the final world kingdom. Their great power will derive from the ten horns, which will be ten economic spheres ruled by Satan, and will be driven by global monetary dynamics — earth's great financial engine. It will be the *love of money* taken to the ultimate degree.

John saw the rise of this composite beast and another beast he described as a man who will take authority over all of this governmental monstrosity. The beast that arose from the sea is the total amalgamation of all of the world governments since the empire headed by Nebuchadnezzar. It is the Babylonian system of humanistic control, the final, man-made empire like that Nimrod tried to construct at Babel as given in Genesis chapter 11. The man who will reign over the latest and greatest attempt to usurp the throne of God, empowered by Satan, will be the one who is most often called Antichrist.

There are forces today that are doing all within their power to bring the world under global governance. Let us examine this preparation taking place that will one day give Antichrist his prophetic opportunity to establish Satan's kingdom on planet earth.

One expert observer of the developments toward a changed world order of biblical proportions frames where this generation stands.

> Those thinking the world will get better and better are victims of wishful thinking and sentimental reasoning. Their whimsical visions of a rosy future are almost the exact opposite of what God's always-accurate prophets foretold in the Bible. Global governance is bearing down on the whole world like a fast-moving, killer tsunami that cannot be stopped. But many in the church — and the vast majority of those on the outside — are asleep or in total darkness.
>
> As absurd as it sounds, some of the so-called intellectual elite . . . are actually trying to restructure the world. Most seem to honestly believe they are doing a good thing by laying the foundation for a coming socialist utopia. Nothing could be further from the truth.
>
> Global governance will evolve into a global disaster that will kill billions and cause the living to envy the dead. This coming hell

on earth will wax worse and worse until Jesus returns because the dangers are not seen by those who don't have a biblical worldview. Extreme havoc is coming, and it is clearly accelerating every time the big, beautiful, bright sun rises in the eastern sky.[1]

The New World Order

Never-ending efforts to bring about changed world order that is intended to be controlled by the very few are indeed accelerating. It is *climate change,* which has evolved from *global warming* as a crisis mantra, that I believe is the centerpiece around which the would-be globalist masters will continue to rally while the time of Antichrist approaches. Environmental issues feed their fanatic, religious-like fervor. We will look at their blueprint for this pursuit of new world order. A highly detailed dissection of their plans follow for the reader who wants a thorough understanding of precisely what I believe is the luciferically influenced design for planet earth.

Environmental Agenda

Agenda 21 is a United Nations blueprint to establish a one-world government through the advancement and enforcement of environmental policy known as sustainable development. Using environmentally noble language, it seeks to have centralized control over all human activity. The term "sustainable development" has been attributed to Gro Harlem Brundtland, vice president of the World Socialist Party and prime minister of Norway, in her 1987 report titled *Our Common Future.* In the *Brundtland Report,* she defined sustainable development as "meeting today's needs without compromising future generations to meet their own needs."[2] Building on the concept of sustainable development, the United Nations launched its Earth Summit conference in 1992 to advance Agenda 21, apparently named for 21st-century global environmental policy. According to Agenda 21:

> The objective is to provide for the land requirements of human settlement development through environmentally sound physical planning and land use so as to ensure access to land to all households

1. Daymond Duck, "Grasping for Global Governance," *The Departure: God's Next Catastrophic Intervention into Earth's History* (Crane, MO: Defender, 2010) chapter 13, p. 246.
2. "Sustainability — ED. Important Milestones in Sustainable Development," *The Brundtland Report,* http://www.sustainability-ed.org.uk/pages/what1-4brundt.htm, accessed June 18, 2015.

and where appropriate, the encouragement of communally and collectively owned and managed land. Particular attention should be paid to the needs of women, and indigenous people for economic and cultural reasons.[3]

The United Nations website defines Agenda 21 as "a comprehensive plan of action to be taken globally, nationally and locally by organizations of the United Nations System, Governments, and Major Groups in every area in which human impacts on the environment."[4] It was officially adopted by 179 world governments during the United Nation's Conference on Environment and Development, also known as the Earth Summit, held in Rio de Janeiro in June 1992. Then President George H.W. Bush signed the agreement on behalf of the United States.

In 1993, President Bill Clinton signed Executive Order 12852 establishing his Council on Sustainable Development. He did so in order to "harmonize" environmental policy in the United States with policies outlined in Agenda 21.[5] In 2011, President Barack Obama signed Executive Order 13575, establishing the White House Rural Council, in which he targets "sustainable rural communities." The order states that 16 percent of the American population resides in these communities, and Obama admits he wants federal government intervention into these lands due to their production of "food, fiber, and energy," and also because these are the locations of many of our "natural resources." He further asserts that his council will "coordinate Federal efforts directed toward the growth and development of geographic regions that encompass both urban and rural areas, and identify and facilitate rural economic opportunities associated with energy development, outdoor recreation, and other conservation-related activities."[6]

Agenda 21 has emerged as a matter of policy in the urban, suburban, and rural communities of the United States. These executive orders, directing federal agencies to work with state and local governments, have been

---

3. "Promoting Human Settlement Development," United Nations Environment Programme, Section 7.28, http://www.unep.org/Documents.Multilingual/Default.Print. asp?DocumentID=52&ArticleID=5, accessed June 18, 2015.

4. "United Nations. Sustainable Development Knowledge Platform," https:// sustainabledevelopment.un.org/index.php?page=view&nr=23&type=400, accessed June 18, 2015.

5. "Agenda 21," American Policy Center, http://americanpolicy.org/agenda21/, accessed June 18, 2015.

6. "Executive Order 13575," Establishment of the White House Rural Council, http://www. gpo.gov/fdsys/pkg/DCPD-201100431/pdf/DCPD-201100431.pdf, accessed June 18, 2015.

implemented in thousands of cities, and the movement is growing — all through government bureaucracy and without any legislative debate on behalf of the citizens.

The implementation of Agenda 21 began by infiltrating local governments through the International Council of Local Environmental Initiative (ICLEI), the implementation arm of the United Nations, headquartered in Bonn, Germany. The mission of ICLEI "is to build and serve a worldwide movement of local governments to achieve tangible improvements in global sustainability, with a specific focus on environmental conditions through cumulative local actions."[7] The ICLEI receives its funding from community dues, multiple foundations, government grants, environmental groups, financial organizations, and many others. ICLEI was also the recipient of more than $2 million donated by George Soros through his Open Society foundation, and has chapters in more than one thousand cities worldwide, including more than six hundred in the United States.

This kind of massive undertaking will of course have an enormous financial cost and will need much more than monies from dues, donors, and grants. In anticipation of those costs, the preamble to the agreement states:

> The developmental and environmental objectives of Agenda 21 will require a substantial flow of new and additional financial resources to developing countries, in order to cover the incremental costs for the actions they have to undertake to deal with global environmental problems and to accelerate sustainable development.[8]

In other words, these resources are substantial, incremental, and are to come from wealthy countries like the United States for the purpose of redistribution to less wealthy or poor countries.

A discussion about sustainability should also include what the architects of Agenda 21 consider unsustainable. According to Maurice Strong, Secretary General of the United Nations' Earth Summit in 1992, "Current lifestyles and consumption patterns of the affluent middle class — involving high meat intake, use of fossil fuels, appliances, home and work air conditioning, and suburban housing are not sustainable."[9] The United Nations

---

7. IPEEC Project List, http://www.ipeec.org/solutions/projectlist/id/3.html, accessed July 25, 2015.
8. United Nations Environment Programme, *Agenda 21,* Chapter 1, Preamble. Section 1.4, http://www.unep.org/Documents.Multilingual/Default.Print. asp?DocumentID=52&ArticleID=4, accessed June 18, 2015.
9. "Agenda 21," American Policy Center, http://americanpolicy.org/agenda21/, accessed June

Biodiversity Assessment Report defined unsustainability as, "Ski runs, grazing of livestock, plowing of soil, building fences, industry, single family homes, paved and tarred roads, logging activities, dams and reservoirs, power line construction, and economic systems that fail to set proper value on the environment."[10]

Section 28 of Agenda 21 calls upon local authorities in the United States and elsewhere to "enter into a dialogue with its citizens, local organizations and private enterprises and adopt 'a local Agenda 21.' "[11] The goal of these local Agenda 21 groups is to create "local authority programmes, policies, laws and regulations to achieve Agenda 21 objectives [that] would be assessed and modified, based on local programmes adopted. Strategies could also be used in supporting proposals for local, national, regional and international funding."[12]

Interestingly, J. Gary Lawrence, President Bill Clinton's advisor on the Council of Sustainable Development, warned Clinton about calling his policies "Local Agenda 21" (LA21). Lawrence said:

> Participating in a UN advocated planning process would very likely bring out many of the conspiracy-fixated groups and individuals in our society such as the National Rifle Association, citizen militias and some members of Congress. This segment of our society who fear "one-world government" and a UN invasion of the United States through which our individual freedom would be stripped away would actively work to defeat any elected official who joined "the conspiracy" by undertaking LA21. So, we call our processes something else, such as comprehensive planning, growth management or smart growth.[13]

In more than three hundred pages, Agenda 21 describes in detail how the United Nations plans to centrally govern a global society by binding world governments to its plan to control the lives of every human being — all under the guise of being good stewards of Mother Earth. The

18, 2015.

10. Ibid.

11. "Local Authorities' Initiatives in Support of Agenda 21," Section 28.2 (1) and 28.3.

12. Ibid.

13. J. Gary Lawrence, "The Future of Local Agenda 21 in the New Millennium," *Millennium Papers*, issue 2, p. 3, http://www.unedforum.org/publications/millennium/mill%20paper2.pdf, accessed June 18, 2015.

goal of Agenda 21 is to take control of privately owned land under the pretense of "sustainability" by drafting individual governments into this agreement. Once fully implemented and overseen by the United Nations (we will fundamentally have a one-world government), the government will control where we live, what we eat, how we move about and communicate with each other, how land use is designated, and how resources are to be redistributed.

In addition to the United Nations' "smart growth" agenda, our own bloated environmental bureaucracy — the United States Environmental Protection Agency (EPA) — has become one of the most abusive and powerful bureaucracies in the United States.

According to a report issued by the American Legislative Exchange Council (ALEC) titled *The U.S. Environmental Protection Agency's Assault on State Sovereignty*, President Obama's EPA policies "have cost states billions of dollars in compliance fees and millions of jobs lost."

William Yeatman, author of the ALEC report and assistant director of the Center for Energy and Environment at the Competitive Enterprise Institute, stated:

> Congress intended for EPA and states to work together to solve the country's environmental problems. Since 2009, however, EPA has centralized a great deal of environmental policymaking. Even worse, the agency has found a method, known as sue and settle, to effectively replace states input with environmentalist special interests in the regulatory process.[14]

The EPA uses the legal strategy known as "sue and settle," also known as "friendly lawsuits," to replace state regulatory officials' input with extremists and activists from environmental groups. According to the *Washington Examiner*, here's how it works:

> First, the private environmental group sues the EPA in federal court seeking to force it to issue new regulations by a date certain. Then agency and group officials meet behind closed doors to hammer out a deal. Typically in the deal, the government agrees to

---

14. American Legislative Exchange Council, "New Report Reveals Significant Increase in EPA Actions Under the Obama Administration," June 26, 2013, http://www.alec.org/ new-report-reveals-significant-increase-in-epa-actions-under-the-obama-administration/, accessed June 25, 2015.

do whatever the activists want. The last step occurs when the judge issues a consent decree that makes the deal the law of the land. No messy congressional hearings. No public comment period. No opportunity for anybody outside the privileged few to know how government regulatory policy is being shaped until it's too late.[15]

These settlements have:

> ... imposed more than $13 billion in annual regulatory costs since 2009 and [have] drastically increased the power of the EPA at the expense of the states. The EPA had 48 sue and settle agreements during President Obama's first term, representing a 380 percent increase from the average sue and settle rate during the previous three four-year presidential terms.[16]

Further, the taxpayers, as well as the regulatory victims, bear the burden of the legal fees for both conspiring parties. The Governmental Accountability Office (GAO) report in 2011 said the costs between 1995 and 2010 included millions of dollars awarded to environmental litigants and their attorneys, as well as at least $43 million to defend the EPA in court. Millions of taxpayer dollars went into the pockets of those who were on the same side to begin with.

Worse than the collusion with environmental extremists in these "sue and settle" cases is the EPA's fraud, deception, and abuse of power under the guise of global warming, or as it's now called, climate change — to most rational people, "the weather." The EPA has relied upon discredited Intergovernmental Panel on Climate Change (IPCC) reports and discredited computer models to push their fear-mongering climate-change agenda while ignoring all evidence to the contrary. And beyond all of that rhetoric, President Obama claims that climate change is the greatest threat to our national security.

In May 2015, President Obama, under executive order, moved to massively expand the EPA's regulatory power under the Clean Water Act. Under the new act, Waters of the United States, the EPA will now have regulatory

15. "EPA's Back Room 'Sue and Settle' Deals Need Reform," *Washington Examiner*, May 25, 2013, http://www.washingtonexaminer.com/epas-back-room-sue-and-settle-deals-require-reform/article/2530505, accessed June 25, 2013.
16. American Legislative Exchange Council, "New Report," June 26, 2013, http://www.alec.org/new-report-reveals-significant-increase-in-epa-actions-under-the-obama-administration/, accessed June 25, 2015.

power over water — including potholes, puddles, creeks, ditches, ponds, streambeds, tributaries, and any other water that the EPA determines has a "significant nexus" with "navigable waters." James Inhofe, an Oklahoma senator and chairman of the U.S. Senate Environment and Public Works Committee, said the rule is "a measure that hugely expands the ability of this aggressive agency to disregard the conservation efforts of American states and interfere with the daily lives and property of the American people. This will drastically affect — for the worse — the ability of many Americans to use and enjoy their property."[17]

The Global Trade Agenda

The United States of America is currently on the precipice of joining a global trade union known as the Trans-Pacific Partnership (TPP), the biggest free-trade deal in the history of the world. This future deal will represent about 40 percent of global trade. It currently includes 12 nations, including Japan, Australia, Canada, and Mexico, but has many more potential members — including China, known for its currency manipulation, deceptive trade practices, intellectual property theft, and, more recently, the most egregious cyber attack to ever occur in the United States for the purpose of espionage.

While on U.S. public radio, regarding the topic of China and trade, President Obama said, "They've already started putting out feelers about the possibilities of them participating at some point."[18] When Fast Track, or the Trade Promotion Authority (TPA), received its final passing vote in Senate on June 23, 2015, it became clear that the Trans-Pacific Partnership and related agreements will soon become law in the United States. At no time in the history of the United States has a president had fast-track authority without having his trade bills enacted. Interestingly, on the day following the passage of the TPA, several high-ranking Chinese officials met with President Obama in the White House.

According to a White House press release on June 24, 2015:

> The President met today with China's Special Representatives to the U.S.-China Strategic and Economic Dialogue and Consultation

---

17. James Inhofe, "Why Every Property Owner Should Fear EPA's 'Waters of the United States' Rule," Fox News, June 2, 2015, http://www.foxnews.com/opinion/2015/06/02/why-every-us-property-owner-should-be-afraid-very-afraid-epas-waters-united-states-rule.html, accessed June 25, 2015.
18. Dan Steinbock, "A Look Behind the Trans-Pacific Partnership Talks," EconoMonitor, June 8, 2015, http://www.economonitor.com/blog/2015/06/a-look-behind-the-trans-pacific-partnership-talks/, accessed June 25, 2015.

on People-to-People Exchange, Vice Premier Liu Yandong, Vice Premier Wang Yang, State Councilor Yang Jiechi, and the Chinese delegation. The President and the Chinese Special Representatives agreed
to further expand U.S.-China cooperation on climate and clean
energy, and affirmed their unity of purpose in our approach to the
Paris climate negotiations in December. Recognizing the importance
of economic ties to the overall bilateral relationship, the President
expressed support for China's efforts to reform and rebalance its
economy, and for our ongoing bilateral investment treaty negotiations, while urging China to address major economic challenges in
the areas of its currency, technology and investment policies.[19]

The Trans-Pacific Partnership is only one of several global trade pacts secretly
being discussed. The Transatlantic Trade and Investment Partnership (TTIP)
and the Trade in Services Agreement (TiSA) together incorporate 75 percent
of the global economy and up to 90 percent if other countries being enticed
agree to join these secret trade deals.

The president's trade representative, Michael Froman, has also stated
that no trade agreement will be put forth without provisions for environmental governance. He said:

> We will insist on a robust, fully enforceable environment chap-
> ter in the TPP or we will not come to agreement. . . . Our proposals
> would enhance international cooperation and create new oppor-
> tunities for public participation in environmental governance and
> enforcement. . . . The United States reiterated our bedrock position
> on enforceability of the entire environment chapter.[20]

Senator Jeff Sessions has been one of the most outspoken representatives
against these secret agreements. In response to Michael Froman's comments,
Senator Sessions responded by saying:

---

19. The White House Office of the Press Secretary, "Readout of the President's Meeting with
China's Special Representatives to the U.S.-China Strategic and Economic Dialogue and
Consultation on People-to-People Exchange," https://www.whitehouse.gov/the-press-
office/2015/06/24/readout-presidents-meeting-chinas-special-representatives, accessed
June 30, 2015.
20. Rick Wells, "Sen Sessions — Obamatrade Centered On Oppressive Climate Rules,
Creating 'Pacific Union' Ruling America," *Constitution Rising*, June 15, 2015, http://
rickwells.us/sen-sessions-obamatrade-centered-on-oppressive-climate-rules-creating-
pacific-union-ruling-america/, accessed July 5, 2015.

Well, that's a powerful statement. There is no doubt that this "president" is intent on utilizing this agreement to drive his environmental agenda, whether the American people or the U.S. Congress agrees with it or not.[21]

Despite the fact that the perpetrators of Agenda 21 have managed to inflict their controls to one extent or the other upon the nations of the world — including the United States — they were disappointed. They aren't satisfied.

Therefore, the would-be masters of the planet met in New York City on September 25–27, 2015, in an effort to generate more dynamic movement in bringing in their new world order. The new nomenclature given the effort is "Transforming Our World: The 2030 Agenda for Sustainable Development." They intend to change the planet to meet specifications demanded by the United Nations by the year 2030.

Bear Nation on Scene

The one nation-state that most evokes the image of an animal is that vast behemoth to the far north of Israel: Russia. I can remember when the chairman of the Communist Party under the regime of the Soviet Union was Leonid Brezhnev. He was a big, burly man with a scowl and bushy hair and thick, menacing eyebrows. He was often depicted in political cartoons as a bear, with that somber, intimidating countenance. It was a quite striking — and appropriate — characterization, both of Brezhnev the man and of the USSR (Union of Soviet Socialist Republics).

Russia reclaimed its name with the dissolution of the Soviet Union in 1989–1990. It has, however, long been referred to as "the Russian Bear." One of its major nuclear bombers is called the "Bear Bomber."

Whether as the Soviet Union or as Russia, its history is one of war-like fierceness. From the times of the Kahns to the Cossaks, to more modern times when they defeated Hitler's Nazi invasion campaign termed Barbarossa in World War II, the Russian military has upheld its namesake by its bear-like ferocity.

Today's Russian leader — a man not at all bear-like in appearance, rather known as physically trim and athletic — nonetheless harbors an aggressive behavior. But his years as a cagey former KGB operative for the Soviets have

---

21. Ibid.

developed a less gruff, more patient demeanor than his Soviet predecessors.

The new, more diplomatically polished version of the top bear brought Russia to the brink of invading Ukraine, one of the USSR's former states. He abruptly went into his diplomatically nuanced mode when it benefited himself to do so.

> Moscow (AFP) — Russia is not a threat to the West, President Vladimir Putin insisted in an interview published on Saturday, saying he was still committed to a Ukraine peace deal after a fresh flare-up in the country's east.
>
> "I would like to say — there's no need to be afraid of Russia," Putin told Italian newspaper *Corriere della Sera* in an interview published Saturday, ruling out a major conflict between Russia and NATO member countries.[22]

For those of my age bracket, this shmoozing by Mr. Nice Guy is a far cry from the bellicose rants of Soviet Premier Nikita Khrushchev, who crudely pounded his shoe on the table at the United Nations and on another occasion threatened that he would bury America. However, for we who lived through those sometimes terrifying days of the Cold War — like during the Cuban missile crisis of October 1962 — the hard realities of dealing with the "evil empire," as President Ronald Reagan called the Soviets, remains fresh in our minds. America and the world should not just *listen* to what Mr. Putin says, but *look* constantly and closely at what he *does*.

That prescription for dealing with the Russian bear is not just sound geopolitical advice. It is good advice gleaned from advance warning given to the world by the very Word of God. We are given a heads-up that there will come just such a leader to the very land upon which today's Russia sits. He will be a thinker first and foremost. His actions that follow will be among the most dastardly ever conceived or attempted.

> And the word of the LORD came unto me, saying, Son of man, set thy face against Gog, the land of Magog, the chief prince of Meshech and Tubal, and prophesy against him, and say, Thus saith the Lord GOD; Behold I am against thee, O Gog, the chief prince of Meshech and Tubal: and I will turn thee back, and put hooks into

---

22. Daymond Duck, "Grasping for Global Governance," *The Departure: God's Next Catastrophic Intervention into Earth's History* (Crane, MO: Defender, 2010), p. 246.

thy jaws, and I will bring thee forth, and all thine army, horses and horsemen, all of them clothed with all sorts of armour, even a great company with bucklers and shields, all of them handling swords. . . .

Thus saith the Lord GOD; It shall also come to pass, that at the same time shall things come into thy mind, and thou shalt think an evil thought (Ezekiel 38:1–10).

At some point in what I believe to be near-history, a Russian leader will think an "evil thought." It will consist of the lust to take by military force the riches that a neighbor to the south of Russia (land of Magog) possesses. We know from much research by Bible and even secular scholars that the land of Magog sat where present-day Russia resides for the most part. The land to the south that will be assaulted for robbing it of its riches can be none other than Israel.

Israel, of course, was scattered to the four winds of the earth around A.D. 135, when the Roman Emperor Hadrian forced all Jews to flee their homeland. The Jews remained exiled into the many nations of the world until 1948, when Israel again became a nation following World War II.

The return of the Jews and the re-establishment of the nation on May 14, 1948, set in motion the alignment of nations for the wrap-up of this dispensation — the Age of Grace or Church Age. It is the dispensation that will see the coming again of the Lord Jesus Christ to put an end to war and devastation on earth.

There will be two phases to Christ's Second Coming, or Second Advent.

The first will be the Rapture of the Church, when, as we've seen a number of times in these chapters, Jesus will step out on the clouds of heavenly glory and call all born-again believers to Himself above earth (Revelation 4:1; 1 Corinthians 15:51–55; 1 Thessalonians 4:13–18).

The second phase will take place when the Lord descends all the way to the planet to stop man's deadliest conflict, the war called Armageddon (Revelation 19:11).

The primary reason I believe that this Gog-Magog assault by Russia and a coalition of countries against modern-day Israel is set to take place in the near term is because the Russian Bear and all other nations in that prophesied coalition of nations are now in configuration exactly as given by Ezekiel in his Gog-Magog prophecy.

That prophecy foretells the makeup of this evil coalition, and the thought that is foremost in their plans.

Persia, Ethiopia, and Libya with them; all of them with shield and helmet: Gomer, and all his bands; the house of Togarmah of the north quarters, and all his bands: and many people with thee. . . .

After many days thou shalt be visited: in the latter years thou shalt come into the land that is brought back from the sword, and is gathered out of many people, against the mountains of Israel, which have been always waste: but it is brought forth out of the nations, and they shall dwell safely all of them.

Thou shalt ascend and come like a storm, thou shalt be like a cloud to cover the land, thou, and all thy bands, and many people with thee (Ezekiel 38:5–9).

My purpose here is not to present a study on the identity of all these nations in modern terms. I have made such presentations in some of my books before, and so have many good scholars within their own works. If interested in checking on the authentication of the nations and their modern-day counterparts who will be involved in the attack on Israel, I suggest you look into some of these very in-depth books on the subject.

Here I will simply say that these nations basically involve Russia, Iran, Turkey, and some parts of far Eastern Europe, as well as nations of people whose history shows their forebearers — and now they, themselves — have harbored hatreds against Israel for thousands of years.

Here, of course, I'm thinking of the many Arab-Muslim nations that are Israel's immediate neighbors.

Although Iranians aren't Arabs for the most part — they are Persian and speak Farsi, not Arabic — it is fascinating to watch, for example, ancient Persian hatreds so out front in today's headlines against modern Israel. We all know of the efforts of Iran, which is the heart of where ancient Persia sat, to develop nuclear weaponry. They threaten practically on a daily basis to destroy Israel and every Jew they can. All of the nations that are foretold to join Russia and Iran in the attack also have vowed to kill every Jew and to push the nation into the Mediterranean Sea.

The invasion, when it occurs, will be truly catastrophic. God has foretold, through His prophet, Ezekiel, just how profound will be His intervention when His *chosen people,* Israel, are threatened with annihilation.

And it shall come to pass at the same time when Gog shall come against the land of Israel, saith the Lord GOD, that my fury shall come up in my face. For in my jealousy and in the fire of my wrath have I spoken, Surely in that day there shall be a great shaking in the land of Israel. . . .

And I will call for a sword against him throughout all my mountains, saith the Lord GOD: every man's sword shall be against his brother. And I will plead against him with pestilence and with blood; and I will rain upon him, and upon his bands, and upon the many people that are with him, an overflowing rain, and great hailstones, fire, and brimstone. . . .

Therefore, thou son of man, prophesy against Gog, and say, Thus saith the Lord GOD; Behold, I am against thee, O Gog, the chief prince of Meshech and Tubal: and I will turn thee back, and leave but the sixth part of thee, and will cause thee to come up from the north parts, and will bring thee upon the mountains of Israel: and I will smite thy bow out of thy left hand, and will cause thine arrows to fall out of thy right hand. Thou shalt fall upon the mountains of Israel, thou, and all thy bands, and the people that is with thee: I will give thee unto the ravenous birds of every sort, and to the beasts of the field to be devoured (Ezekiel 38:18–39:4).

So, there will be *beasts* of the carrion sort to clean up the carnage left of the terrible governmental militaries that seek to destroy God's chosen nation. It is a frightening prospect that today's anti-Semites and Israel-hating hordes face. It is all setting up at this very moment for fulfillment, as we watch on our television and computer monitor screens.

There is no doubt whatsoever in my mind that this cataclysmic event will take place following the Rapture of the Church. Here's why.

Again, we must go back to Jesus' words about when He will next catastrophically intervene into the affairs of rebellious mankind. Remember that, as pointed out several times, business will be going on pretty much as usual when that intervention comes. At the time of Armageddon, when Christ comes to earth (Revelation 19:11), times will be anything but normal. Perhaps as much as three-fourths of mankind will have been killed from the judgments of the Tribulation period at the time when Christ returns at Armageddon.

People will not be buying, selling, building, planting, marrying, etc., as they will be at the time Jesus says He will next break in upon an unsuspecting world.

To refresh your memory on the "days of Noah" and the "days of Lot," read again Matthew 24:36–42 and Luke 17:26–30.

Jesus foretold in these accounts that He will next intervene into mankind's history in a catastrophic way when business is going along in a relatively normal way. It will come as a complete surprise to most people, just like what happened in the days of Noah when the torrential rains began and the deep broke open. It will be much as the day when fire and brimstone fell upon Sodom and Gomorah. When Noah went into the ark and Lot went out of Sodom, judgment began — that very day. Jesus promised it will be just exactly like those times when He next intervenes. That will be the Rapture!

The point to consider here is that because the Gog-Magog attack will be such a staggering cataclysm in its own right, with God Himself literally devastating all but one-sixth of the no doubt millions who will come against Israel, it will *not* be "business as usual" anywhere on the planet.

That means that it would take away the possibility of the Rapture occurring, with all of the carnage taking place. It would not be like Jesus described for the time of that event — people carrying on with normal activities, etc.

When the Gog-Magog assault takes place, it will be worldwide disaster. There is even mention of something akin to nuclear fire falling on nations around the world in the prophecy.

So the Gog-Magog attack by the Russian bear and his cohort beasts will take place *following* the Rapture, not *before*. The only way I can see the Gog-Magog attack being launched before the Rapture is if the Rapture would, after the great upheaval caused by the destruction of Israel's enemies, not occur for many years — perhaps decades — i.e., world conditions would again have to get into configuration like they are now, with things moving along pretty much in a normal ebb and flow fashion to make conditions right for the sudden Rapture event to occur as Jesus prophesied.

The Dragon Nation

There is at least room for debate about whether the "bear nation" will lead the Gog-Magog attack on Israel before or after the Rapture. However, in my view, there can be little doubt that the country long known as the "dragon nation" is prophetically scheduled for an even more horrendous action during the Tribulation, well after the Rapture of the Church.

China, the most massive country on earth, with a population currently of more than 1.4 billion, has long been likened to a dragon. We are familiar with the Chinese Year of the Dragon zodiac designation. This is purported to be a sign in the heavens that, according to ancient Chinese lore, occurs periodically. This belief holds that anyone in the Chinese culture born under this sign is destined for a future of good luck. As a matter of fact, a number of other nations consider the Chinese Year of the Dragon such a favorable sign that they report a spike in birth rates in those countries, based, apparently, upon people wanting to be "blessed" by such timely births as being born under the designation.[23]

The world, however, won't be blessed by the dragon nation, according to John's great apocalyptic vision. Quite the opposite is predicted.

China has grown from a country known for its dynasties, which for the most part were inward turned, only coming out from behind their curtain of inscrutability to establish occasional trade dealings with other nations. The Great Wall of China — a structure the astronauts reported could be seen from space — is a tangible proof of the Chinese desire to keep the world out of their business.

Today's China now threatens to establish its own global, economic hegemony.

China's Prophetic Action

I outlined the current push by China in a weekly column I write for www.raptureready.com. I believe it reflects the astounding changes in this once almost invisible culture.

> Sino-American interaction — or perhaps better put, the lack of America's interaction — might have just taken on prophetic relevance. The nation, symbolized by the dragon, we know, will likely be one of the key players while rebellious mankind carries out the final acts of human history. There is some well-founded conjecture that China has made preparations to fire the powerful volley that could eventually prove to help bring America down as the greatest economic power on earth.
>
> The story has yet to take on major emphasis by mainstream news, but look for it to grow in the near future. The news is not insignificant.

---

23. United Nations Environment Programme, *Promoting Human Settlement Development*, Section 7.28, http://www.unep.org/Documents.Multilingual/Default.Print.asp?DocumentID=52&ArticleID=5, accessed June 18, 2015.

BEIJING — At least 35 countries will join the China-led Asian Infrastructure Investment Bank (AIIB) by the deadline of March 31, the bank's interim chief, Jin Liqun, said on Sunday. Currently, India, Indonesia and New Zealand have expressed interest in joining the bank, he told a conference in Beijing, following a request by Britain, France, Italy and Luxembourg to become founding members. "By deadline, (we believe) 35 countries, or more, will become founding members of the bank," he said. (Source: Reuters, 3/23/15)

The Chinese government has been rumored for many months to be working to undermine U.S. top-nation economic status and the American dollar's position in the monetary world. That there is a grab by China to secure as much gold as possible is no secret. They are making deals with Russia and others for buying gas and oil, thereby, it is thought, working to marginalize U.S. involvement and influence. It is believed they are attempting to set up an economic system, which they would, of course, head — totally separate from American interaction.

It is worrisome to many within the world of economics that China holds so much of America's debt. Fears are that their manipulation of a tremendous amount of U.S. Treasury bonds will one day be used to help crash America's economy.

One concern that China is doing all it can to gather world economic power to itself is its reaching out to traditional enemies such as South Korea and Japan. The three nations met recently, ostensibly to work out territorial and diplomatic disputes. They agreed to continue to establish a trilateral series of meetings, and it is thought that the purpose of the meetings will be to secure stronger economic ties.

The dragon nation has proven to be one that is among the worst in the area of human rights. Its many atrocities show the leadership is led and inspired by a dragon of even more virulence — the great, red dragon, Satan.

Again, when considering the often-examined fact that America is mentioned nowhere in Bible prophecy, we must ask whether this current push by China to garner economic power at America's expense is yet another element of the end-times formula for bringing the U.S. down.

China, of course, is not mentioned by name in Bible prophecy. However, is there much room for doubt that the dragon nation is there by inference to the student who studies carefully?

I believe that China as the major end-times prophetic nation from the Orient is presented primarily in two places in the Book of Revelation. The first of the relevant passages is found in the ninth chapter:

> And the sixth angel sounded, and I heard a voice from the four horns of the golden altar which is before God, saying to the sixth angel which had the trumpet, Loose the four angels which are bound in the great river Euphrates. And the four angels were loosed, which were prepared for an hour, and a day, and a month, and a year, for to slay the third part of men. And the number of the army of the horsemen were two hundred thousand thousand: and I heard the number of them (Revelation 9:13–16).

The prophet John, through the prophecy given him by God, expanded upon the foretelling in chapter 16:

> And the sixth angel poured out his vial upon the great river Euphrates; and the water thereof was dried up, that the way of the kings of the east might be prepared. And I saw three unclean spirits like frogs come out of the mouth of the dragon, and out of the mouth of the beast, and out of the mouth of the false prophet. For they are the spirits of devils, working miracles, which go forth unto the kings of the earth and of the whole world, to gather them to the battle of that great day of God Almighty (Revelation 16:12–14).

The king of the kings of the east — unless something very dramatic happens to change the configuration of things east of the Euphrates — has to be China. It could, by itself, have manned a two-hundred-million soldier army even as far back as the 1970s. Today, with the other nations of Asia and their massive populations, the two-hundred-million figure presents no problem at all so far as potential for fulfillment of the prophecy is concerned. And, certainly, China exerts hegemony over all of the other nations of its oriental sphere. Many within secular news media are beginning to recognize the same things those who watch Bible prophecy and current events have been recognizing for some time: China indeed looks like a major influence on factors that might bring about profound changes in the world.

Ironically, it is America and its rapidly fading wealth that has in effect funded the outfitting of that massive army that will one day destroy one-third of the world's population.[24]

The dragon nation's intentions to dominate the world recently became manifest with a display of aggression that some within U.S. government and the business community are calling "an act of war."

China's spying isn't limited to economic interests. On June 4, 2015, the Associated Press reported that China was behind a cyber attack stealing the personal identifying information of some four million federal employees across multiple agencies. "This is an attack against the nation," said Ken Ammon, chief strategy officer of Xceedium, a network security software company.[25] The attack fit the pattern of those carried out by nation states for the purpose of espionage. The information stolen, he said, "could be used to impersonate or blackmail federal employees with access to sensitive information."[26]

According to U.S. officials who spoke to the *Washington Post*, "China is building massive databases of Americans' personal information by hacking government agencies and U.S. health-care companies, using a high-tech tactic to achieve an age-old goal of espionage: recruiting spies or gaining more information on an adversary."[27]

Some top-ranking military officers who have now retired are wondering aloud as TV pundits whether China's cyber attacks might be a precursor to an attack on America's electric grid. Such an assault, if successful, could

---

24. United Nations. Sustainable Development Knowledge Platform, https://sustainabledevelopment.un.org/index.php?page=view&nr=23&type=400, accessed June 18, 2015.

25. Fox News, "US Believes China behind Cybersecurity Breach Affecting at Least 4M Federal Employees," http://www.foxnews.com/politics/2015/06/04/us-officials-massive-breach-federal-personnel-data.html, accessed March 5, 2016.

26. Ibid.

27. Ellen Nakashima, "With a Series of Major Hacks, China Builds a Database on Americans," *Washington Post*, June 5, 2015, https://www.washingtonpost.com/world/national-security/in-a-series-of-hacks-china-appears-to-building-a-database-on-americans/2015/06/05/d2af51fa-0ba3-11e5-95fd-d580f1c5d44e_story.html, accessed March 5, 2016.

destroy U.S. ability to carry on life as usual, if not permanently, certainly on a temporary basis that could last for months or years.

These military experts are wondering if World War III has already begun.

Beast State Almost Set

Daniel and John's identical prophetic visions are materializing — merging into what will become the end-times empire Antichrist will dominate. It will be more wicked than the tyrannical dictatorships of Hitler, Stalin, Mao Tse-Tung, and all the other diabolical monster regimes of human history. All the nations of prophecy being in perfect alignment is a sure signal that the Tribulation is about to begin.

It cannot fully develop until one event takes place. The Rapture must first take all believers in Christ from planet earth. This is because God the Holy Spirit is living within each believer, and He is the omnipotent force who is keeping absolute evil from bursting forth in full fury upon the world.

Rapture Ready . . . or not . . . the occurrence of that earth-rending event is as near as the next blink of the eye.

CHAPTER 7

RECALL OF HISTORY'S MOST DEADLY PRODUCT

Reason #7: The incessant call for peace and safety because of nuclear threat is an important reason to believe that this is the generation that will be left behind.

In 2015, Chrysler Corporation recalled many of its Ram pickup trucks due to defects, at a very high, bottom-line cost. Automakers fear lawsuits pointing to defective vehicle parts claimed to cause injurious or deadly accidents. They recall any product that might be defective by the thousands, costing millions of dollars to the automakers. This is because the lawsuits from accidents, plus damage to their corporate reputations, might cost in the billions of dollars if steps to remedy the potential for accidents aren't taken.

We hear of these recalls consistently. Some of us have had our own cars or trucks recalled. We usually don't mind too much, because the automaker pays for the corrective measure at our local dealership. The biggest gripe is usually the time and inconvenience involved in taking the vehicle to get it fixed. The main concern is that those we love and we, ourselves, aren't harmed because of a defective product. We usually endure the time and inconvenience in trade for peace of mind.

The recall process is, of course, the same across the whole line of products, including the foods on the shelves of grocery stores throughout the country.

Peace of mind and safety go hand in hand in the thinking of industries that produce things we consumers purchase. They know that if the consumer doesn't feel safe with the products they offer, they will soon be out of business. This is their primary motive for their concern for our peace and safety.

There is one producer of goods today that I believe is inexorably linked to end-times Bible prophecy. Further, this industry is directly involved in the creation and distribution of products that constitute a primary signal that the Church of Jesus Christ is on the very brink of being called into heaven.

A president of the United States, in giving his last address to the nation as chief executive, brought this industry into focus.

> A vital element in keeping the peace is our military establishment. Our arms must be mighty, ready for instant action, so that no potential aggressor may be tempted to risk his own destruction. . . . This conjunction of an immense military establishment and a large arms industry is new in the American experience. The total influence — economic, political, even spiritual — is felt in every city, every State house, every office of the Federal government. We recognize the imperative need for this development. Yet we must not fail to comprehend its grave implications. Our toil, resources, and livelihood are all involved; so is the very structure of our society. . . .
>
> In the councils of government, we must guard against the acquisition of unwarranted influence, whether sought or unsought, by the military-industrial complex. The potential for the disastrous rise of misplaced power exists and will persist.
>
> We must never let the weight of this combination endanger our liberties or democratic processes. We should take nothing for granted. Only an alert and knowledgeable citizenry can compel the proper meshing of the huge industrial and military machinery of defense with our peaceful methods and goals, so that security and liberty may prosper together. . . . Yet, in holding scientific research and discovery in respect, as we should, we must also be alert to the equal and opposite danger that public policy could itself become

the captive of a scientific technological elite. . . . Disarmament, with mutual honor and confidence, is a continuing imperative. Together we must learn how to compose differences, not with arms, but with intellect and decent purpose. Because this need is so sharp and apparent I confess that I lay down my official responsibilities in this field with a definite sense of disappointment. As one who has witnessed the horror and the lingering sadness of war — as one who knows that another war could utterly destroy this civilization which has been so slowly and painfully built over thousands of years — I wish I could say tonight that a lasting peace is in sight.[1]

President Dwight Eisenhower — who had been the Supreme Allied Commander during World War II — in warning about the powerful military-industrial complex that had developed framed for the world the profound truth of Bible prophecy's number one issue as indicator of Christ's soon return. His successor, John F. Kennedy, further expressed a warning about the danger posed.

Finally, to those nations who would make themselves our adversary, we offer not a pledge but a request: that both sides begin anew the quest for peace, before the dark powers of destruction unleashed by science engulf all humanity in planned or accidental self-destruction.

We dare not tempt them with weakness. For only when our arms are sufficient beyond doubt can we be certain beyond doubt that they will never be employed.

But neither can two great and powerful groups of nations take comfort from our present course — both sides overburdened by the cost of modern weapons, both rightly alarmed by the steady spread of the deadly atom, yet both racing to alter that uncertain balance of terror that stays the hand of mankind's final war.[2]

Duck and Cover!

Many today who see the old public-service-type announcements laugh and mock the ludicrous idea. "Did they really believe someone could dive

1. "Eisenhower's Farewell Address to the Nation, January 17, 1961," http://mcadams.posc.mu.edu/ike.htm, accessed March 5, 2016.
2. "Inagural Address of President John F. Kennedy, Washington, D.C., January 20, 1961," http://www.jfklibrary.org/Research/Research-Aids/Ready-Reference/JFK-Quotations/Inaugural-Address.aspx, accessed March 5, 2016.

behind a park bench or simply cover their heads with their arms while in the fetal position — that ducking and covering — would save them?" That, or other questions with amused voice inflection in offering the query is today's reaction to those long-ago instructions on how to avoid injury in a nuclear explosion.

I laugh, too, when I "watch" that commercial. (I'm now blind, remember, so can no longer "see" it.) But it wasn't quite so funny to people who lived through the time of the Cold War.

As a youngster myself in the early days when the public service announcements were shown, I honestly didn't pay much attention. I imagine that most of my generation — as children — felt about the same as I did. But our parents did have fears of what would happen to us, to America and our way of life, while they watched the proliferation of nuclear weaponry and threats the Soviet Union and "Red" China posed.

The politicians of the time placed a premium on assuring the American public that their foremost priority was to keep us safe from the Soviet bear and the Chinese dragon. At the same time, they wanted to appear to be the ones who would prevent nuclear war from destroying the world. The most prominent of examples in this regard was the political commercial that was the most accredited with totally destroying any chances of an opposition candidate as any ever aired.

Perhaps even the younger readers have seen reruns many times of the commercial. The networks — liberals all — love to run the old spot many times, particularly during presidential election seasons, as a documentary educational piece, of course, I say with tongue firmly in cheek.

The commercial, created by operatives of the Democrat Party, showed a beautiful little girl on a sunny day in a field picking flowers and counting them, as I recall. The narrator then, in an ominous, echoing tone, picked up the count, counting down toward zero.

Then, of course, the hydrogen bomb ignited. We are to surmise that that was the end of the little girl's day of flower picking in the field — and the end of the rest of us as well!

With the airing of that TV spot, Barry Goldwater, Lyndon Johnson's opponent in that 1964 election, was as much toast as we would have all been if in actuality we would have been under that mushroom cloud.

It was a landslide for Johnson's re-election. Conservatism and, in my opinion, all socio-economic sensibility went out the proverbial window.

President Johnson, in the wake of the assassination of John F. Kennedy, and basking in the light of his own overwhelming victory, ramrodded through his Great Society program, with its slogan that declared a war on poverty.

Since the implementation of that spending orgy in 1964, the U.S. government has thrown more than $22 trillion at social programs, including funding a welfare system in which 50 percent of Americans are now receiving largesse from taxpayers. The nation is broke, with a national debt of more than $19 trillion plus as of this writing. The only way things keep going is to keep printing money — dollars that are backed by nothing but faith in America's ability to repay credit debt. All of this portends economic doom sooner or later.

Daggers for Defense

Mainstream news and entertainment media support the ludicrous thinking within the political realm that proclaims it is the U.S. defense complex, alone, that has caused the spending problems. The thinking goes, if the defense budget were cut to the bare bone, there would be much more for the social programs. Johnson's Great Society might still come to fruition, if that were to happen.

There needs to be a redistribution of the wealth of the rich from within the military-industrial complex. That is where resides the pool of wealth that could otherwise be drained and used to finally have enough money to fund adequately the social needs.

So goes the insane thinking of the social engineers — of the *let's-get-it-done-like-the-European-socialist* crowd. I say "insane thinking" because the definition of "insanity," as we mentioned earlier, is to keep doing the same thing over and over even though it fails every time. The social engineers in media, academia, and government have been complicit in spending $22 trillion on creating a welfare state that is worse off now than ever. That means billions upon billions — trillions — of dollars have been thrown time after time at trying to end poverty, actions that have brought about the opposite results.

Yet these left-leaning social architects want to tear down the American military, which admittedly often spends unwisely, in my view, take the "savings," and throw those dollars again at a problem that obviously more and more money will never resolve.

This debate is for another book at another time. The point that should be made in consideration of these things for our purposes in this chapter is quite clear. The present desire to build a humanistic, poverty-free heaven on earth — totally apart from God's influence — fits precisely within the developing of what I believe to be the number one, specific, prophetic indication that Christ's call to His Church in the Rapture must be very near.

Let me explain.

We have seen that the greatest of all prophets, Jesus Christ — who is God — prophesied that He will next intervene into human history at a sudden "think not" time (see Matthew 24:44), when business is going on pretty much as usual. His coming at that unknown, unanticipated-by-the-world moment will be just like things were at the time when Noah and his family went into the ark. It will be just like it was when Lot and his family members were removed from Sodom.

The very day Noah went into the ark and Lot went out of Sodom, judgment fell and destruction began.

We look next at what another prophet foretold. The Apostle Paul spent time writing to the Thessalonian believers. His letters to them, like his letters to the Corinthians, include a great deal of writing about the Rapture of the Church. Chapter 4 of 1 Thessalonians is where we learn much about that sudden, most stunning event.

Paul then continues with prophecy about the Rapture as recorded in the following chapter — chapter 5.

> But of the times and the seasons, brethren, ye have no need that I write unto you. For yourselves know perfectly that the day of the Lord so cometh as a thief in the night. For when they shall say, Peace and safety; then sudden destruction cometh upon them, as travail upon a woman with child; and they shall not escape (1 Thessalonians 5:1–3).

Paul was talking in this instance about the same event that Jesus prophesied of in the Matthew 24: 36–42 and Luke 17: 26–30 passages.

The Apostle had just laid out the Rapture prophecy to the Thessalonians, the same basic teaching he presented in his first letter to the Corinthians, telling them that believers will be changed in the twinkling of an eye. That will come at an unknown moment, like a thief breaking in on an unsuspecting world.

Paul then said that as the time of that thief-in-the-night moment approached, people would be calling for "peace and safety."

Now this is the thing I want to emphasize. It is a dramatic point for understanding that Jesus and Paul were both talking about the stupefying moment of Rapture that will literally stagger the world of people who will be left behind.

Paul says that when "they" — and this is a pronoun indicating the world of unbelievers, not believers — "will be saying peace and safety," sudden destruction will come . . . and they will not escape that destruction. He indicates that the great convulsions — like those of a woman about to give birth — will begin. This will be the Tribulation period of which Jesus spoke in the Olivet Discourse and which John saw in his Revelation visions on Patmos.

This "sudden destruction" is the same sudden destruction that Jesus said would begin the moment He next intervenes into the affairs of man. It will be just like in the days of Noah and the days of Lot.

The Peace-and-Safety Mantra

"Recall of History's Most Deadly Product" is the title of this chapter. This will, I hope, explain why that title was chosen. The meaning is inexorably tied to the prophecy both Jesus and Paul gave for the very end of the Church Age (Age of Grace).

Both the Lord and Paul presented the same, most profound forewarning: sudden destruction will happen with one stupendous event that will be totally unanticipated by those who are unbelievers, who haven't accepted Christ as their Savior. We have looked at the scriptural proof that that event is the Rapture.

Jesus indicated that destruction will come the very day the Rapture occurs. Paul prophesied destruction will follow a plea by unbelievers for peace and safety as part of the thief-in-the-night coming of the day of the Lord, another term for God's time of judgment on a rebellious world.

So it seems clear that a strongly expressed, worldwide desire for peace and safety might well be a key signal of just how near is that moment of the Rapture.

Recalling the Nukes

We are thus brought back to the point of today's socialist engineers and all politically leftist-leaning ideologues wanting to tear down the military-industrial complex's capability to make war. They want the weapons of war-making to be scrapped and the money spent for killing to instead be allocated to more social programs so Utopia can finally be achieved. Their chief rant involves the demand that all nuclear arsenals be reduced until they are completely eliminated.

It all sounds so noble and so reasonable, doesn't it? As the late John Lennon of The Beatles fame would say, "Let's give peace a chance."

However, the prophet Jeremiah gave the war-like condition within mankind's fallen minds when he said people say "peace, peace; when there is no peace" (Jeremiah 8:11). The Neville Chamberlains of the species are still among us. So are the Adolf Hitlers!

The desire to recall history's deadliest product, as our title has it, isn't just foolishness. To do so would be an insane death wish.

Beside the staying hand of God, the geopolitical doctrine that kept nuclear war from destroying mankind during the Cold War was the one termed Mutually Assured Destruction (MAD).

The present call for peace and safety is wrapped up in the fear that nuclear conflict could break out, particularly in the Middle East. The diplomats of the world know, like Lyndon Johnson's re-election planners knew, that to keep their power and authority over the rest of us, they must at least appear to be doing all they can to allay our fears. And our greatest fear is that hydrogen bombs on the tips of ICBMs could put an end to us. We are far beyond "duck and cover"!

Therefore they are seeking to bring about arms reduction in a campaign that is never ending. They are pretending to try to convince us that they can somehow recall that nuclear genie that escaped at Alamagorda, New Mexico, in August of 1945. Such a recall will never be accomplished, but they are making their greatest show of how they intend to achieve peace and safety with a loosely knit process they call the "Roadmap for Peace."

Roadmap for False Peace

There is not a more specific indicator of where this generation stands on God's prophetic timeline than the diplomatic design wrapped up in the Roadmap for Peace developed in recent decades. Today we constantly hear a call for peace and safety like none in history.

Never before has there existed at the same time such weaponry with potential for ending all human life and such volatility in terms of probable ignition points within the millennia-long racial and ethnic hatreds of the

Middle East. With Iran's seemingly unstoppable effort to produce nuclear weapons and the missiles to deliver them, and that regime's constant proclamations that it wants Israel completely destroyed, the quest for peace is front and center at all times.

To achieve perspective on developments about this biblically prophetic plea for peace and safety at this critical juncture, we must consider the ancient roots of the evil the Bible says are at the center of the anger and hatred in the region.

Middle East End-Times Evil

Iran, the nation that is at the center of ancient Persia, seems almost without question to harbor the nucleus of the evil that threatens to start the next world war. This observation, of course, has a scriptural basis.

Daniel the prophet was told about an evil force that inhabits that geographic region. He was informed about that "prince" by one of God's emissaries — an angel — who was sent to give the prophet answers to his prayers about Israel's future.

> But the prince of the kingdom of Persia withstood me one and twenty days: but, lo, Michael, one of the chief princes, came to help me; and I remained there with the kings of Persia. Now I am come to make thee understand what shall befall thy people in the latter days: for yet the vision is for many days (Daniel 10:13–14).

Our hourly newscasts testify to the fact that the areas near Israel are inflamed with satanic rage that threatens not only Israel but the world as a whole.

The intention of the evil forces of the region — like ISIS — is to establish a worldwide caliphate, an Islamic rule over the entire earth. Iran's mullahs want the same thing as ISIS, even though they are of a different sect of Islam. Israel is known to have a powerful military and a nuclear arsenal and will fight to the death to prevent any of the forces surrounding them from defeating them in war. Therein is the crux of the diplomatic cries for peace and safety.

The Prince of Persia, we who believe in the Bible as foretelling the future are certain, will continue to fan the embers of war until the region and world are engulfed in the flames of Armageddon.

Let us look at the details of Middle Eastern issues and events of these volatile times that are leading to man's final war — those danger-fraught matters of war and peace that are causing the ever-increasing call for peace and safety by earth's diplomats. Every signal on the scene today, whether considering geopolitics, socio-economics, religion, or natural upheaval, is caught up in an unstoppable, titanic end-times storm. At the center of the vortex is the eye around which all other things swirl — the nation Israel.

The incessant call for peace — manifest in the Roadmap to Peace process — has been for a time obscured by the dark cloud of global distress and perplexities, but now is returned to the radar screens of the world's diplomats. Israel, of course, is viewed by those diplomats as the holdup to peace in the Middle East. It is the region of planet earth prophesied by the Word of God to be at the center of the great humanity-endangering storm at the very end of the age. Observers of these goings-on, especially those who watch for the unfolding of Bible prophecy, should take notice with an increased level of fascination. The Middle East is the region of the world that God, the ultimate forecaster, says will produce the most destruction in human history.

That brewing storm is undeniably upon this generation, as the Bible prophecy student knows, and the tornadic winds that it is beginning to produce are vacuuming all of humanity in every aspect into its massively expanding vortex. All is being drawn toward the valley of Megiddo and the land God promised would be Israel's forever. The last-days storm continuously has fuel added to its dynamic by players on the world's diplomatic scene. One example follows.

> JERUSALEM, June 18, 2013 (UPI) — "The only choice for Israel to remain a Jewish and democratic nation is to work toward a two-state solution," former U.S. President Bill Clinton said. Clinton was in Israel to attend celebrations marking the 90th birthday of Israeli President Shimon Peres.
>
> "You have to cobble together some kind of theory of a two-state solution, and the longer you let this go, just because of sheer demographics, the tougher it's going to get. I don't see any alternative to a Palestinian state," the former U.S. President said in a speech before the Peres Academic Center in Rehovot Monday night.[3]

Mr. Clinton, we remember, was at the helm of the U.S. ship of state during the Oslo Accords, in which Yasser Arafat was offered most anything he

---

3. "Clinton Urges 2-State Solution for Israel," UPI, June 18, 2013, http://www.upi.com/Top_News/World-News/2013/06/18/Clinton-urges-2-state-solution-for-Israel/12751371553339/.

wanted if he would agree to simply acknowledge Israel's right to exist and vow to get along. Arafat refused, leaving it all sitting on the table — demonstrating to the sane thinkers of the world that the rage at the center of the Middle East storm has nothing to do with rationality or desire to live peaceably with God's chosen nation.

Practically every Islamist country, and certainly every terrorist organization of the region, has declared at every opportunity that it wants to erase Israel from the earth.

When Anwar El Sadat, the president of Egypt, shook hands with Israeli President Menachem Begin during the Camp David Accords in 1978 as President Jimmy Carter looked on, Sadat's fate was sealed. He was soon assassinated by his Islamist brothers for wanting to make peace with the hated Jewish state.

The storm is a supernatural one, and God has told us what its course will be as we proceed deeper into history.

> For, behold, in those days, and in that time, when I shall bring again the captivity of Judah and Jerusalem, I will also gather all nations, and will bring them down into the valley of Jehoshaphat, and will plead with them there for my people and for my heritage Israel, whom they have scattered among the nations, and parted my land (Joel 3:1–2).

Again, the nuclear genie is out of the bottle. It cannot be recaptured, no matter how much the diplomats of the world squeal for its recall. America and the world face a deadly future because of their treacherous dealings with God's chosen people.

CHAPTER 8

WANNA SEE SOME NASTY END-TIME PICTURES?

Reason #8: Paul's perilous-times prophecy of 2 Timothy 3 headlines our news daily. Those characteristics of end-times man constitute a sure reason to believe that this will be the left behind generation.

It is hard to imagine living during times historians call the Dark Ages. That era encompassed, basically, the 10th and 11th centuries, a time following the final dissolution of the Roman Empire. The time was also termed the Middle Ages, and is referred to as medieval times.

It has also been characterized as the era from the 6th century through the 13th century. The reason it is so hard to define is because there was little information about the period that survived those oppressive times. As a matter of fact, this is one reason it's called "the Dark Ages." The era followed what was considered the intellectual light, or enlightenment, of Rome, and was followed by the time known as the Italian Renaissance in the 14th century.

The cerebral pictures that the imagination conjures from that time include the brutal Inquisitions carried out by the Catholic Church, which saw heresy and demonic evil in most every human activity. The Catholic ecclesiastical authorities began to do their brutish work of oppression and torture around 1184, proceeding on an increasingly tyrannical path for several centuries.

Much of Europe was immersed in the determination to stamp out what the Church inquisitors saw as apostasy, demonism, and witchcraft of every sort. Some historians of modern vintage, many coming from within the Catholic system itself, have written on those dark times in what others consider a revised fashion. Today, it is claimed that the Catholic Church had as its goal the noble purpose of saving the souls of the perpetrators of evil. But the real record seems to indicate a more sinister modus operandi.

The revisionists have it that in most cases those found guilty were relatively few, and their punishments for the most part much lighter than what is given in the picture we have had presented to us by writers of books and producers of films dealing with the period.

Like within every evil governing authority — and the medieval inquisitors were evil — there have always been those who achieve great pleasure from their own involvement in torture of their victims. There is no doubt that this was particularly true during a time when little light from the outside world could be shined on the brutality inflicted on those who were deemed heretical or worse.

Another beastly element of the time was that those in charge of the Inquisitions — like the Nazi thugs who removed Jews from their businesses during Hitler's rise to power — grabbed for themselves and the Church the possessions of those they persecuted, tortured, and murdered. Thus it is in every period of human history. The evil, when given the authority, unchecked and unbridled, not only do away with their hapless victims, they enrich themselves in the process.

We began by saying that it is hard to imagine living in those times. But there is a generation of people yet to come who will see times infinitely more brutal, believe it or not.

We are told in prophetic Scripture that this sort of evil will continue until Christ returns at Armageddon. The images those prophecies present are graphic. We have seen the images through a very brief glimpse at one period of man's history. The picture is foretold to get much, much worse. Jesus said the worst time in history is still future from our time today:

For then shall be great tribulation, such as was not since the beginning of the world to this time, no, nor ever shall be (Matthew 24:21).

More Pictures from the Past

History tells of horrific periods of atrocities. Jesus' words are thus made even more thought-provoking. The Lord foretells of a time unprecedented in the history of fallen mankind. That forewarning portrays a troubling future indeed!

Perhaps if we look in some detail through a photo album of man's past, so to speak, we can get an inkling of what the future might hold before human history finally runs its course at Christ's return to establish His millennial reign.

Man's Horrid History

The Roman Catholic Church established judicial institutions in order to carry out the Inquisitions against those thought to be guilty of heresy. Historically, the Inquisitions have been divided into four different time frames and locations: the Medieval or Episcopal Inquisition (1184), the Spanish Inquisition (1478), the Portuguese Inquisition (1536), and the Roman Inquisition (1542).

Excommunication was the typical punishment for heresy among Christians prior to the establishment of the Roman Catholic Church. However, once Catholicism became the state religion of the Roman Empire in the 4th century, heretics were considered enemies of the state. As such, they were hunted down, tortured, and sometimes punished unto death. This initially occurred under the authority of local bishops.

By the 12th century, the Roman Catholic Church developed a structure for and officially sanctioned the Inquisitions. The inquisitors were then given special jurisdiction and the authority of the papacy, whereby the pope would appoint them and give them the power to investigate and excommunicate even the most rich and powerful in the empire, providing the inquisitors vast powers. Numerous tribunals were initiated to organize the authorized eradication of heretical groups within the Holy Roman Empire.

These inquisitors were known for subjecting people to the cruelest methods of torture and punishment, which was formally authorized by the Church as a means of extracting confessions. A common method of torture and execution was to bind the accused to a stake and burn him alive. The rack was another gruesome method, whereby the accused was placed on a table with his ankles and wrists tied to pulleys at either end. The body was then pulled in opposite directions until all joints were dislocated, sometimes tearing the victim in half. The heretic's fork was popular during the Spanish Inquisition. This was a metal instrument with forks on either end that were used to pierce the victim at the base of the neck and under the jaw. It was held in place by a collar around the neck. The victim's hands were bound behind the back, forcing him to keep his head erect and preventing him from talking. Also used was the head crusher, which was a modified vice designed to secure the skull and chin in place. Tightening of a screw forced the cranium toward the chin, crushing the teeth, facial bones, eyes, and brain.

In 1326, Pope John XXII expanded the authority of the Inquisition to include the persecution of suspected witches as heretics. And in 1484, Pope Innocent VIII authorized the Inquisition to pursue witches using any means necessary to extract confessions and to kill them. Under torture, they were interrogated and asked to name others who practiced witchcraft, causing widespread panic among the population because they would name anyone and everyone to avoid further pain. Common methods of torture included sleep deprivation and dunking. In the latter, the victim would be bound to a chair and lowered into a tank of water or a pond until completely submerged until the victim was about to pass out, then the victim was pulled back up and given a chance to confess. A confession was usually followed by a death sentence. Sexual humiliation was another form of torture, including having the victim sit naked in a red-hot metal chair or having one's breasts mutilated with a red-hot iron. Those who were executed were usually killed by being burned alive at the stake, being hung in the gallows, or by being beheaded.

The Enlightenment in the 18th century led to the banning of torture in the legal codes of Europe. However, the 20th century saw its revival. In Stalin's gulags, a popular form of extracting confessions from those deemed to be enemies of the state were repeated beatings using rubber straps, sand bags, and wooden mallets. The assaults could go on for days, with the perpetrators taking shifts. Another form of torture was to truss a prisoner using a long, rough-fibered towel that was placed between the jaws like a horse's bridle, then strung over the shoulders and tied to the feet, flexing the spine to the point of nearly breaking it. Prisoners would be left like that on a cold stone floor without food or water for days on end. Execution by a firing squad was likely a welcome end to the pain and humiliation of the gulag prisoners.

Another sadist came on the scene in 1933 Germany: Adolf Hitler. Torture of the Jews and other prisoners of the Holocaust was commonplace. Victims were exposed to the elements, starved, and worked until death if they were not gassed first. Human medical experiments were brutal. Women were sterilized by having chemicals injected into their reproductive organs, and some were killed so an autopsy could be performed to confirm the success of the procedure.

To study the effects of hypothermia on the body, victims were dunked into ice-cold water where they were kept for up to five hours at a time if they survived the experience.

Dr. Josef Mengele had a fascination with twins and experimented on them in an attempt to discover the cause of blond hair, blue eyes, and multiple births. Doing so would give him the ability to rapidly advance the Aryan race. These children had organs removed, including their eyes; amputations of limbs; and castrations — all performed without anesthesia. One twin would be injected with a disease such as tuberculosis or typhus, then both twins were killed and autopsied to study the effects of those diseases. Some were killed by an injection of chloroform to the heart, causing the blood to coagulate, resulting in death. Other prisoners also suffered amputation as an experiment to see if limbs and joints could survive a transplant.

Heinrich Himmler ordered the artificial insemination of women prisoners through a variety of experimental techniques. These women were tied down naked on tables and mocked and taunted by the experimenters who would tell them they had been inseminated by an animal and would give birth to a monster. There seemed no limit to human depravity.

No sooner did Hitler commit suicide in 1945 then genocidal maniac and Marxist, Mao Tse-tung, founder of the communist Peoples Republic of China, come on the scene in 1949. Mao takes the title for the greatest mass murderer of all time. Although the numbers are debatable, many credit Mao with the deaths of more than 70 million of his own people — during peace time — in his quest for world dominance. This compared to Stalin's 40 million and Hitler's 30 million, both during times of war. The 20th century should be known as the century of genocide.

Mao was no stranger to torture, either. In addition to murder, rape, beatings, forced labor, and starvation, his victims suffered atrocities such as being buried alive, having their ears sliced off, tendons cut, being led around by wire that had pierced their nose or ears, being publicly humiliated, and being executed.

Cambodia's Pol Pot pales in comparison, having killed 1.7 million of his political enemies between 1975 and 1979. His forms of torture included burning prisoners with cigarettes and electric shocks, ripping out their fingernails, force feeding them feces, beating them with wire, sticks, and fists, or covering them with an enraged batch of scorpions or centipedes.

Iraq's Saddam Hussein deserves mention, having killed some 600,000 Kurds, Shi'ites, and Kuwaitis between 1979 and his overthrow in 2003, and torturing countless more. He killed masses of Kurds by gassing them with nerve agents such as Sarin and mustard gas. Others were gunned down in mass graves. Hussein's methods were especially sadistic, as he tortured and killed children in front of their parents and fed their bodies to wild dogs. Prisoners were beaten without mercy, fingers and toes shattered with their nails yanked out. Some were buried alive up to their necks and left to die in the heat if wild animals didn't kill them first.

Since then we have seen the rise of Al Qaeda, Hamas, Hezbollah, and the notoriously barbaric ISIS. Video footage of beheadings soon turned to the burning alive of prisoners in cages, the drowning of prisoners in cages, mass shootings into shallow graves, and ISIS children as young as nine or ten shown executing prisoners by both beheading and shooting. Horrific stories from women fortunate enough to escape tell of the brutal rapes and humiliation of Christian and Yazidi young girls and women — victims of sexual slavery at the hands of ISIS.

And as chants of "Death to America" and "Death to Israel" echoed all over the Middle East, President Barack Obama was telling the world to proceed with a global agreement that will surely put nuclear weapons and ICBMs into the hands of Iran in a decade or less. These are indeed perilous times.

The foregoing unfathomable evil that man has perpetrated on his fellow man, believe it or not, is merely a warm-up for things to come, according to the Lord Jesus Christ. The Tribulation era will far surpass anything the likes of Hitler and Stalin have been able to conjure from the pits of their demonically inspired minds. Jesus gave the following speech while sitting atop the Mount of Olives just before facing His crucifixion. He was speaking of the last seven years of the age leading up to His Second Advent.

> For then shall be great tribulation, such as was not since the begin-
> ning of the world to this time, no, nor ever shall be (Matthew 24:21).

That era is yet future from our perspective today. The Bible has something
to say about our present time as precursor to that Tribulation era that will be
the most horror-filled period of all human history.

Paul Pictures Perilous Times

While Jesus and the prophets of the Old and New Testaments gave sometimes vivid descriptions of things to come in the horrific future period
known as the Tribulation, it is the great Apostle Paul who gives specific
depictions of end-times mankind. He characterizes in detail precisely how
people who make up the very end of the age will comport themselves. It is a
series of pictures that is especially disturbing because of the reality that Paul's
portrayal looks like the world around us at this very moment.

Let's look closely at these end-of-the-age characterizations. Paul begins
with the introduction of 2 Timothy 3:1–5:

> This know also, that in the last days perilous times shall come.
> For men shall be lovers of their own selves, covetous, boasters,
> proud, blasphemers, disobedient to parents, unthankful, unholy,
> without natural affection, trucebreakers, false accusers, incontinent,
> fierce, despisers of those that are good, traitors, heady, highminded,
> lovers of pleasures more than lovers of God; having a form of godli-
> ness, but denying the power thereof. . . .

Men shall be lovers of their own selves

Psychologists and sociologists have for years planted in the minds of Americans that self-esteem is something that is important to making a successful
life. These point to the fact that at the center of most every problem of the
human condition resides the feelings of inadequacy and self-loathing.

We are told that the radical Islamists who attacked on September 11,
2001, did so because they felt inferior due to U.S. treatment that looked
down upon them. The whole matter involving the attacks that took the lives
of more than three thousand that day therefore convinced those in charge
of the U.S. State Department to employ a study group designed to help
determine how to make those who hate us, particularly in the Middle East,
no longer hate us.

So ingrained is self-love in our nation that, in delusion, we covet the admiration of those who hate us with satanic rage born out of our support for Israel, not out of envy and low self-esteem on the terrorists' part.

The terrorists, murderers, gang members, rapists, and all other of those who commit crimes these days are analyzed by the woolly-minded psychologists and sociologists based upon the premise that the perpetrators hate themselves, thus all others who they see as deserving of their victimization.

God's Word says, "For no man ever yet hated his own flesh" (Ephesians 5:29). In other words, self-loathing is not part of our DNA. Quite the opposite is true. The Bible says that those who have not the Holy Spirit are of their father, the devil. Satan is the ultimate example of self-love.

The social engineers tell us the secret to ultimately producing a healthy cultural environment is high self-esteem. A sense of self-worth will make man live up to his own great expectations.

Rather than love of self, however, God's Word tells us to love others, to esteem others more than ourselves, to humble ourselves before God. This generation is obviously doing none of these.

Men shall be . . . covetous

One of the most obvious pictures of this ugly, end-times characteristic is presented when we consider how the U.S. federal government has created class envy as part of the political process. The politicians promise government care from cradle to grave, with guarantees to a welfare base of ever-growing proportions, paid for on the backs of those who are responsible and work hard to sustain their own families. The bureaucracy in Washington, D.C., grows more massive by the year and feeds on this untenable structure that will one day come tumbling down from its own weight.

This is not to denigrate those who are incapable of working because of mental or physical problems. Certainly, these people must have help. Their needs are legitimate. But statistics show that more than 94 million who are sound of mind and body are out of work as of this writing, a high percentage of that number having voluntarily dropped out of the workforce to accept government largesse in one form or the other. The politicians drive the wedge deeper and deeper between the workers and non-workers in order to provide themselves ever-increasing numbers of voters who will continue to put their idle hands out for taxpayer earnings.

Too many governmental leaders covet all the power and treasure the gargantuan American vaults can provide. They thus, in most cases, will leave what they consider their personal power perches only when the voting public gets fed up with them. Many then go on to lobbyist or other jobs of wealth-provision they have carved for themselves while posing as public servants.

Class envy (or covetousness) therefore is a permanently ingrained societal ill that the Bible says will be part of the days leading up to Christ's return.

Men shall be . . . boasters, proud

These two disturbing images reflecting back as we peer into the mirror of this generation are things I have presented before in a volume on Bible prophecy. I can't improve on my previous depiction. I find these characteristics haven't changed for the better. Here they are again, edited and excerpted to some extent.

> Following closely on the heels of covetousness — actually an outgrowth of it — are the dual vanities within the heart of end-time man. These people are boasters; they are extremely proud.
>
> Jesus said, "Blessed are the meek [humble] for they shall inherit the earth [the millennial earth]."
>
> The father of those whose characters exhibit the antithesis of humility is Satan. Lucifer was the greatest boaster of them all. "I shall put my star above the throne of the most high," he said in his supremely prideful arrogance. He seduced Eve in the Garden of Eden with the same prideful boast and promise. "Ye shall be as God," he told her. When Adam yielded, all humankind became genetic heirs to the great pride that first welled in Lucifer's heart.
>
> Again, we see the boasting and the pride in our children. We can remember our own childhood experiences. We made claims, each having to be bigger and better or farther or faster than the boast that went before.
>
> Politicians are living, breathing proof of boastfulness and pride, while they vie for a chance to "serve" us. How quickly the boasts turn bitter and ring hollow when they become inaccessible and self-willed after election time. They become little lords; we become

revenue producers for the wastefulness of bureaucracy. The rhetoric of the campaign stump, whether on the courthouse lawn, door to door, or in media propaganda, is a strange alchemy of prideful boasting and humble exhortation.

Yet we who are victimized time after time have no room to complain; it is the American political process in action. It is the process we have allowed to stray far from the noble designs of the founding fathers, a process we perpetuate through our acquiescence. This is not cynicism — it is fact.

Such pride has given the Supreme Court a de facto authority. They execute, legislate, and adjudicate such marvelously innovative things as: 1) the forbidding of prayer in public schools; 2) abortion on demand; 3) in effect, evolution as a religion; 4) the softening of the legal system to the extent that criminals now feel they have a green light to plunder, rape, and murder; 5) interpreting homosexuality as deserving moral and legal status equivalent to that given heterosexual marriages; 6) made a mockery of the First Amendment by pampering pornographers in film and other entertainment venues at every juncture, while at the same time banning Bible reading and all mention of the true, living God from classrooms in public schools and calling "hate speech" anything that pushes back against the gross immorality rampant today.

Like Satan himself, our judiciary over recent decades has ascended to such heights that it serves as documented proof that we have little to be prideful or boastful about as a people who have allowed it to happen.[1]

Men shall be . . . blasphemers

This generation has witnessed an attempt to remove the name of Jesus Christ from every public forum, especially when federal government has a say on matters involved. There are numerous attempts to remove the name of God from most every governmental building. The Ten Commandments are under fire by the God-haters, with a continuous effort to have them removed from public places. The declaration "In God we trust" is under growing assault.

---

1. Terry James, "Characteristics of End-Time Man," *Storming Toward Armageddon* (Green Forest, AR: New Leaf Press, 1992), p. 27–28.

So blasphemy against the God of heaven isn't anything new in America. But blasphemy has taken on a whole new level of activist effort in very recent days.

The following news story gives evidence of how blasphemy — the effort to express man's hatred for God — is on the rise.

A crowd of several hundred gathered Saturday night to see Detroit's newest resident: a 9-foot, 2,000-pound statue of a goat-headed occult idol named Baphomet.

The Satanic Temple unveiled the bronze figure to an estimated 700 attendees at an undisclosed location. The group's initial venue canceled after local religious groups protested.

The group's approach to secrecy with the second venue led to little opposition on Saturday, Director of the Detroit Satanic Temple chapter and national spokeswoman Jex Blackmore told Fox News.

"Protesters arrived for a short time at our first ticketing location, but retreated after only about 30 minutes," Blackmore said. "One woman attempted to block the event entrance and was removed by the police in cooperation with the building's owner."

Guests were washed in red light shining down from the rafters at the venue as "dark punk" bands played and DJs performed from a stage located beneath a lighted, upside-down crucifix. Satanic Temple officials delivered speeches and a pair of shirtless men held candles on either side of the statue, prior to its unveiling.

Despite the dark pageantry, however, the Temple says its concept of Lucifer is as a literary figure. "The mission of The Satanic Temple is to encourage benevolence and empathy among all people," the group's website states.

The statue will now be stored out of public view until the Temple can find it a permanent home. The group hopes to display it at the Arkansas State Capitol, next to a monument of the Ten Commandments.[2]

God's name has been all but officially removed from public education in America — in itself a blasphemous thing. But His name is at the same time

---

2. Cody Derespina, "Satanic Temple Unveils Goat-Headed Statue in Detroit," FoxNews.com, July 27, 2015, http://www.foxnews.com/us/2015/07/27/for-one-night-devil-is-in-detroit/, accessed August 8, 2015.

in practically every theater in America. Jesus Christ is unmentionable in public forums because His holy name represents a narrow-minded viewpoint and would offend. Religion, if it is to be mentioned, must represent an eclectic view — must encompass an ecumenical theological viewpoint.

In almost every film above the rating of G, the name of Jesus Christ is repeated frequently. It seems as if screenwriters are required to use His Holy Name blasphemously a minimum number of times per scene. Always, the name of God, the name of Jesus, is used in one of two ways: 1) as an expression of frustration, exasperation, or anger; or 2) to portray the fanaticism of one religious zealot or another, usually a character who is dangerously insane.

Is it any wonder that a blasphemous generation of young people rejects discipline and self-control, when adults have spent decades producing an anti-God language? Even Christian parents have slowly become desensitized, thereby giving into this blasphemous language's insidious, venomous effects.

Men shall be . . . disobedient to parents

Almost daily, reports assault our eyes and ears telling of children committing crimes of the most heinous sort. In my own state recently, a 14-year-old boy was arrested for having bludgeoned his grandfather and grandmother to death because he resented being what was reported to be proper discipline.

According to *The Daily Telegraph*, children are increasingly being investigated for violent crimes against their parents, crimes including robbery, murder, and assault. Violence against a parent by a child under the age of 18 increased 61 percent in a two-year period, including children as young as 7. "The Metropolitan Police figures showed 1,417 children under 18 were treated as suspects in violent crimes against parents in 2014, up from just 895 in 2012."[3]

God's Word says there will come a time in human history when children will betray parents. This has already come to pass in one instance. The Hitler youth movement, dissatisfied with the perceived weakness of German parents, removed the children and trained them in Nazi ways for the purpose of

---

3. David Barrett, "Children as Young as Seven Accused of Violent 'Crime' on Parents," *The Telegraph*, May 6, 2015, http://www.telegraph.co.uk/news/uknews/crime/11586949/ Children-as-young-as-seven-accused-of-violent-crime-on-parents.html, accessed August 8, 2015.

properly educating them. The children became tools of the state for spying on those who resisted the regime. When parents refuse to accept responsibility, government, ostensibly to preserve the order of things and promote the general welfare, will.

During the soon-to-come Tribulation, Antichrist and associates will no doubt use the same tactics as Hitler did. It will be relatively easy to institute such a system because uncaring or too-busy parents will have paved the way by handing the most horrendous dictatorship in history a generation of children ripe for the picking.

Jesus said in Luke 18:16: "Suffer little children to come unto me, and forbid them not."

Sunday school rooms remain more than half-empty while parents selfishly seek other things to do on Sundays. By so doing, they forbid children from coming to the One who can make them truly productive people. A primary command to parents by God is given by the Apostle Paul in Ephesians 6:4: "Provoke not your children to wrath: but bring them up in the nurture and admonition of the Lord."

Parents who refuse these commands of the living God risk reaping a bitter harvest of disobedience. We can look around us today and see the terrible consequences of rebellion taking their toll on this generation of young people.

Men shall be . . . unthankful

Although President Abraham Lincoln officially instituted a national day of Thanksgiving in April of 1863, Americans already had a long tradition of showing thankfulness to the God of heaven for blessings bestowed. As far back as the autumn of 1621, William Bradford, governor of Plymouth Colony, called for a day of thanksgiving and prayer for a bountiful harvest, a celebration that was eventually adopted by other colonies in New England.

It is sad to have to say that today there is not only a lack of such thankfulness, but much of pop culture now looks at God's blessings with increasing disdain.

Ariana Grande is a 21-year-old American pop singer worth a reported $5 million. She wandered into a donut shop on the Fourth of July where several trays of fresh donuts decorated with red, white, and blue frosting were on the counter. To show her thankfulness to this country and the

Americans who buy her products, she first acted like she was licking the donuts, then had this to say: "What the f— is that? I hate Americans. I hate America. That's disgusting!"[4]

To be seen as a spoiled brat is considered hip and cool in these closing days of the age. We only have to remember reports of the deportment of some of the nation's and world's youthful celebrities to understand that this end-times characteristic is a major part of this generation.

Men shall be . . . unholy

Paul's end-times characteristic, unholy, is front and center in American society today. The most holy of institutions — given by God Himself — has been summarily dismissed as no longer valid. The Supreme Court's letting the Lord know that He is no longer relevant is the most stinging representation of this characteristic I can fathom. The court's decision has opened up a floodgate to all sorts of perversions of God's created order.

Five days after the Supreme Court ruling on same-sex marriage, polygamist Nathan Collier filed an application at the Yellowstone County Courthouse in Montana, seeking a state-sanctioned marriage license so that he could marry a second wife, Christine. He and Christine were married in a religious ceremony in 2007. He legally married his first wife, Victoria, in 2000. Collier cited marriage equality, and believes if same-sex marriage is now legally considered equal to heterosexual marriage, polygamy or plural marriages deserve the same recognition. "We just want to add legal legitimacy to an already happy, strong, loving family," Collier said.[5]

Unthankfulness and unholiness go hand in hand, in my view. To be truly thankful to God, one must be holy, that is, a believer that God is the provider of all things good. This is a generation of unthankful, unholy people. They know neither the God of the Bible nor seek to know Him. The only way to know the Father is to know the Son, Jesus Christ, who said as recorded in John 14:6: "I am the way, the truth, and the life: no man cometh unto the Father, but by me."

4. Peter Sblendorio, "Ariana Grande Will Not Face Charges for Donut-Licking Incident," *New York Daily News*, July 13, 2015, http://www.nydailynews.com/entertainment/music/ariana-grande-not-face-charges-for-donut-licking-incide-article-1.2290969, accessed August 8, 2015.
5. Randy DeSoto, "Western Journalism, Right after the Supreme Court's Gay Marriage Ruling, This Man Attempted Something Shocking," July 20, 2015, http://www.westernjournalism.com/right-after-the-supreme-courts-gay-marriage-ruling-this-man-attempted-something-shocking/, accessed August 8, 2015.

The world today views the biblical truth that Jesus Christ is the only way to God as a narrow or closed-minded concept that cannot and will not be tolerated by an enlightened people of the 21st century.

A holy, thankful people in the eyes of God must desire to worship and serve Him. In Joshua 24:15, God commands: "Choose you this day whom ye will serve."

This subsequent passage records God's command for not only the children of Israel, but for all mankind: "Fear the Lord [reverence, worship Him], and serve him in sincerity and in truth: and put away [all other gods]" (Joshua 24:14). One quick glance around us tells the story. Man is obsessed with many things other than the God of the Bible. These are the days of a truly unholy, unthankful generation.

Men shall be . . . *without natural affection*

There is no greater love in nature than a mother for her young. At least God created things to be that way. America has allowed the anti-God forces in this nation to pervert God's natural order. Babies are murdered in the wombs of their mothers — with their mothers' full cooperation in most cases. More than 57 million children have thus been slaughtered since *Roe v. Wade* in 1973.

In 2015, explicit proof of the beastly nature of this wanton killing of helpless little ones came to light. The pro-life group, Center for Medical Progress, spent 30 months obtaining undercover video footage of meetings with senior executives, including Planned Parenthood Rocky Mountains vice president and medical director, Savita Ginde. The group began releasing the footage to the public in July 2015. In those videos, representatives of Planned Parenthood, including Ginde, are shown discussing the sale of aborted baby parts for profit, one such discussion occurring over lunch while swilling wine.

In the fifth video, director of research for Planned Parenthood Gulf Coast, Melissa Farrell, openly discussed how abortion procedures could be adjusted in such a way that the entire five and one-half month-old fetus' body could be delivered intact, presumably to best afford the infants' body parts for sale.

"We can get creative about when and where, and under what conditions we can um, interject something that is specific to the tissue procurement needs. . . . If we alter our process, we are able to obtain intact fetal cadavers, then we can make it part of the budget that any dissections are this, and splitting the specimens in different shipments in this. I mean, that's, it's all just a matter of line items," said Director Farrell.[6]

In the seventh video, Holly O'Donnell, a licensed phlebotomist formerly working as a tissue procurement technician for biotech company StemExpress, gives testimony of her assignment to harvest a brain from a late-term aborted male baby whose heart was still beating.

> "Hey Holly, come over here, I want you to see something kind of cool, kind of neat," O'Donnell says her supervisor told her. "And she just taps the heart, and it starts beating. And I'm sitting here and I'm looking at this fetus, and its heart is beating, and I don't know what to think."[7]

The medical technician was quite pleased that the baby was intact, allowing her to "procure a lot from it. We're going to procure a brain." The technician then instructed Holly to do the unthinkable. She told her that in order to procure that brain, they would have to cut through the baby's face. The technician proceeded to cut through the baby's jaw and mouth, instructing Holly to finish the job by cutting through "the middle of the face" to get to the brain.[8]

> "I can't even describe what that feels like," Holly said. She then had to dispose of the remains in a biohazard bag and "then I realized I was the only person ever to hold that baby. . . . That was the moment I realized I couldn't work for them anymore," she said.[9]

This casual attitude about human life — considering the unborn as non-entities, as nuisances to be eliminated, or as tissue to be utilized — is also precisely the mindset that God's Word says will pervade the generation alive in the era immediately preceding the Apocalypse, Armageddon, and the return of Jesus Christ to earth.

6. Katie Pavlich, "Fifth Video Shows Planned Parenthood Official Willing to Sell Whole Baby Bodies For Intact Parts," Townhall.com, August 04, 2015, http://townhall.com/tipsheet/katiepavlich/2015/08/04/breaking-fifth-planned-parenthood-video-shows-n2034355, accessed August 8, 2015.
7. "Human Capital, Episode 3: Planned Parenthood's Custom Abortions for Superior Product," The Center for Medical Progress, https://www.youtube.com/watch?v=FzMAycMMXp8, accessed August 20, 2015.
8. Ibid.
9. Ibid.

People have been convinced by humanists — the social engineers who claim to want to save planet earth through human effort, apart totally from God Almighty — that these little ones are not people, that the unborn are not yet human. But God — whom the humanists in their critical-thinking, values-clarifying, no-moral-absolutes philosophizing consider to be dead — says something diametrically different.

God told Jeremiah the prophet,

> Before I formed thee in the belly I knew thee; and before thou camest forth out of the womb I sanctified thee, and I ordained thee a prophet unto the nations (Jeremiah 1:5).

The Psalmist wrote under God's inspiration:

> For he knoweth our frame; he remembereth that we are dust (Psalm 103:14).

God's Word records in Luke 1:41–44 that the child within the womb is indeed fully a person. Elizabeth, the mother of John the Baptist, said upon greeting Mary, the mother of Jesus, while both were pregnant with those babies:

> For, lo, as soon as the voice of thy salutation sounded in mine ears, the babe leaped in my womb for joy (Luke 1:44).

God Himself tells us that the embryo, the fetus, the unborn child, is every bit as much a living human being as the child who has taken breath.

Paul the Apostle says that the last generation before Christ's return will be marked by the trait "without natural affection" — or without love — for the most basic kind of relationship such as the mother for her baby still in the womb. People of that generation will, God's Word says, prefer convenience to responsibility. Millions upon millions of abortions, the vast majority of them nothing less than contraception after the fact, have marked this as the generation that has perpetrated the worst infanticide in recorded times.

Men shall be . . . trucebreakers

Geopolitical Truce-breaking

Communism of the Soviet and Chinese kind, as well as every other variety, presents in microcosm and typifies the last-days' characteristics termed by the Apostle Paul as trucebreakers. The number of incidents of Communists lying and going back on their word is legendary, though the liberal-minded of the West just don't seem to get it. Today's Western diplomats — especially those within the United States presidential administration since 2008 — seem to get it even less than did other administrations during the Cold War era.

The Obama administration has observably been outplayed by the Persian chess-masters at every point during Iran's ongoing development of nuclear weapons capability. This process represents the best example of this characteristic as given in Paul's perilous-times prophecy.

The stated goal of the multilateral Non Proliferation of Nuclear Weapons Treaty (NPT) is to prevent the spread of nuclear weapons, to eventually achieve nuclear disarmament, and to promote cooperation in the peaceful use of nuclear energy by allowing equal access to nuclear technology for all States parties. A total of 190 parties have signed on to the treaty, including all five of the nuclear-weapon States. Iran signed on in 1968 and ratified the agreement in 1970. It remains in effect today. The NPT established a safeguard system to build confidence and assure compliance by assigning inspections responsibility to the International Atomic Energy Agency (IAEA). The IAEA was given the authority to conduct inspections of nuclear facilities to make sure fissile materials were not being diverted for weapons use.

In January 1993, concern for Iran's compliance was first reported to Congress. Again in 2003, and every year following, State Department reports to Congress have found Iran to be in violation of the treaty. Beginning in 2006, the IAEA has made multiple reports regarding Iran's noncompliance to the United Nations Security Council. As a result, numerous resolutions demanding Iran cease its nuclear activities have passed, and harsh economic sanctions against Iran have been imposed by the European Union, the United Nations, and the United States.

In spite of this long, deceptive, and dangerous history revealing Iran's ambitions for obtaining nuclear weapons, and after extensive secret negotiations, on July 14, 2015, the Joint Comprehensive Plan of Action (JCPOA) between Iran and the P5+1 nations (United States, Britain, China, France, Germany, and Russia) was signed. This agreement reportedly will not only reduce the inspection rights of the IAEA, but also limit the United States' ability to respond to Iranian violations, and will put Iran on the path to obtaining a nuclear weapon in as little as ten years. It will also put over $100 billion in the hands of the world's largest State sponsor of terrorism, which

Secretary of State John Kerry freely admits will likely be used to fund terrorism against the West.

Trucebreakers of a truly dangerous sort are front and center in these closing days of this Church Age. The fact that Persian nuclear weapons will soon threaten Israel, the United States, and every other nation on earth makes Iran a chief reason this generation has entered perilous times.

Russia continues in the style of Soviet truce-breaking. The present presidential administration appears as inadequate to deal with the likes of Russian leadership as with the Iranian ayatollahs.

The Intermediate Nuclear Forces Treaty (INF) was signed by General Secretary Mikhail Gorbachev, of the former Soviet Union, and United States President Ronald Reagan in December 1987. It came in to force in June 1988. It was an agreement to not test, produce, or possess nuclear or conventional ground-launched ballistic and cruise missiles with an intermediate range as defined by 300 to 3,400 miles.

While Russia disputes the charges, the United States began suspecting Russia of INF violations as early as 2008, and by 2011 thought them to be a serious compliance concern. The State Departments senior arms control official, Rose Gottemoeller, formally raised this concern with Russian officials in 2013 without resolution. By January 2014, American officials reported to the North Atlantic Treaty Organization allies (NATO) that Russia had tested a ground launch cruise missile, yet the Obama Administration refused to call it a violation of the INF treaty.

Perhaps this is one thing Obama was talking about when he was caught on a hot mic just prior to the 2012 election telling then Russian President Dmitry Medvedev that he would have more flexibility after the election. Medvedev assured Obama that he would let Vladimir know.

Michaela Dodge, senior policy analyst, defense and strategic policy expert for the Heritage Foundation, criticized the Obama administration for its failure to act against Russia in its blatant violation of the INF treaty. Dodge said:

> The President, the State Department, and the Chairman of the Joint Chiefs of Staff raised the INF violations with their Russian counterparts to no avail. The Administration did not properly communicate deadlines to Russia for coming back into compliance with the treaty, and has failed to hold Russia accountable.

As a consequence, Russian violations have gone unreported and unpunished for years. . . .

The President must exercise leadership and recognize that his benevolent approach to Russia has emboldened Russia's aggression rather than encouraging a more constructive relationship.[10]

Marriage Truce-breaking

There is an epidemic of truce-breaking in arenas other than geopolitics. It is estimated by some sociologists that as many as one out of two marriages in the United States — that is, people now being married, not necessarily including marriages made in past decades — end in divorce. The most basic truce, treaty, or pact is that made between man and woman to be husband and wife. God ordained marriage to be monogamous and to last a lifetime.

Hollywood has represented the contemporary marriage as a contract to be broken at any time or one to be ignored whenever expediency demands a one-night stand or weekend getaway with someone other than one's husband or wife. Young people now have what seems almost a legitimate excuse to avoid marriage or to at least have an experimental live-in relationship before marriage. "Why have marriage," they can ask, "when the commitment of the marriage vow is so lightly treated in practice?" The widespread practice of divorce in this culture has been based on the wishful thinking of adults while its tragic cost has been borne by children.

Barbara Dafoe Whitehead, co-director of Rutgers' National Marriage Project and director of Civil Society Studies at the Institute for American Values, is a well-known author on the topics of marriage, family, and the well-being of children. In her book *The Divorce Culture*, she analyzed the social significance and history of divorce, as well as the ethical problems of divorce when it comes to its effects on children.

The rate of divorce doubled in the United States between 1965 and 1975 before reaching its peak in 1979 and then leveling out in 1994 when 20 out of every 1,000 women were divorced. Today, nearly half of all children will become victims of divorce before reaching the age of 18.

---

10. Morgan Chalfant, "Report Slams Obama Administration for Doing Nothing to Punish Russian Violation of INF Treaty," *The Washington Free Beacon*, August 3, 2015, http:// freebeacon.com/national-security/report-slams-obama-administration-for-doing-nothing-to-punish-russian-violation-of-inf-treaty/, accessed August 8, 2015.

This cultural shift reflects a changing view of marriage from one in which American adults began to see marriage as about their own self-fulfillment instead of subordinating their personal desires to the needs of their children. Personal happiness of the adults is now the standard as it relates to marriage, and the happiness and well-being of children comes in a distant second.

According to Whitehead, this changing cultural attitude can be attributed to the sexual revolution of the 1960s and 1970s, which changed "the locus of divorce from the outer social world to the inner world of the self . . . the family, once the realm of the fettered and obligated self, [became] a fertile realm for exploring the potential of the self, unfettered by roles and obligations."[11]

Whitehead wonders whether our general acceptance of divorce without placing any blame or responsibility on the divorcing adults has muted any critical ethical discussion on the impacts divorce is having on our society. Whitehead writes:

> The truth is that divorce involves a radical redistribution of hardship, from adults to children, and therefore cannot be viewed as a morally neutral act.[12]

Truce-breaking has become a profoundly American characteristic, made so based upon unfaithfulness to the marriage vow.

Men shall be . . . false accusers

If one wishes to look to a single area within American life where false accusation runs unchecked, it is best exemplified by the political process at all levels. False accusations and false accusers are generally accepted as normal in today's society as a whole, but in politics — as is said of love and war — all is fair.

False accusation is nothing more or less than lying in order to seek and to gain advantage for one's self — to the denigration of the one being accused. Lies, then, are at the heart of that described in 1 Timothy 3 by Paul.

Lying to avoid punishment or to gain advantage has always been the human thing to do. Corporations and kingdoms have been built on

---

11. William C. Spohn, "The American Myth of Divorce," Santa Clara University, Markkula Center for Ethics, http://www.scu.edu/ethics/publications/iie/v9n2/divorce.html, accessed August 8, 2015.
12. Ibid.

deception of every sort. The trait of lying — of falsely accusing for personal gains — the Scripture says, is a heart problem:

> The heart is deceitful above all things, and desperately wicked (Jeremiah 17:9).

One of the most blatant examples of false accusation I can think of took place as part of the 2012 American presidential campaign.

During the 2012 presidential campaign between former Republican Massachusetts Governor Mitt Romney and Democrat incumbent President Barack Obama, then Senate majority leader Harry Reid took to the podium on the floor of the United States Senate and openly accused the republican challenger, Mitt Romney, of failing to pay his taxes for a period of ten years. Reid cited an anonymous source at Bain Capital, a private equity and venture capital firm cofounded by Romney from which he had retired in 2002, ten years previously.

Romney eventually released his tax returns from the previous two years and submitted a letter from his tax advisers summarizing the taxes he had paid over the prior 20 years, proving Leader Reid's accusations completely false.

In a 2015 interview with Dana Bash of CNN, who recalled the incident and mentioned that some had characterized his false accusations as "McCarthyite," Bash questioned him on the matter, wondering if he had any regrets. His smug response? "Well, they can call it whatever they want . . . Romney didn't win, did he?"[13]

False accusations are hurled by those who push the homosexual agenda in today's America. The news and entertainment industry are more than willing to pick up on the invective and magnify it at every opportunity.

Many other instances of false accusations come to mind, especially in the current political climate of radical progressivism. For example, if one disagrees with the policies of the progressives when it comes to welfare, immigration, or a variety of other issues, that individual is labeled a racist. Or, if one supports natural marriage, and believes — according to mountains of social science evidence — that children do best and deserve to be raised by their married, biological parents, well, those individuals are now falsely accused of being homophobic bigots. And it doesn't stop at a false

---

13. Alex Rogers, "Harry Reid: No Regrets over False Romney Charges," *Time*, March 31, 2015, http://time.com/3765158/harry-reid-mitt-romney-no-taxes/, accessed August 8, 2015.

accusation. Those false accusers have rapidly become persecutors of anyone who dissents — they seek to destroy their businesses, their reputations, and even threaten their lives.

Take for example the case of a young Christian family living in the small town of Gresham, Oregon, who owned and operated their own small business, Sweet Cakes by Melissa. Yes, *owned*, past tense. They have now gone out of business after refusing to bake a wedding cake for a lesbian couple and being sued for $135,000 as a result. They not only lost the case, they were slapped with a gag order, forbidding them to speak about their Christian beliefs as the reason for their refusal.

According to Paul Kengor, author of *Takedown: From Communists to Progressives, How the Left Has Sabotaged Family and Marriage*, "The Klein family will be among the first victims in the cultural left's crusade against people who refuse to redefine their faith's 2,000-year standard for natural, traditional, biblical marriage. . . . Prepare yourself to watch a lot of hate and anger and intolerance from the forces [of] 'tolerance.' I warned people: do not trust the left with same-sex marriage!"[14]

Men shall be . . . incontinent

Webster's Third Dictionary defines "incontinent" as: "marked by lacking control, unrestrained evil appetites; inability, disinclination to resist impulse [as in alcoholism]."

Every major civilization in recorded history has ultimately come to a time when the symptoms wrapped up in tile term "incontinent" overwhelmed society. Perhaps Edward Gibbons' *Decline and Fall of the Roman Empire* is the most complete account of such a deterioration. The Apostle Paul tells us that the last generation of human history will also come to be predominantly incontinent, not only in conduct but in its very character.

A lack of self-discipline and self-control is a growing monster straining at the tethers of law, order, and common sense. These restraints are themselves perpetually under the abrasive, corrosive attacks of luciferic agencies that seek to replace all traces of godly influence with humanism. We have witnessed this perilous time's manifestation played out through rioting in American streets recently.

---

14. Paul Bremmer, *World Net Daily*, " 'Gay Marriage' All about Attacking Christianity, Says Author," August 1, 2015, http://www.wnd.com/2015/08/gay-marriage-all-about-attacking-christianity-says-author/, accessed August 8, 2015.

The most recent wave of race-based mass violence occurred in Ferguson, Missouri, and Baltimore, Maryland, which both experienced riots and looting — Ferguson over the shooting death by a police officer of African-American 18-year-old Michael Brown, and in Baltimore over the death of 25-year-old Freddie Gray, also an African-American, who died while in police custody. On the one-year anniversary of Michael Brown's death, violent riots again erupted in Ferguson, causing St. Louis officials to declare a state of emergency. Although Obama promised to heal race relations when he was elected in 2008, we have seen quite the opposite, some say at his very hands, stoking racial tension and division with his anti-police public statements.

The increase in violent riots in recent years in the United States are not all race related. The anti-capitalism and class warfare movements, Occupy Wall Street and the May Day protesters rioted in multiple major U.S. cities between 2010 and 2013. Occupy Wall Street even reached London in 2011. College campuses also saw their share of rioting at alcohol-saturated fraternity parties and sporting competitions.

This is a generation of growing incontinence. Society and culture are convicted by news headlines that continue to report perilous times comportment.

Men shall be . . . fierce, despisers of those that are good

We have only to look to the Middle Eastern terrorism conducted by the likes of ISIS to understand that this is a time of fierceness as evil as any in history. And that evil has invaded America, to be added to our own brand of fierceness. Consider the woman who was beheaded in Texas by a Muslim who worked in the same company as his victim.

In America (in the city of Chicago, for example), youths slaughter each other at a rate that should shame any people, yet there is little coverage by mainstream news reporters, unless there is a racial component to the killings. And these are reported with enthusiasm only if it is white on black atrocities being committed, for the most part.

ISIS and other terrorist organizations particularly go after Christians, as the hordes of Islamists cut their swath of death and destruction in their Jihadist pursuit of establishing the much-desired caliphate. They behead women and children — as well as infants — to demonstrate their hatred for Christians and Jesus Christ, whom the martyrs worship.

One who looks at human life as sacred from God's viewpoint must ask whether these perilous times characteristics — fierce and despisers of those that are good — should apply to the murder of the more than 57 million babies in the wombs of their mothers in America. Anyone who has looked at video of an abortion being performed cannot deny that it is a violent act that ends the life of the preborn. These infants in the womb are considered "good" by the Lord of heaven, their Creator. They are considered sinless until they reach the age when they are capable of making the decision to accept or reject Christ for salvation.

To my thinking, these characteristics of these perilous times in which we live fit within the intents and purposes of those of Planned Parenthood and other abortionists who carry out such infanticide. Those who murder babies in the womb seem to me not that much different in attitude to those of the Middle Eastern madmen who rampage against their victims.

Men shall be . . . heady, high-minded

The powerful and elite, would-be new world order builders fit well within this perilous times category. They sell out their nations and even their families for the sake of building the new world they desire — apart from any governance by God. Psalm 2 calls out these earth-dwellers as the KJV of the Bible defines them. They are driven by the powers and principalities outlined in Ephesians 6.

This self-uplifting, while ascending on the misfortune of others, is symptomatic of headiness or high-mindedness. Satan was and is the highest-minded of all. He sought and still has the audacity to believe he can lift himself to a position above the one, true, eternal God. Those who reject the truth of Jesus Christ are, through omission, heirs to the fallen ones — Lucifer's great high-mindedness.

All who seek, through their great intellect, their desire, or their superiority in the realm of power-brokerage, to put themselves upon the pinnacle of god-likeness in the world they have chosen to conquer are inheritors of Satan's pridefulness. They are exhilarated by the cutthroat struggle to vanquish all obstacles, all foes.

The high-minded intellectuals of academia, of the sciences, or of the liberal clergy seek more than at any time in history to erase all mention of God the Almighty, even at the temporary expedient of tolerating many religions and allowing those religions their many various ways to godhood.

With the intellectual exercise of plotting the planet's physical and social salvation, they are sacrificing their eternal souls on the altar of "evolutional theory." God's Word tells that the last generation will be as was the generation that perished in the Flood of Noah's day. Of that people God says:

> Because that, when they knew God, they glorified him not as God, neither were thankful; but became vain in their imaginations, and their foolish heart was darkened. Professing themselves to be wise, they became fools, and changed the glory of the uncorruptible God into an image made like to corruptible man, and to birds, and fourfooted beasts, and creeping things (Romans 1:21–23).

What is this, if not a description of modern intellectual man and his attempts to rationalize away all vestiges of the true God? It perfectly describes the writings of Charles Darwin and those who have reworked, reformulated, and totally fallen for, in one form or another, the evolution lie. These, like the antediluvians, "changed the truth of God into a lie, and worshipped and served the creature more than the Creator" (Romans 1:25). These foolish, soul-darkened "intellects" join forces with those they would once have termed superstitious idiots, the occultists, and New Age adherents, to deify Mother Earth for the sake of ecological purity.

Headiness and high-mindedness are encapsulated within the climate change, radical environmentalism that is being used to destroy national sovereignty and autonomy, thus to bring all within one-world rule. The Antichrist regime will be the penultimate outgrowth of that drive toward global order.

Men shall be . . . lovers of pleasures more than lovers of God; having a form of godliness, but denying the power thereof

My friend Wilfred Hahn addressed this characteristic of end-times man in a recent article, an excerpt of which follows.

> Jesus Christ clearly said that one can only love one master, God or Mammon. ("No man can serve two masters: for either he will hate the one, and love the other; or else he will hold to the one, and despise the other. Ye cannot serve God and mammon" Matthew 6:24; KJV.)
>
> But, did Jesus really say that? Wouldn't it be nice if one could sup at both tables . . . to worship both God and Money? Wouldn't

that be a pleasurable perspective, and one that will suit itching ears (2 Timothy 4:3)?

Implicitly, this commingling of fealty to both God and Money is exactly what the Bible prophesies will occur. "People will be [. . .] lovers of money" (2 Timothy 3:2) and "lovers of pleasure rather than lovers of God" (verse 4), while at the same time "having a form of godliness but denying its power" (verse 5). Jesus describes this duality . . . really a duplicity: "[. . .] on the outside you appear to people as righteous but on the inside you are full of hypocrisy and wickedness" (Matthew 23:28; NIV).

Here we see a society that thinks its love of money is compatible with godliness.[15]

---

15. Wilfred Hahn, "End-time Wickedness: Consorting with Mammon," www.raptureready. com, "Newest Articles" section.

CHAPTER 9

YES. THEY'RE THE GREAT PRETENDERS

*Reason #9: Deceivers, false prophets, and false christs
are on the scene today, just as Jesus predicted. It is a sure
reason to believe that this generation is prophetically
scheduled to be left behind.*

It is good to pause here to remind that we are looking at issues and events in light of Bible prophecy. Our book title also reminds that whether we are *Rapture Ready . . . or Not,* that great event is on the brink of snatching millions of believers into heaven. If what we now see unfolding all around us is, as I believe, indicating that this generation is bumping up against the very end of the Church Age (Age of Grace), time is very short to do what needs to be done for the great cause of Jesus Christ.

Our subtitle has it that we are also going through *15 Reasons This Is the Generation That Will Be Left Behind.*

The very first sign Jesus foretold as an end-times signal in His Olivet Discourse just before His crucifixion is at the forefront of life in America today. It surely is a primary reason we can know that this is the generation that is about to be left behind.

Christ's words on this first indicator of His Second Coming were, of course, given while He sat with His disciples atop the Mount of Olives overlooking the Temple Mount in Jerusalem.

> And as he sat upon the mount of Olives, the disciples came unto him privately, saying, Tell us, when shall these things be? and what shall be the sign of thy coming, and of the end of the world?
>
> And Jesus answered and said unto them, Take heed that no man deceive you. For many shall come in my name, saying, I am Christ; and shall deceive many (Matthew 24:3–5).

There are at least two ways of looking at the heads-up the Lord gives in this prophecy. Jesus was saying that there will come at the very end of the age dangerous deceivers and great deception.

1. These deceivers will say that they are actually Christ, themselves.
2. Others will be saying that Jesus is Christ (they will identify themselves as believers in Him), but they will be, in fact, deceivers — not true believers.

We will look at these two groups, beginning with those who claim to be Christ. These don't necessarily have to claim to be Christ to be in this category. They might claim to be prophets in the Old and New Testament sense, for example. They claim to have special revelation beyond that given in God's Holy Word.

Some claim they are prophesying through dreams and visions that they are given on a regular basis. They are false prophets and false teachers.

How can I say this with such authority in the declaration? Because their claims don't come true. Every prophecy that is truly of God — who is *omniscient* (all-knowing) — is 100 percent accurate. In Old Testament times and in the times of the New Testament prophets, these prophets had to have a perfect track record. Their prophecies always came true in the short term, and also, in many cases — such as in the Revelation — they had a long-term or distant future fulfillment that had to be shown as accomplished.

If prophets were proven false — if the prophecies didn't come true in a short-term time frame — they were subject to being stoned to death.

God's Word says:

> But the prophet, which shall presume to speak a word in my name, which I have not commanded him to speak, or that shall speak

in the name of other gods, even that prophet shall die. And if thou say in thine heart, How shall we know the word which the LORD hath not spoken? When a prophet speaketh in the name of the LORD, if the thing follow not, nor come to pass, that is the thing which the LORD hath not spoken, but the prophet hath spoken it presumptuously: thou shalt not be afraid of him (Deuteronomy 18:20–22).

A prophecy writer whom I respect greatly as one who was an authority, who has now gone to be with his Lord, wrote the following:

> When God speaks through a prophet, that prophet will prophesy what is to actually occur in the future. There will be no doubt as to who is speaking as these prophesies come to pass, since only God can see the future. Thus this person would be considered a true prophet of God. . . . In the days of the recorded prophets of God, there were also false prophets who were determined to do damage to God and His Word. But God had a remedy for this type of chicanery. In days of old, these false prophets weren't merely dismissed as crackpots, nor were they given another chance to prophesy correctly. They were stoned to death for their evil deeds.[1]

Why such a severe punishment? Because that false prophet is claiming to speak for God. It is God who suffers the consequences when those prophecies fail. God will not be mocked or blasphemed, and His Word is true 100 percent of the time.

In modern times, these false prophets face no such punishment; therefore, their deception continues. One must remember that Satan has a vested interest in deceiving people and will do so through false prophets, including clairvoyants, spirits, and mediums such as Jeane Dixon and Edgar Cayce.

"Prophets" Aplenty!

False christs and false prophets have been a part of human cultures since the early days of man's history. Soothsayers of every sort have always been able to delude. The human mind, since the fall in Eden, has always seemed to gravitate toward false promises rather than toward truth.

We can see this again most clearly by considering how an entire nation was led into World War II by promises of Hitler's false prophet or propagandist

---

1. Ron Graham, "Stoning False Prophets," Rapture Ready, https://www.raptureready.com/featured/graham/g162.html, accessed August 8, 2015.

Josef Goebbels. The German people eventually fell for the lies and accepted another devastating war, even though the nation had just come out of World War I, which had decimated the people's lives.

But that was deception and false promises of a different sort. The sort we are exploring is even more destructive, because it involves the eternal soul — where men, women, and children will spend eternity.

There were many false prophets and false messiahs before the time of Jesus Christ. There have been many since. Here are some of those who have in later centuries claimed to be the reincarnation of the Christ, or to be the Second Coming of Jesus Christ.

Eighteenth Century

Ann Lee (1736–1784), the founder and leader of the Shakers. Lee's followers referred to her as "Mother," believing that she was the female incarnation of Christ on earth.

John Nichols Thom (1799–1838), a Cornish tax rebel who claimed to be the "saviour of the world" and the reincarnation of Jesus Christ in 1834. He was killed by British soldiers at the Battle of Bossenden Wood on May 31, 1838, in Kent, England.

Nineteenth Century

Arnold Potter (1804–1872), schismatic Latter-Day Saints leader; he claimed the spirit of Jesus Christ entered his body and he became "Potter Christ," Son of the living God. He died in an attempt to "ascend into heaven" by jumping off a cliff. His body was later retrieved and buried by his followers.

Jones Very (1813–1880), American essayist, poet, literary scholar, and Greek tutor at Harvard who befriended several prominent American Transcendentalists and suffered a nervous breakdown in 1837 after which he claimed to have become the Second Coming of Jesus.

Bahá'u'lláh (1817–1892), born Shiite, adopted Bábism later in 1844; he claimed to be the prophesied fulfillment and Promised One of three major religions. He founded the Bahá'í Faith in 1863.

Twentieth Century

William W. Davies (1833–1906), leader of a Latter-Day Saints schismatic group called the Kingdom of Heaven located in Walla Walla,

Washington, from 1867 to 1881. He taught his followers that he was the archangel Michael, who had previously lived as the biblical Adam, Abraham, and David. When his son Arthur was born on February 11, 1868, Davies declared that the infant was the reincarnated Jesus Christ. When Davies' second son, David, was born in 1869, he was declared to be God the Father.

Mirza Ghulam Ahmad of Qadian, India (1835–1908), claimed to be the awaited Mahdi as well as (Second Coming) likeness of Jesus the promised Messiah at the end of time. He claimed to be Jesus in the metaphorical sense, in character. He founded the Ahmadiyya Movement in 1889, envisioning it to be the rejuvenation of Islam, and claimed to be commissioned by God for the reformation of mankind.

John Hugh Smyth-Pigott (1852–1927). Around 1890, Smyth-Pigott started leading meetings of the Agapenomite community and recruited 50 young female followers to supplement its aging population. He took Ruth Anne Preece as his second wife and she had three children named Glory, Power, and Hallelujah. By 1902, his fame had spread as far as India, from where Mirza Ghulam Ahmad warned him of his false teachings and predicted his miserable end.

Haile Selassie I (1892–1975) did not claim to be Jesus and disapproved of claims that he was Jesus, but the Rastafari movement, which emerged in Jamaica during the 1930s, believes he is the Second Coming.

Ernest Norman (1904–1971), an American electrical engineer who cofounded the Unarius Academy of Science in 1954, was allegedly Jesus in a past life and his earthly incarnation was as an archangel named Raphael.

Krishna Venta (1911–1958), born Francis Herman Pencovic, in San Francisco, founded the WKFL (Wisdom, Knowledge, Faith, and Love) Fountain of the World cult in Simi Valley, California, in the late 1940s. In 1948, he stated that he was Christ, the new messiah, and claimed to have led a convoy of rocket ships to earth from the extinct planet Neophrates. He died on December 10, 1958, after being suicide-bombed by two disgruntled former followers who accused him of mishandling cult funds and having been intimate with their wives.

Marshall Applewhite (1931–1997), an American who posted a famous Usenet message declaring, "I, Jesus — Son of God — acknowledge on this date of September 25/26, 1995. . . ."

Yahweh ben Yahweh (1935–2007), born as Hulon Mitchell Jr., was a black nationalist and separatist who created the Nation of Yahweh in 1979 in Liberty City, Florida. His self-proclaimed name means "God, Son of God." He could have only been deeming himself to be "son of God," not God, but many of his followers clearly deem him to be God Incarnate.

Laszlo Toth (1938–2012) was a Hungarian-born Australian who claimed he was Jesus Christ as he vandalized Michelangelo's Pietà with a geologist's hammer in 1972.

Wayne Bent (1941–) is also known as Michael Travesser of the Lord Our Righteousness Church. He claims, "I am the embodiment of God. I am divinity and humanity combined."

Ariffin Mohammed (1943–) is also known as "Ayah Pin," the founder of the banned Sky Kingdom in Malaysia in 1975. He claims to have direct contact with the heavens and is believed by his followers to be the incarnation of Jesus.

Mitsuo Matayoshi (1944–) is a conservative Japanese politician who in 1997 established the World Economic Community Party based on his conviction that he is God and Christ, renaming himself Iesu Matayoshi. According to his program, he will do the Last Judgment as Christ but within the current political system.

José Luis de Jesús Miranda (1946–2013), Puerto Rican founder, leader, and organizer of Growing in Grace based in Miami, Florida, claimed that the resurrected Christ "integrated himself within me" in 2007.

Inri Cristo (1948–), a Brazilian who claimed to be the second Jesus reincarnated in 1969, is considered by Inri Cristo and his disciples as the New Jerusalem of the Apocalypse.

Thomas Harrison Provenzano (1949–2000), an American convicted murderer who was possibly mentally ill, compared his execution with Jesus Christ's crucifixion.

Shoko Asahara (1955–) founded the controversial Japanese religious group Aum Shinrikyo in 1984. He declared himself Christ, Japan's only fully enlightened master, and the Lamb of God. His purported mission was to take upon himself the sins of the world. He outlined a doomsday prophecy, which included a Third World War, and described a final conflict culminating in a nuclear Armageddon, borrowing the term from Revelation 16:16.

Hogen Fukunaga (1945–) founded Ho No Hana Sanpogyo, often called the "foot reading cult," in Japan in 1987 after an alleged spiritual event in which he claimed to have realized he was the reincarnation of Jesus Christ and Gautama Buddha.

Marina Tsvigun (1960–), or Maria Devi Christos, is the leader of the Great White Brotherhood. In 1990 she met Yuri Krivonogov, the Great White Brotherhood founder, who recognized Marina as a new messiah and later married her, assuming in the sect the role of John the Baptist, subordinate to Tsvigun.

Maurice Clemmons (1972–2009) was an American felon responsible for the 2009 murder of four police officers in Washington state, and referred to himself in May 2009 as Jesus.

Twenty-First Century

Apollo Quiboloy (1950–) is the founder and leader of a Philippines-based Restorationist church, the Kingdom of Jesus Christ, The Name Above Every Name, Inc. He has made claims that he is the "Appointed Son of God."

Alan John Miller (1962–), more commonly known as A.J. Miller, is a former Jehovah's Witness elder and current leader of the Australia-based Divine Truth movement. Miller claims to be Jesus Christ reincarnated with others in the 20th century to spread messages that he calls the "Divine Truth." He delivers these messages in seminars and various forms of media along with his current partner Mary Suzanne Luck, who identifies herself as the returned Mary Magdalene.

David Shayler (1965–) was a former MI5 agent and whistleblower who, in the summer of 2007, proclaimed himself to be the Messiah. He has released a series of videos on YouTube claiming to be Jesus, although he has not built up any noticeable following since his claims.

Oscar Ramiro Ortega-Hernandez (1990–) in November 2011 fired nine shots with an Romanian Cugir semi-automatic rifle at the

White House in Washington, D.C., believing himself to be Jesus Christ sent to kill U.S. President Barack Obama, whom he believed to be the Antichrist.

Lightning Deng is a woman whom the Chinese Eastern Lightning cult believe to be the reincarnation of Christ.[2]

There are many more that could be included in this end-times category. Certainly, the proliferation of false christs is a sure sign the end of the age approaches.

False Christs, False Prophets, Great Deception

The most prominent people and organizations propagating religious false prophecy and claiming they alone either are Christ or have the only truth about God's way to salvation constitute the ones I wish to examine in this chapter. Dr. Ed Hindson's chapter in one of my books explored the depth the cults have gone to in order to make their pernicious effects felt in these latter days. I've excerpted a portion of his excellent treatment of these end-times deceivers.

The Cultic Paradigm

All cult logic is built on the same faulty premise: "We alone know the truth." Believing themselves to have discovered truth that is unknown to others, cultists assume they have a corner on that truth. The cultic paradigm works like this: We alone know the truth of God, therefore, of God. We alone are the people other variations of the cultic paradigm derive from this original premise. For example, if we alone know the truth, then all others are in error. If we alone are the people of God, then all others are heretics. If people reject our message, they are rejecting God's message. If people persecute us, they are persecuting the cause of God because our cause is God's cause. Since we are right, and others are wrong, our church is the only true church.

Basic Traits

While schismatic cults exist in every religion from Lubavitcher Jews to Muslim extremists, they all have certain characteristics in common.

2. "List of People Who Claim to Be Jesus," Wikipedia, https://en.wikipedia.org/wiki/List_of_people_claimed_to_be_Jesus.

Every religious cult has a sacred book translation, set of writings, key to interpretation, and perhaps visions, dreams, or voices to validate its beliefs. Muslims believe the Koran is God's final revelation to man through the Prophet Muhammed. Mormons look at the Book of Mormon as equally inspired as the Bible. Jehovah's Witnesses recognize only their New World Translation of the Bible. Seventh-Day Adventists recognize Ellen G. White as an inspired prophet of God. Christian Science reveres Mary Baker Eddy's Science and Health with Key to the Scriptures as divinely inspired. . . .

Satan, the great deceiver, convinces the cult leader that he has found the truth no one else has ever discovered. Armed with this egotistical ammunition, the cultist begins to weave a web of religious deception. He first falls victim to it himself, then he convinces others that he is right and manipulates their resources to further spread his message. In time, this leads to oppressive organizational controls to ensure that this process continues.

God is against false prophets whose spiritual delusion causes them to invent their own message apart from God's truth. The Bible presents them in seven categories:

1. Self-deceived. Some false teachers may be sincere, but they are still wrong. They have deceived themselves into believing their messages are true. As Jeremiah points out, their messages come psychologically from within their own minds and are not from God.

2. Liars. Some false prophets are deliberate liars who have no intention of telling the truth. The apostle John says, "Who is the liar? It is the man who denies that Jesus is the Christ. Such a man is the Antichrist — he denies the Father and the Son" (1 John 2:22).

3. Heretics. These are people who preach heresy (false doctrine) and divide the church. Of them John said, "They went out from us, but they did not really belong to us" (1 John 2:19). The apostle Peter said, "There will be false teachers among you. They will secretly introduce destructive heresies. . . . These men blaspheme in matters they do not understand" (2 Peter 2:1, 12).

4. Scoffers. There are some who do not necessarily promote false teaching so much as they outright reject the truth of God. Of them the Bible warns, "In the last days scoffers will come, scoffing and following their own evil desires" (2 Peter 3:3). The apostle Paul calls them "lovers of themselves . . . boastful, proud . . . conceited" (2 Timothy 3:2, 4). Jude calls them "grumblers and faultfinders" (verse 16).

5. Blasphemers. Those who speak evil of God, Christ, the Holy Spirit, the people of God, the kingdom of God, and the attributes of God are called blasphemers. Jude calls them godless men who "speak abusively against whatever they do not understand. . . . They are clouds without rain . . . trees, without fruit . . . wild waves of the sea . . . wandering stars" (Jude 10, 12, 13). The apostle Paul says that he himself was a blasphemer before his conversion to Christ (1 Timothy 1:13).

6. Seducers. Jesus warned that some false prophets will appear with miraculous signs and wonders to seduce or deceive the very elect "if that were possible" (Mark 13:22). Our Lord's implication is that spiritual seduction is a very real threat even to believers. This would account for the fact that a few genuine, but deceived, believers may be found among the cults.

7. Reprobates. This term means "disapproved," "depraved," or "rejected." Paul refers to those who have rejected the truth of God and turned to spiritual darkness. Consequently, God has given them over to a "reprobate mind" (Romans 1:28). They have so deliberately rejected God that they have become "filled with every kind of wickedness" (verse 29). As a result, they are "God-haters" (verse 30) whose behavior is "senseless, faithless, heartless, ruthless" (verse 31). These people are so far gone spiritually that they know it and don't care!

In Jesus' own prophetic message, the Olivet Discourse (Matthew 24–25), He warned, "Watch out that no one deceives you. . . . Many will turn away from the faith . . . and many false prophets will appear and deceive many people. . . . False Christs and false prophets will appear and perform great signs and miracles" (Matthew 24:4, 10, 11, 24). Our Lord warned His disciples — and us — of the possibility of spiritual seduction by false prophets and teachers, especially as the end of the age approaches.[3]

Although this chapter hasn't dealt with the *great pretenders* within the confines of Christ's Body — the True Church — these are the most dangerous. These have proliferated in this late hour of the Church Age, and have brought this generation into the Laodicean era.

Here is what the prophet Jude has to say about the wolves in sheep clothing:

> Beloved, when I gave all diligence to write unto you of the common salvation, it was needful for me to write unto you, and exhort you that ye should earnestly contend for the faith which was once delivered unto the saints.
>
> For there are certain men crept in unawares, who were before of old ordained to this condemnation, ungodly men, turning the grace of our God into lasciviousness, and denying the only Lord God, and our Lord Jesus Christ. . . .
>
> These are spots in your feasts of charity, when they feast with you, feeding themselves without fear: clouds they are without water, carried about of winds; trees whose fruit withereth, without fruit, twice dead, plucked up by the roots (Jude 1:3–12).

Never has there been a greater number of pretenders among the rank of true believers. These will be examined in a later chapter. Rapture Ready — or not — the evidence is mounting that Christ's any-moment call to His Church is about to occur!

---

3. Ed Hindson, "False Christs, False Prophets, Great Deception," *Foreshadows of Wrath and Redemption*, William T. James, ed. (Eugene, OR: Harvest House, 1999), p. 36–48.

CHAPTER 10

THE HUMPTY–DUMPTY DUMBING DOWN FOR A GREAT FALL

Reason #10: Apostasy — departure from truth — abounds today at every level. According to 2 Thessalonians 2, this is a strong reason to believe that this is the generation that will be left behind at the time of Rapture.

One of the most prominent reasons I believe this might well be the generation that will be left behind when the Rapture takes place is found today within secular as well as religious worldviews. It is literally taking place more quickly than the observer of prophetic issues and events can analyze and report. "Apostasy" is the word that properly encapsulates this dramatic signal that this generation has reached the end of this dispensation. The word "apostasy" is most often applied to the arena of religion. However, it can be equally applied to the secular world.

"Apostasy" is defined, according to the *Random House Dictionary*, as a "total desertion of or departure from one's religion, principles, party, cause, etc." In other words, it applies to any departure from previously acceptable standards embraced by a culture, be it religious or other.

The Bible predicts such a departure as one of the key signals that Christ's Second Coming is near. Paul wrote, as recorded in his second letter to the Thessalonians, regarding the day of the Rapture of the Church:

> Let no man deceive you by any means: for that day shall not come, except there come a falling away first, and that man of sin be revealed, the son of perdition (2 Thessalonians 2:3).

Paul was saying that there would first come an apostasy before Antichrist could come to prominence on the world stage. He wrote further:

> Now the Spirit speaketh expressly, that in the latter times some shall depart from the faith, giving heed to seducing spirits, and doctrines of devils (1 Timothy 4:1).

Paul, in both of those Scriptures on people departing from truth, is addressing mostly those within the Body of Christ. He is addressing the religious realm and how the deception and departure or apostasy will happen.

In writing to the church at Rome, the Apostle addressed the question of the secular world being caught up in a specific departure or apostasy. That total pulling away from God, the Creator, had taken place before in the past, was taking place at the time Paul wrote the letter to Christians at Rome, and it will continue to take place until it is finally and forever dealt with in holy judgment.

> Because that, when they knew God, they glorified him not as God, neither were thankful; but became vain in their imaginations, and their foolish heart was darkened. . . . And even as they did not like to retain God in their knowledge, God gave them over to a reprobate mind, to do those things which are not convenient (Romans 1:21–28).

Devil's Dumbing-Down Diatribe

Lucifer the fallen one — Satan — is at the core of the apostasy taking place at every level of human activity. Again, the results of his never-ending effort to turn the creation called man away from the Creator has produced the profound signal that the end is not just near, but is here, now. It is an indicator that we are about to experience the catastrophic intervention into the affairs of mankind by Christ's call to the Church in the Rapture.

Although the word "apostasy" can affect both the religious and secular realms of human interaction individually, that is, separately, Satan has managed to convince man, through the combining of both religious and secular apostasy, to try to shake off God's restraint. That restraint will indeed be removed one day. All hell will then break loose on a planet which will receive the incremental judgment and wrath of God.

> For the mystery of iniquity doth already work: only [The Holy Spirit] who now [restrains] will [restrain], until [the Holy Spirit as Restrainer] be taken out of the way. And then shall [Antichrist] be revealed, whom the Lord shall consume with the spirit of his mouth, and shall destroy with the brightness of his coming (2 Thessalonians 2:7–8).

For now, Satan's man, Antichrist, lurks somewhere in the shadows, awaiting his moment in history's spotlight. Lucifer the fallen one continues to pave the way for that son of perdition through a never-ceasing diatribe against all things godly. Satan began this planting of doubt regarding God's truth at the time of man's earliest days on earth. The encounter is recorded in the first Book of Moses — Genesis.

> Now the serpent was more subtle than any beast of the field which the LORD God had made. And he said unto the woman, Yea, hath God said, Ye shall not eat of every tree of the garden?
> And the woman said unto the serpent, We may eat of the fruit of the trees of the garden: But of the fruit of the tree which is in the midst of the garden, God hath said, Ye shall not eat of it, neither shall ye touch it, lest ye die.
> And the serpent said unto the woman, Ye shall not surely die: For God doth know that in the day ye eat thereof, then your eyes shall be opened, and ye shall be as gods, knowing good and evil (Genesis 3:1–5).

Mankind has pulled away from the Lord's loving, nurturing hand ever since sin entered the garden and the world when Adam partook of the forbidden fruit. That rebellion reached its fruition when all the earth became corrupt before God's holy eyes. The Lord destroyed all but Noah and seven members of his family with the worldwide Flood.

The earth is again filled with corruption, and all of the signals that God's wrath is about to again be released is all around us at this present time. This "falling away" or "apostasy," as it is termed, has produced iniquity that requires another cleansing of God's creation. The build-up to the present state of corruption has been one that warrants explanation.

I will begin by again addressing something mentioned earlier. At the opening of this section, I presented the following thought: Although the word "apostasy" can affect both the religious and secular realms of human interaction individually, that is, separately, Satan has managed to convince man, through the combining of both religious and secular apostasy, to try to shake off God's restraint.

The *father of lies* has worked diligently — and has been largely successful — in bringing rebellious mankind to the point of *departure* from the governance of God. This he has accomplished with willful compliance by a nation and world caught up in the age-old preference of doing "what is right in their own eyes" (Judges 17:6). Satan has, as the chapter title implies, dumbed down humanity as a whole, through diverting their minds and spiritual hearts from biblical truth.

I believe it is the United States of America that offers the most vivid picture of this dumbing-down process. To begin looking at how this has happened, first let us consider America's founding. Despite many accusations against America's founders, the evidence indicates that they, though flawed human beings like all of us, were nonetheless obviously a group of individuals chosen for a special purpose. They were selected to bring into being the most unique experiment in liberty ever to be instituted upon the earth.

These founding fathers had at the center of their thinking a special perspective. We get an understanding of that perspective by considering their own words.

John Adams, second president of the United States, said:

> The general principles on which the fathers achieved independence were the general principles of Christianity. I will avow that I then believed, and now believe, that those general principles of Christianity are as eternal and immutable as the existence and attributes of God.
>
> Without religion, this world would be something not fit to be mentioned in polite company: I mean hell.

The Christian religion is, above all the religions that ever prevailed or existed in ancient or modern times, the religion of wisdom, virtue, equity and humanity.

Suppose a nation in some distant region should take the Bible for their only law book and every member should regulate his conduct by the precepts there exhibited. . . . What a Eutopia — what a Paradise would this region be!

I have examined all religions, and the result is that the Bible is the best book in the world.

John Quincy Adams, sixth president, said:

My hopes of a future life are all founded upon the Gospel of Christ and I cannot cavil or quibble away [evade or object to] . . . the whole tenor of His conduct by which He sometimes positively asserted and at others countenances [permits] His disciples in asserting that He was God.

The hope of a Christian is inseparable from his faith. Whoever believes in the Divine inspiration of the Holy Scriptures must hope that the religion of Jesus shall prevail throughout the earth. Never since the foundation of the world have the prospects of mankind been more encouraging to that hope than they appear to be at the present time. And may the associated distribution of the Bible proceed and prosper till the Lord shall have made "bare His holy arm in the eyes of all the nations, and all the ends of the earth shall see the salvation of our God" [Isaiah 52: 10].

In the chain of human events, the birthday of the nation is indissolubly linked with the birthday of the Savior. The Declaration of Independence laid the cornerstone of human government upon the first precepts of Christianity.

Samuel Adams, governor of Massachusetts, signer of the Declaration of Independence, and ratifier of the U.S. Constitution, stated:

I . . . [rely] upon the merits of Jesus Christ for a pardon of all my sins.

The name of the Lord (says the Scripture) is a strong tower; thither the righteous flee and are safe [Proverbs 18:10]. Let us secure

His favor and He will lead us through the journey of this life and at length receive us to a better.

I conceive we cannot better express ourselves than by humbly supplicating the Supreme Ruler of the world . . . that the confusions that are and have been among the nations may be overruled by the promoting and speedily bringing in the holy and happy period when the kingdoms of our Lord and Savior Jesus Christ may be everywhere established, and the people willingly bow to the scepter of Him who is the Prince of Peace.

Benjamin Franklin, signer of the Declaration of Independence, diplomat, printer, and scientist, said the following:

As to Jesus of Nazareth, my opinion of whom you particularly desire, I think the system of morals and His religion as He left them to us, the best the world ever saw, or is likely to see.

The body of Benjamin Franklin, printer, like the cover of an old book, its contents torn out and stripped of its lettering and guilding, lies here, food for worms. Yet the work itself shall not be lost; for it will, as he believed, appear once more in a new and more beatiful edition, corrected and amended by the Author. [Franklin's self-authored eulogy.]

John Hancock, signer of the Declaration of Independence, president of Congress, Revolutionary War general, and governor of Massachusetts, called on the entire state to pray:

. . . that universal happiness may be established in the world [and] that all may bow to the scepter of our Lord Jesus Christ, and the whole earth be filled with His glory.

He also called on the State of Massachusetts to pray:

. . . that all nations may bow to the scepter of our Lord and Savior Jesus Christ and that the whole earth may be filled with his glory, that the spiritual kingdom of our Lord and Savior Jesus Christ may be continually increasing until the whole earth shall be filled with His glory. To confess their sins and to implore forgiveness of God through the merits of the Savior of the World. To cause the benign religion of our Lord and Savior Jesus Christ to be known, understood, and practiced among all the inhabitants of the earth. To confess their sins before God and implore His forgiveness through the merits and mediation of Jesus Christ, our Lord and Savior. That He would finally overrule all events to the advancement of the Redeemer's kingdom and the establishment of universal peace and good will among men. That the kingdom of our Lord and Savior Jesus Christ may be established in peace and righteousness among all the nations of the earth.

Patrick Henry, Revolutionary War general, legislator, "The Voice of Liberty," ratifier of the U.S. Constitution, and governor of Virginia, said:

> Being a Christian . . . is a character which I prize far above all this world has or can boast.
>
> The Bible . . . is a book worth more than all the other books that were ever printed.
>
> Righteousness alone can exalt [America] as a nation. . . . Whoever thou art, remember this; and in thy sphere practice virtue thyself, and encourage it in others.

John Jay, president of Congress, diplomat, author of the Federalist Papers, original chief justice of the U.S. Supreme Court, and governor of New York, stated:

> Condescend, merciful Father! to grant as far as proper these imperfect petitions, to accept these inadequate thanksgivings, and to pardon whatever of sin hath mingled in them for the sake of Jesus Christ, our blessed Lord and Savior; unto Whom, with Thee, and the blessed Spirit, ever one God, be rendered all honor and glory, now and forever.
>
> Unto Him who is the author and giver of all good, I render sincere and humble thanks for His manifold and unmerited blessings, and especially for our redemption and salvation by His beloved Son. . . . Blessed be His Holy Name.

Thomas Jefferson, signer of the Declaration of Independence, diplomat, governor of Virginia, secretary of state, and third president of the United States, stated the following:

> The doctrines of Jesus are simple, and tend all to the happiness of man.
>
> The practice of morality being necessary for the well being of society, He [God] has taken care to impress its precepts so indelibly on our hearts that they shall not be effaced by the subtleties of our brain. We all agree in the obligation of the moral principles of Jesus and nowhere will they be found delivered in greater purity than in His discourses.
>
> I am a Christian in the only sense in which He wished anyone to be: sincerely attached to His doctrines in preference to all others.
>
> I am a real Christian — that is to say, a disciple of the doctrines of Jesus Christ.

James Madison, signer of the Constitution, author of the Federalist Papers, framer of the Bill of Rights, secretary of state, and fourth president of the United States, said:

> A watchful eye must be kept on ourselves lest, while we are building ideal monuments of renown and bliss here, we neglect to have our names enrolled in the Annals of Heaven.
>
> I have sometimes thought there could not be a stronger testimony in favor of religion or against temporal enjoyments, even the most rational and manly, than for men who occupy the most honorable and gainful departments and [who] are rising in reputation and wealth, publicly to declare their unsatisfactoriness by becoming fervent advocates in the cause of Christ; and I wish you may give in your evidence in this way.

George Washington, judge, member of the Continental Congress, commander-in-chief of the Continental Army, president of the Constitutional Convention, first president of the United States, and "Father of his Country," said:

> You do well to wish to learn our arts and ways of life, and above all, the religion of Jesus Christ. These will make you a greater and happier people than you are.
>
> While we are zealously performing the duties of good citizens and soldiers, we certainly ought not to be inattentive to the

higher duties of religion. To the distinguished character of Patriot, it should be our highest glory to add the more distinguished character of Christian.

The blessing and protection of Heaven are at all times necessary but especially so in times of public distress and danger. The General hopes and trusts that every officer and man will endeavor to live and act as becomes a Christian soldier, defending the dearest rights and liberties of his country.

I now make it my earnest prayer that God would . . . most graciously be pleased to dispose us all to do justice, to love mercy, and to demean ourselves with that charity, humility, and pacific temper of the mind which were the characteristics of the Divine Author of our blessed religion.[1]

With these quotes from a few of the founding fathers of America and hundreds upon hundreds more that could be included above, it should be crystal clear to even the most hardened "progressive" contrarian that Jesus Christ and the gospel was at the center of their thinking when forming this government. Of course, I'm not so naive as to think all the proof that would fill a thousand volumes would deter the liberal's contentions that America is founded upon wrong precepts.

These are devoted to deconstructing even the fully documented history of the republic — i.e., rewriting it — to either (1) prove the founding fathers didn't intend to establish a nation based upon godly, Judeo-Christian principles, or (2) convince that that founding was so bigoted and mean-spirited that it must be torn down, that is, that the nation must be taken apart and reconstructed so as to make it a strictly secular, humanistic entity, with all thoughts and direction by any deity expunged from the hearts and minds of the people.

Thus, the dumbing down has been underway at full speed for many years. The secular apostasy — departure from the intentions and principles established by the founders set in long ago, and now the infection of humanism's vileness — is in process of destroying from within.

We will first look further into this dumbing down/apostasy at the secular level before looking into the even more despicable apostasy — that predicted by the Apostle Paul, and even the Lord Jesus, Himself.

---

1. David Barton, "The Founding Fathers on Jesus, Christianity and the Bible," May 2008, WallBuilders, http://www.wallbuilders.com/LIBissuesArticles.asp?id=8755.

Treachery of Time

Time was created for man. It is linear. That is, time has a beginning point, and will have an end time point. "History" is the term used for the encapsulation of time. Between the starting and ending points on history's timeline, there is a mystery that is perplexing, but blatantly obvious.

Man's progress along this timeline reached a certain point that saw the acceleration of human-generated activity. Man's inventiveness exploded, spawning all manner of work-saving devices. This inventiveness and resultant progress has produced effects beyond those that could have been anticipated at the conceptual level of their creation. Bible prophecy presents this explosion in one verse. The prophet Daniel, through divine inspiration, foretold the following:

> But thou, O Daniel, shut up the words, and seal the book, even
> to the time of the end: many shall run to and fro, and knowledge
> shall be increased (Daniel 12:4).

The beginning of the 20th century brought with it an acceleration of mankind's inventiveness. America was the nucleus out of which sprang a fantastic array of devices and gadgets that would forever change living standards for mankind.

The example for the explosion of knowledge — thus technology — that is usually given when saying Daniel 12:4 is prophecy fulfilled is the horse and buggy. Until the late, late 1800s, man could travel no faster than a horse could run on land. Of course, a wind-driven ship might go faster during a violent storm, if the sails weren't furled. But that could last but a few minutes before the ship would be torn apart.

The invention of steam locomotion changed that. The *iron horse* — the noisy, smoke-belching locomotive — moved things along, and was instrumental in expansion of America across the North American continent. That, of course, was only the beginning. Automobiles and even airplanes came along, and the human *race* was really on in earnest.

The instruments for making war proliferated also. Ability to produce war on a worldwide scale indeed eventuated in two such conflagrations, with other almost as horrific conflicts to follow.

Mixed in between all of the fast-track inventiveness that physically moved mankind at ever-increasing speeds came the truly world-changing innovations — especially for Americans. Labor-saving devices of every sort quickly began to be developed. Washing clothing and cooking foods became ever-lessening labor-intensive chores. Food production, distribution, and packaging, and more efficient machinery with which to prepare those foods, cut tremendous amounts of time and work for people in the United States.

Communication technologies brought even more time saving and productivity. Those amazing inventions brought about, then, an ever-increasing level of pleasurable entertainment technologies.

Movies enthralled audiences in theaters, while radio programs entertained in the homes. Then, the truly phenomenal invention called television exploded on the scene, and America was fundamentally and forever changed. Families, I believe, began to disintegrate significantly from the point the TV entered American life. Home life no longer was centered around the dinner table, where families had talked and socialized on a regular basis. Now there came a hurried effort to finish the meal and get to whatever the evening's TV fare included.

Soon, TV dinners took the place of many traditional table settings, and microwave ovens were introduced to make that convenience even more . . . well . . . convenient.

Television began to make its impact on church attendance. I remember in 1956 or so wanting desperately to stay home on Sunday night and watch the *Ed Sullivan Show*. That's right, ol' Elvis — a very young Elvis, actually — was the guest. My sweet mom, reluctantly, relented finally. She was wrong — as were so many moms and dads of the time.

The disintegration of home life had begun in earnest, and we all know the rest. The computer and all of the devices, most of which I couldn't even begin to intelligently discuss, have literally made the entire country a nation of *one*. Of course, I mean by that, not a unified nation, but a totally divided nation, with each young person, singularly, deeply engrossed within his or her own electronic/cyberspace device. And the not-so-young in many cases are equally so singularly preoccupied.

The smartphone, as so much of the technologies that have burst onto civilization's horizon, has so dumbed down humanity to truth presented in God's instructions to humankind that the present generation has likely reached the point of no return. While the proponents of the cyberspace wonders would argue that we have become much closer together because of these technologies, I believe the opposite is true.

But, if there is a coming together through these fantastic new devices, it is in one particular way. All are more and more tending toward moving away from thoughts of the God who created them, and toward the pleasure-seeking that Lucifer, the ultimate provocateur and seducer, has supernaturally engineered for the fallen minds of humanity. In this sense, all are becoming *one.*

My contention is that while people — particularly the young — are diverted in their attention to their cyberspace pursuits, those who remain with attentions firmly affixed upon bringing about a system of governance that will ultimately enslave, are full-bore into their efforts. Those who aren't paying attention are playing directly into Lucifer's ill-intentioned hands.

Our recent presidential elections and the cultural rot that has set in are glaring testimony to the truth of my contention. The culture hasn't just *drifted* toward godlessness. It has *exploded* in a frightening burst toward societal cataclysm.

Everyone who is of the fallen mindset that he or she can do "what is right in their own eyes" (Proverbs 12:15, 21:2) are not a part of a new thinking. This form of rebellion is as ancient as humanity itself. And this is what caused the Lord to intervene catastrophically in the past into the affairs of man.

Genesis 11 tells of the Tower of Babel, and of Nimrod and the people of that time. They determined they didn't need the God of heaven. They would achieve godhood themselves — just like Lucifer was still telling men was their destiny. Man had become *dumbed down* to the truth of God. It was a deliberate act of rebellion.

Here is what God said, when looking upon what was going on upon the plains of Shinar:

> And the Lord said, Behold, the people is one, and they have all one language; and this they begin to do: and now nothing will be restrained from them, which they have imagined to do (Genesis 11:6).

The agent-architects of "change" are the globalists that are intent on building the new Tower of Babel. Part of their blueprint — again, given them by Lucifer, Satan — includes a concerted effort to dumb down the people in the area of God's truth. This has been masterfully accomplished to a large extent, as can be witnessed by the dismantling of the American culture since the explosion of knowledge and technologies. The deconstruction of Judeo-Christian values as given by the founding fathers has accelerated exponentially within the past decade.

Merging Secular and Religious Apostasy

Dumbing down of America began with the secularization of the culture, as described above. The great explosion of knowledge and ability to move swiftly through transportation, the airwaves, and cyberspace dismantled the home environment for the most part, so far as concerns the nurturing incubator for life God intended the home to be.

Church attendance became less and less a priority, and now the assault began in earnest upon the churches themselves, and on the Bible. The emphasis Satan put at that point on dumbing down the American populous switched from the secular departure or *apostasy* to the *spiritual apostasy.*

He convinced the politicians and the Supreme Court to remove prayer and Bible reading from public schools in 1962 and 1963. The Humpty-Dumpty tumble downward began in a major way from that point.

The Lord of heaven didn't let it happen without warnings that it was the wrong course the nation was taking. A president was assassinated the very year Bible reading was removed. The sexual revolution began shortly thereafter, and America's moral fabric began to come apart. Films like *Deep Throat* became acceptable, almost mainstream, and even were lauded by universities as good for the culture.

Other leaders were assassinated during the era, like Martin Luther King Jr. and Robert F. Kennedy. America became embroiled in the quagmire of Vietnam, where more than 50,000 young American lives would be lost.

The cultural and societal downward spiral has accelerated to the point that speaking from the Bible against moral depravity is becoming more and more railed against. Obviously, it will one day be made illegal as "hate speech." Not only is it frowned upon, but any expression of opposition to the moral decay taking place is made the focus of scorn by mainstream news media journalists and even by the president of the United States. As a matter of fact, a president has bathed the White House and Washington, D.C. monuments in the rainbow colors of an organization that champions homosexuality — a thing God's Word calls an "abomination." The flag of that organization has flown above the nation's government buildings. The *departure* — the *apostasy* of the secular and the spiritual —

has set in, and it is a great, prophetic sign of just how near must surely be Christ's return.

And, the proof of that fact is that the churches of America, even fundamentalist, evangelical churches that once held strongly to the essentials of the faith, are caving day by day to the pressures of the God-haters to just shut up speaking against sin outside the confines of the church buildings. The preachers and teachers more and more stay within any subject but condemnation of sin. They concentrate on the nonconfrontational topics, preferring to stick to the "love" message within the Bible. The most popular preacher in America is exactly this kind of preacher. He has the largest church in attendance and contributions, and receives even the accolades of the secularist apostates. But, God has a prophetic Word for exactly this type of presentation in the last days — the time just before Christ's return:

> I charge thee therefore before God, and the Lord Jesus Christ, who shall judge the quick and the dead at his appearing and his kingdom; preach the word; be instant in season, out of season; reprove, rebuke, exhort with all longsuffering and doctrine. For the time will come when they will not endure sound doctrine; but after their own lusts shall they heap to themselves teachers, having itching ears; and they shall turn away their ears from the truth, and shall be turned unto fables (2 Timothy 4:1–4).

From this departure from truth has come the joining of some of the mainline denominations to an amalgamation of belief systems within Christianity that can be described as nothing more or less than *apostate*. And many of those who claim Christ as the central figure of their worship have joined with all sorts of religions and pagan worship systems. All of this, of course, is building toward the great apostasy prophesied by the Apostle Paul in 2 Thessalonians 2. The ultimate result of this ecumenism will be the bringing forth of the false prophet and the Antichrist of Revelation 13.

This last-days coming together of these false systems of worship are built around the true god of their affection: *mammon,* that is, wealth or money. Riches there are aplenty for the gurus of these apostate belief systems that are amalgamating at an unbelievable rate.

The following speaks to the financial aspects of some of these organizations that are seeking to establish one-world religion.

There are numerous channels and multiple feedback loops in this present-day progression. Such relatively new organizations as the International Interfaith Investment Group (3IG), which claims to wield some $10 trillion in wealth and 7 percent of the inhabitable real estate on the planet, are pushing for a purer and better world with the power of money. This is a group of some seven world religions.

There are many other organizations that seek to bridge the powers of religion, politics and money. Some of these include the Alliance of Religions and Conservation (ARC), the Coalition for Renewal (COR), and the Ecumenical Council for Corporate Responsibility (ECCR), to name a few. A sense of the spirit of these initiatives is evident in this quote from the ARC secretary-general: "The world's major faiths are starting to discover the power of their collective purse. Worldwide . . . they own trillions of dollars of shares, estimated by Citigroup to be in the region of 8–10 percent of the world's equity market."

There are many, many more such initiatives, and naming them would shock in some cases. . . .

This blurring of wealth worship (materialism) and institutionalized "godliness" is pictured in the figure of the whore shown in Revelation 17. She is bedecked in fine clothes, "glittering with gold, precious stones and pearls," and has "a golden cup in her hand" (Revelation 17:4). She represents religion that is in a lucrative league with the worldly kings of the earth. Here it appears that the two orbs of commerce (money) and religion co-exist comfortably. The reality is that materialism, greed, and the worship of wealth alone has won the hearts of mankind, though the Bible expressly states that "man does not live by bread alone, but man lives by everything that proceeds out of the mouth of the Lord" (Deuteronomy 8:3; Matthew 4:4).

This apparently unbridgeable gap between God and mammon offers one of the biggest, exploitable marketing opportunities ever known to mankind (and is also an important key to Satan's last-day strategy). How can one not pass up the chance for rich comfort and lucre from the wealth of mammon, while at the same time have the assurance of being righteous and spiritual?

If one can figure out a way to convince people that they can both worship God and sup with mammon at the same table, they or their businesses will meet with certain success. This is not a new discovery. It is a ruse that has worked in past history every time. Today it is an institutionalized strategy and unfolds on a global scale.

Mammon has masterfully honed its alluring appeals to the fleshly affections of mankind.

It is therefore no surprise that secular observers comment on the wealth of religious organizations. Says David Silverman of American Atheists, "Churches have a tremendous amount of power and a stupid amount of money."[2]

The financial power is now available to give the fiscal energy needed to fund Antichrist's satanic worship system of Revelation 13. The Antichrist spirit seems available in overwhelming numbers of anti-God adherents to give the dark, spiritual energy necessary to bring the satanic worship system into being when the Church goes to Christ in the Rapture.

My friend, the late Dave Hunt, wrote the following some years ago. It is even more timely at this present hour.

> Christ warned His disciples that "the time cometh, that whosoever killeth you will think that he doeth God service" (John 16:2). This is a most remarkable prophecy. Obviously Christ is not referring to persecution by atheists. He did not have in mind the slaughter of Christians by the Caesars or by Mao or Stalin or Hitler, for they did not believe they were serving God thereby. Of course, when the Jews killed the early Christians, they thought they were serving God; and so did the Roman Catholics when they slaughtered the true Christians before and after the Reformation, and so did the Muslims when they killed Christians. But none of these killings was the complete fulfillment of Christ's prophecy.
>
> That word "whosoever" is the key. Neither the Pharisees nor the popes were alone in killing Christians. Others were pursuing them to the death at the same time. But Christ is saying that a time is coming when whosoever, in other words, everyone who kills Christians will think he is serving God. That can only mean that a world

---

2. Wilfred Hahn, "End-time Wickedness: Consorting with Mammon," www.raptureready. com, "Newest Articles" section.

religion to which everyone must belong is coming, a religion that will seek to exterminate true Christians in the name of God. John saw the same scene in the future:

> And it was given unto him [Antichrist] to make war with the saints, and to overcome them. . . . And I beheld another beast. . . . he exerciseth all the power of the first beast . . . and causeth the earth and them which dwell therein to worship the first beast. . . . And he had power to . . . cause that as many as would not worship the image of the beast should be killed (Revelation 13:7–15).

Not Revival, But Apostasy

Even more solemn is an added dimension to Paul's declaration concerning the coming apostasy. Whereas Christ warned of deception, Paul said it is essential: "for that day [of the Lord] shall not come except there come a falling away [apostasy] first." This statement, as we have noted, is preceded by the strange warning, "Let no man deceive you."

Clearly, Paul, by the leading of the Holy Spirit, anticipated the very delusion we find in our day: the rejection of the biblical teaching concerning apostasy and the insistence that we are in the midst of or at least are building up to the "greatest revival in the history of the church." Such is the prevailing teaching today among charismatics and even noncharismatics. The promise of revival will be a deception, he warns, so beware. Instead of a great revival in the last days directly preceding the Rapture, there will be a great apostasy — a falling away from the faith.

Christ refers again to this falling away more subtly when He raises the question, "When the Son of man cometh, shall he find [the] faith on the earth" (Luke 18:8)? While the definite article is not included in most translations, it is obviously implied here and is found in other exhortations, such as in Jude. Christ is not referring to just any "faith" but to "the faith which was once [for all] delivered unto the saints" (Jude 3) and for which we are to "earnestly contend." This is the faith from which great numbers (seemingly even the vast majority) will fall away. . . .

Paul presents yet another characteristic of the apostasy: "For men shall be lovers of their own selves" (2 Timothy 3:2). This false teaching is rampant in the Church today through Christian psychology. It came from a godless psychologist named Erich Fromm who called "belief in God . . . a childish illusion." He claimed that when Christ said, "Love your neighbor as yourself," He meant that we must learn to love ourselves before we can love our neighbors or God. In fact, the Church had always interpreted that verse to mean that we love ourselves too much and need to give some of that love to our neighbors, not that we don't love ourselves enough.[3]

Certainly, we find ourselves in a time of self-delusion. It is a time that tells us that God doesn't condemn, but offers only "love." The woolly minded, left-leaning progressives believe that if we just tear down American hatred for those who want to live life as they see fit — apart from any governance by God — the whole world will love us in return. Even the Islamists will begin to stop beheading and doing the other horrendous atrocities they commit daily. Christians need to be shut up in our "hate speech."

All of this is a sure signal Christ is about to step out onto the clouds of glory and say to believers, "Come up here!" (Revelation 4:1).

3. Dave Hunt, "Flashes of Falling Away," *Forewarning*, Terry James, ed. (Eugene, OR: Harvest House, 1998), p. 27–51.

CHAPTER 11

THE ROMAN EMPIRE STRIKES BACK

Reason #11: The Roman Empire reforming, and geopolitical, economic, and religious prophetic indicators converging, is a dramatic reason to know that this will be the generation that will be left behind.

Historian Edward Gibbons wrote a number of volumes called *The Decline and Fall of the Roman Empire.* The vast scope of the work portrayed in minute detail how that great empire never was defeated by and taken over by military enemies. It became corrupt, rotted inwardly, and collapsed of its own over-stretched size and bloated bureaucracy. Its culture became debauched at every level. Homosexuality and pedophilia were among the final dominant societal features during its ultimate collapse.

I personally believe that the entire six volumes of analyzing the fall of that great empire is boiled down into one expression by Gibbon:

> But how shall we excuse the supine inattention of the Pagan and philosophic world to those evidences which were presented by

the hand of Omnipotence, not to their reason, but to their senses? During the age of Christ, of his apostles, and their first disciples, the doctrine which they preached was confirmed by innumerable prodigies. The lame walked, the blind saw, the sick were healed, the dead were raised, demons were expelled, and the laws of Nature were frequently suspended for the benefit of the church. But the sages of Greece and Rome turned aside from the awful spectacle, and, pursuing the ordinary occupations of life and study, appeared unconscious of any alterations in the moral of physical government of the world.[1]

To repeat scriptural truth we have seen before, the Apostle Paul — who lived during the time of Rome's power, and who suffered death at its hands — gave God's Word on any human culture, society, or government that ignores and/or opposes Him:

> For the wrath of God is revealed from heaven against all ungodliness and unrighteousness of men, who hold the truth in unrighteousness; because that which may be known of God is manifest in them; for God hath shewed it unto them. For the invisible things of him from the creation of the world are clearly seen, being understood by the things that are made, even his eternal power and Godhead; so that they are without excuse: because that, when they knew God, they glorified him not as God, neither were thankful; but became vain in their imaginations, and their foolish heart was darkened (Romans 1:18–21).

Reviving Roman Empire

The similarities should be apparent to anyone paying attention. America, in its decline, seems to be following the same downward pathway that took, arguably, history's most world-dominating empire into dissolution. The chief cause of our nation's moral dissipation, I believe, is like that Gibbon described for the ancient Roman Empire.

America is the most blessed of all nations with light from God's Word. Yet there is more and more a deliberate turning away from that light toward anything and everything other than toward that which is godly. A major

---

1. Edward Gibbon, *The History of the Decline and Fall of the Roman Empire* (Paris: Baudry's European Library, 1840), p. 109.

question to be asked is: *Will the United States of America simply go up in a ball of judgmental fire, or will it, like the Roman Empire, dissolve to be reborn in a form unrecognizable as the beloved nation we have known?*

The influence of that ancient empire of the Caesars, as it melted away, seeped and flowed into cultures around the globe, as many observers of the process of history have expressed. God's Word predicts that the ancient Roman system will *revive* and grow to be the most powerful and dominant governing force the world has ever known. It will be ruled by the most terrible tyrant ever to step foot upon a platform of power.

All one has to do is to walk the environs of Washington, D.C. to see the influence of Rome. The architecture reflects the ancient Greek and Roman influence at every turn. We get an interesting perspective on other ancient influence from the following.

> The English historian Peter Salway notes that England under Roman rule had a higher rate of literacy than any British government was able to achieve for the next fourteen centuries. One of the most important documentary legacies the Romans left behind was the law — the comprehensive body of statute and case law that some scholars consider our greatest inheritance from ancient Rome.
>
> The idea of written law as a shield — to protect individuals against one another and against the awesome power of the state — was a concept the Romans took from the Greeks. But it was Rome that put this abstract notion into daily practice, and the practice is today honored around the world. Ancient Rome was also concerned with the liberties of its citizens.

Innocent Until Proven Guilty

> The emperor Justinian's monumental compilation of the Digests, the Institutes, and the Revised Code, completed in A.D. 534, has served as the foundation of Western law ever since. Two millennia before the Miranda warnings, the Romans also established safeguards to assure the rights of accused criminals.
>
> We can see this process at work in the case against the Christian pioneer St. Paul, as set forth in the New Testament in the Acts of the Apostles. America's democratic system is clearly modeled after the Roman Republic.

Rome — U.S.A.

The Roman process of making laws also had a deep influence on the American system. During the era of the Roman Republic (509 to 49 B.C.) lawmaking was a bicameral activity. Legislation was first passed by the comitia, the assembly of the citizens, then approved by the representative of the upper class, the senate, and issued in the name of the senate and the people of Rome.

Centuries later, when the American Founding Fathers launched their bold experiment in democratic government, they took republican Rome as their model. Our laws, too, must go through two legislative bodies. The House of Representatives is our assembly of citizens, and, like its counterpart in ancient Rome, the U.S. Senate was originally designed as a chamber for the elite (it was not until the 17th Amendment, in 1913, that ordinary people were allowed to vote for their senators).

Impressed by the checks and balances of the Roman system, the authors of American government also made sure that an official who violated the law could be "impeached," a word we take from the Roman practice of putting wayward magistrates in *pedica*.

The reliance on Roman structures at the birth of the United States was reflected in early American popular culture, which delighted in drawing parallels between U.S. leaders and the noble Romans.

There was a great vogue for marble statues depicting George Washington, Alexander Hamilton, even Andrew Jackson in Roman attire. A larger-than-life statue of Washington in a toga and sandals is still on exhibit at the National Museum of American History in Washington, D.C.

These few quotations offer overwhelming proof that our modern world, regardless of where we reside, is based, built, and directed by Roman European principles that will lead to the solidifying of all the nations of the world, regardless of race, national origin, religion, or whatever else may be considered. All nations and peoples must become one under a one-world government.[2]

We learn of this Bible prophecy about the Roman Empire reviving to world power through the prophet Daniel. We have looked before in this book at

2. Arno Froese, "European Union on the Brink," *Foreshadows of Wrath and Redemption*, William T. James, ed. (Eugene, OR: Harvest House, 1999), p. 191–218.

Daniel's prophecy regarding the succeeding world powers that would come upon a constantly war-torn planet throughout human history. It is necessary that we look at them again here and again in future portions of this book to solidify understanding of the prophetic future. Let's review the prophecy very briefly.

Daniel, a captive in Babylon, was one of King Nebuchadnezzar's fortune tellers — as the king looked at him during Daniel's youngest years in captivity. Daniel, of course, was described as "greatly beloved" by the Lord. He was a prophet with a direct line to God's throne, it seemed.

Daniel interpreted Nebuchadnezzar's dream after first telling the king what he had dreamed. None of the other fortune tellers could tell the king the dream he had forgotten, or its meaning. The dream was of a metallic image of a man made of metals of descending value downward through the image's body, with the head being of gold and the feet being made of iron mixed with clay. The image represented, Daniel told the king, the succeeding world empires of history that would follow Nebuchadnezzar, who was the head of gold.

The last empire would be the two feet of iron and clay, with ten toes that would be part of the final form of government. These toes would be part of the same power structure, but would not "cleave to one another." They would be separate in their governing of the world's geographical areas, apparently.

Later, as was recorded in chapter 7 of the Book of Daniel, the prophet was given a vision of this end-times governmental system in the form of a strange, composite beast. It would have ten horns, again representing these final power-wielding entities. There would be a "little horn" that had eyes like a man and a mouth speaking great things, that would dominate and rule this composite beast — which represented an amalgamation of the four world empires combined into one, final, governmental beast-state.

Daniel later was given a prophecy that presented history yet future concerning the rebuilding of the Jewish Temple in Jerusalem and Israel's leaving captivity in Babylon. Gabriel the angel told Daniel that a total of 70 prophetic weeks was given to bring in God's everlasting Kingdom. Each prophetic week equaled seven years, for a total of 490 Jewish calendar years that will conclude with the Messiah putting an end to transgressions as He rules from the Temple in Jerusalem.

Gabriel said the Messiah would be "cut off" after 69 of those prophetic weeks. So the 69th prophetic week (at the 483rd year), the Messiah would be "cut off," or die. He would voluntarily give up His life, not because He had done anything wrong, but as sacrifice for the sins of all of mankind.

The Scripture reads:

> Know therefore and understand, that from the going forth of the commandment to restore and to build Jerusalem unto the Messiah the Prince shall be seven weeks, and threescore and two weeks: the street shall be built again, and the wall, even in troublous times.
>
> And after threescore and two weeks shall Messiah be cut off, but not for himself: and the people of the prince that shall come shall destroy the city and the sanctuary; and the end thereof shall be with a flood, and unto the end of the war desolations are determined (Daniel 9:25–26).

The prophecy covered an unknown number of years from the time Jesus Christ would die and ressurect to life through the time that a specific people would destroy Jerusalem and the Jewish Temple atop Mount Moriah — and a vast amount of years well beyond that event. The prophecy includes the mention of the "prince that shall come," who will be the progeny, the offspring, of those people. The rest of that prophecy gives further information on this coming *prince* and his future role in earth's history:

> And he shall confirm the covenant with many for one week: and in the midst of the week he shall cause the sacrifice and the oblation to cease, and for the overspreading of abominations he shall make it desolate, even until the consummation, and that determined shall be poured upon the desolate (Daniel 9:27).

This prince who will someday come on the scene and confirm a covenant is from the people who, from Daniel's perspective, would destroy Jerusalem and the Temple. We know this prophecy was fulfilled in A.D. 70 when Roman Emperor Vespasian sent his son, General Titus, and the Roman legions to put down insurrection in Jerusalem. The city and the sanctuary (Temple) were indeed destroyed.

Just as Jesus had prophesied some 40 years earlier, not one stone was left upon another atop the Temple Mount. (Read Matthew 24:2.)

So this prince who is yet to come, even from our perspective today, will be out of that people who accomplished the predicted destruction in A.D.

70. He will be a Roman, or one who comes from the region of Rome — the center of the ancient Roman Empire.

This is the man we have come to call *Antichrist*. He will sign onto a covenant of peace between Israel and its enemy neighbors, assuring that peace is observed by all parties, which, evidently, will include most of the nations of the world at that time.

The confirming of that covenant will begin the final prophetic week (the 70th week) Gabriel gave Daniel in the prophecy. The Jewish people — and all the people of the world — have been within the long parenthesis following the 69th prophetic week since Jesus died on the Cross, was buried and resurrected on the third day as sacrifice for the sins of all mankind. Again, the 70th prophetic week will begin when Antichrist confirms the deadly covenant of peace — the peace that "will destroy many" (Daniel 8:25).

So the *reviving of the ancient Roman Empire* is in process at the present time. When it comes again onto the scene in all its predicted power and authority, it will strike back with all its fury against anything and everything that is godly. It will be Satan's earthly kingdom, ruled over by the most wicked tyrant ever to walk the planet's surface.

The reviving of this final form of the ancient Babylonian Empire and all the empires that followed is a profound signal at just how near the world is at this present hour to Christ calling His Church in the Rapture.

Facts Surrounding the Reviving Empire

The 20th century began with Europe, the heart of what was the ancient Roman Empire, in decline. The upstart, America, was coming on strong as a world leader among nations. This circumstance, some historians propose, was a major factor in setting in motion movement toward World War I. Following that war, Europe was in chaos, but with great determination set about to put its house in order.

Despite fierce nationalism among Europe's nations, by 1954 the recovery was looked at as an economic miracle. Still, there was a major problem in ever achieving the much longed-for unity of purpose so many elite European thinkers coveted for the region. The nations had come together to fight in a common cause against Germany for the most part. However, each country continued to be completely independent from one another, and to maintain impenetrable economic trade-barrier walls. The situation made carrying on trade with other European nations difficult, if not impossible.

Powerful economic dynamics began to move Europe toward its prophetic destiny.

The old Roman Empire, which had fallen apart but was never destroyed, began reforming on May 9, 1950.

French Foreign Minister Robert Schuman contacted West German Chancellor Konrad Adenauer, proposing that the two nations merge their steel and coal production. They would act, the proposal went, as one in dealing internationally in those matters. The governments, however, would remain independent. There would be no joint, intergovernmental authority in the pact. Adenauer and the Germans agreed the same night of the proposal. By May 1952, six nations had ratified the European Coal and Steel Community. The glue that would begin putting the Humpty Dumpty, old Roman Empire, together again had been applied.

Europe's Coal and Steel Community experiment in economic reunification was successful. Other negotiations for further economic integration led to the signing of the Treaties of Rome in March 1957. That established the European Economic Community (EEC), and the European Atomic Energy Commission (EURACOM).

Following another step toward reunification with agricultural integration in 1962, the stage was set for the Brussels Treaty of 1965, also called the Second Treaty of Rome.

All previous treaties were merged into a four-fold structure. The structure consisted of a commission, council, parliament, and court.

The United Kingdom, Ireland, and Denmark joined the other six members of the EEC in 1973. Greece was admitted in 1981, and Spain, then Portugal, joined in 1986.

The European Community (EC) approved the Treaty of Maastricht in December 1991, the third foundational treaty of the drive toward European reunification.

It follows that a unified Europe needs a single currency, so the Maastricht Treaty established the European Monetary Union (EMU) in three stages. The stages took place in 1991, 1994, and 1997. The single European unit of currency, the euro, was created January 1, 2002.

Today, of course, many more nations have been accepted into the EU. Jack Kinsella, writing for *The Omega Letter, Prophecy Update,* April 23, 2003, says: "The European Union consists of more than twenty-five European nations today, but there are only ten full members. The rest are associate members or have observer status. The ten nations of the Western European Alliance have a distinct and separate status from the remaining associates."

Where the number of countries that will ultimately constitute the EU will end is anybody's guess, but the figure that has long fascinated prophecy watchers is the number 10. This fascination stems in part from Daniel 7:7–8 and Revelation 13:1. Both passages describe a beast with ten horns. The prophets Daniel and John apparently saw the same beast in their visions, the beast symbolizing ten heads of ten kingdoms.

Further, a heavenly being tells John in Revelation, chapter 17, that the vision of (apparently) the same beast he saw in Revelation 13:1 and the woman riding upon its back symbolize a religious system riding (receiving its own authority to dominate) on the power and authority of a satanically empowered system headed by ten kings over ten kingdoms. These things are to occur during the future time just before Christ's return to earth to set up His Kingdom.

It isn't surprising, then, that the addition of ten nations to the EU in 2003 sent some prophecy buffs into speculation orbit. An abundance of signals indeed makes the diligent student of God's Word know that ours could well be the generation that will see fulfillment of all things prophesied for this earth age.

No prophecy seems more in view today than the foretelling about the beast that Daniel and John reported seeing in their visions. We must take care not to read into the event's significance that isn't there. Truly, the facts involving current events are astonishing enough! It's not necessary for us to embellish.

The European Union is on the march as never before, despite its family feuding on occasion. For example, the economic problems presented by Greece and other EU states have caused considerable divisions. Despite their often internal bickering, the EU still most often maintains the attitude of superiority in dealings with the rest of the world. They are, after all, the center of intellectual enlightenment for the whole world.

It is just that sort of arrogance that gave the Caesars of the ancient Roman Empire their lust and determination to try to conquer the world. Supreme arrogance will inspire Antichrist, "the prince that shall come," out of the revived Roman Empire to take charge of the ten-horned beast-government and do his deadly worst to enslave the world.

If the EU's arrogant posturing in international matters is somewhat of an indicator that we might be witnessing the forming of the beast-government of Daniel 7, Revelation 13, and Revelation 17–18, then things on the geopolitical horizon surely are irrefutable signs that we are bumping up against the very end of the age.

The two pre-eminent entities of Bible prophecy yet future are emerging and will shortly collide with each other. These prophetic entities are Israel and the people of "the prince that shall come" (Europe). Presently, the conflict within the region where ancient Babylon once sat appears to be shaping up for major prophetic progression; all eyes, cameras, and microphones are turning — as they always do — back toward Israel and Jerusalem.

The European Union is a major entity at the forefront of calling for Israel and the Palestinians to come to the peace table. It will be just such a peace negotiation, according to Daniel 9:26–27, out of which will come the "covenant made with death and hell" (Isaiah 28:15, 18). Antichrist, "the prince that shall come," will personally guarantee that covenant. But the prophetic Word says that "when they shall say, peace and safety; then, sudden destruction cometh upon them, as travail upon a woman with child, and they shall not escape" (1 Thessalonians 5:3).

The Islamic world's hatred for the Jews and the nation Israel is satanic at its core. No amount of negotiating for peace ever will change that. Israel's neighbors want the Jewish state forever done away with — expunged from what they consider their land. The Arab leaders — Iran's (Persia's) leaders, too — all dictators to one degree or another, must keep the region in foment against Israel to assure their dictatorships stay in power.

In terms of Bible prophecy, this is significant on several levels. It is clear that the Islamic world will never accept the existence of Israel. Iran, in fact, is in process of developing nuclear weaponry to make sure the Jewish state doesn't exist.

Daniel speaks of the ten kings who arise out of the ashes of the Roman Empire. Daniel says that out of this alliance will rise the Antichrist, who will confirm a seven-year peace deal between Israel and the many (Israel's enemies all around).

America's part in pushing Israel toward the table of false peace is troubling. President Barack Obama, who has proven to be the least friendly president to Israel in U.S. history, has declared that that nation must bring to the table the idea that a Palestinian state will be created. That future state must, the United States as well as the EU and the others demand, be formed out of land of the West Bank (Judea and Samaria).

The European Union's influence is growing at a phenomenal rate. Soon its economy will, it is predicted, eclipse that of the United States in almost every category. This is expected to eventuate, despite what looks to be at times its overwhelming economic problems. It is a beast just about to be released upon an unsuspecting world.

Understanding that Europe has shed its former robes of Christianity to accept its prophesied economic and governmental role within the end-times Babylonian system of world domination is essential to comprehending its beast nature. Out of this strange mixture of democracy and collusion with the money-masters of international banking, a man will emerge whom Bible prophecy says will be a genius at underhanded dealings such as the world has never known. That Scripture says: "And in the latter time of their kingdom, when the transgressors are come to the full, a king of fierce countenance, and understanding dark sentences, shall stand up" (Daniel 8:23).

Antichrist will, through his satanic genius, know exactly how to get the most for himself and his world-order elitists who assist him in his drive to enslave the world.

The European Union grows rapidly toward its full power that will produce a leader of unprecedented authority. Bible prophecy foretells that seven out of ten "kings" will back a world leader, who will forcibly rip power from the other three and give it to himself. The great question of our time, prophetically speaking, might be: Is the European Union the prophesied governmental body that will eventuate in becoming the ten kingdoms that will provide Antichrist with his beastly power?

No one can say for certain, although some seem to have no problem making such declarations, as if they personally helped God give the prophets the prophecies. All we will say here is that with all other prophetic indicators seemingly in full view upon the immediate geopolitical horizon, another profound ingredient is in process of being added to the fascinating mix. If the EU is not the body that will evolve into that most evil of history's empires, it must be that biblically prophesied empire's twin.

The EU looks to be, at the very least, the prototype union for the global economic power structure — the ten entities — being constructed.

Economics Set the End-Times Stage

We are witnessing economic rearrangements at present like no other generation has seen. Even the United States — as anyone with any sense of what's been going on in the news will attest — is being forced into a mold of one-world economic order. It is all leading toward the mark and numbering system that will give Antichrist his power.

The United States of Antichrist

I think the dramatic upheavals being orchestrated in America demonstrate that these convulsions are being used to diminish America's influence in this world rapidly headed for greatly changed global order. Unless the United States is brought down, that change will be difficult, if not impossible, to effect.

It is obvious to me that forces outside of America and, even more troubling, forces within the ranks of our government at the highest levels, believe it is high time that the United States be brought to account for the perceived wrongs they insanely believe this great nation has perpetrated. The changes they seek will soon allow the master manipulator of all things evil to achieve — at least for a time — the new order of things he desires for humanity.

This gestating global entity I term "the United States of Antichrist."

What we are experiencing is a "change," in my opinion, that is designed to shift the movement of union of this continent — even this hemisphere — into high gear. It is perhaps a move more dynamic than any other of recent years to accelerate a major prophetic development. This alignment is what I term — again — the "United States of Antichrist." The following is how God's Holy Word describes my United States of Antichrist.

The prophecy of which I write is wrapped up in the alignment of nations as they will be at the time Christ's Second Advent nears.

Let us again look closely at the prophet John's words.

> And the ten horns which thou sawest are ten kings, which have received no kingdom as yet; but receive power as kings one hour with the beast. These have one mind, and shall give their power and strength unto the beast (Revelation 17:12–13).

We have seen before that Daniel the prophet, like John to whom the Revelation was given, saw the entity that would emerge at the time near the end. Daniel saw it as the lowest extremities of the great, metallic image of Babylonian King Nebuchadnezzar's prophetic dream.

Again, Daniel told the king the following about what the feet of this prophetic dream-image involved.

> And whereas thou sawest the feet and toes, part of potters' clay, and part of iron, the kingdom shall be divided; but there shall be in it of the strength of the iron, forasmuch as thou sawest the iron mixed with miry clay.
>
> And as the toes of the feet were part of iron, and part of clay, so the kingdom shall be partly strong, and partly broken.
>
> And whereas thou sawest iron mixed with miry clay, they shall mingle themselves with the seed of men: but they shall not cleave one to another, even as iron is not mixed with clay.
>
> And in the days of these kings shall the God of heaven set up a kingdom, which shall never be destroyed: and the kingdom shall not be left to other people, but it shall break in pieces and consume all these kingdoms, and it shall stand for ever (Daniel 2:41–44).

Once again we reflect upon the fact that Daniel, and later, John, saw these ten kings and kingdoms as the last world power that will be ruled over by the first beast of Revelation 13. That strange, composite behemoth is described through John's telling of the Revelation:

> And I stood upon the sand of the sea, and saw a beast rise up out of the sea, having seven heads and ten horns, and upon his horns ten crowns, and upon his heads the name of blasphemy (Revelation 13:1).

This composite monster, although symbolic in its representation of planet earth's final world power, presents a terrifying image of what it is to become once it moves onto the end-times world. Daniel describes the monster further, as well as the personage who will be at its head.

> After this I saw in the night visions, and behold a fourth beast, dreadful and terrible, and strong exceedingly; and it had great iron teeth: it devoured and brake in pieces, and stamped the residue with the feet of it: and it was diverse from all the beasts that were before it; and it had ten horns.
>
> I considered the horns, and, behold, there came up among them another little horn, before whom there were three of the first horns plucked up by the roots: and, behold, in this horn were eyes like the eyes of man, and a mouth speaking great things (Daniel 7:7–8).

There can be no serious contention with the fact that Bible prophecy predicts a final world power that will consist of ten separate, yet unified in some way, entities. Regardless of whether one believes the Bible or not, one cannot deny that such a final world governing monster is prophesied to come on the scene at some point. It is foretold to be all-consuming, and a monstrosity that is headed by the most mesmerizing orator of all time — and the most blasphemous.

Prophetic Empire Emerging

The geopolitical factors for the soon fulfillment of Bible prophecy are in alignment. Israel is again a nation hated by practically all other nations, and Jerusalem, with the Temple Mount at the center of potential for all-out war, is headline stuff daily. Russia and Iran are poised to fulfill their destinies as the nucleus of the Gog-Magog force of Ezekiel 38–39. Just as dramatic as these is the emergence of a number of distinct global economic trading blocs.

I consider these that I term the developing "United States of Antichrist" to be the reviving Roman Empire, from which the beast of Revelation 13 will emerge. Our own once great and sovereign nation is the key factor in ultimately determining how swiftly Daniel and John's composite world government will come into fulfillment.

We can understand just how important the United States is to the rest of the nations of earth by thinking on America's chief Cold War nemesis at this very hour. In very recent times, Russia's president, Vladimir Putin, was threatening to cut off oil and gas to Europe. He blustered in his macho way to tell the West that its sanctions imposed for his bellicosity against Ukraine, etc., would only hurt the West and harden Russia's resolve.

In addition to leading the imposition of sanctions against Putin's saber-rattling, the U.S. administration, it is almost a certainty in my mind, twisted the arms of the Saudi royal family to drop the price of oil through market manipulations. Thus, the powers that be, even above our president's own input, achieved their two-fold purpose: (1) It cut the legs out from under Putin's oil sales because he could not compete with such decreases. Almost overnight, the ruble fell precipitously against the dollar. The fall and its ramification was so great that some heads within European governments wanted sanctions eased or lifted so as to save Russia from possible economic collapse. (2) It greatly set back the burgeoning fracking industry in America's North Dakota and other regions, an action intended to further bring America's economic base to an ever-lessening position of dominance.

So, Lucifer — again, in my opinion — is using the most powerful nation to ever be upon earth to bring all others into his desired one-world configuration — the configuration that was his desire at Babel all of those millennia ago. At the same time, he is managing to diminish America, thereby bringing her into conformation with the new world order he is building. I think his demented genius is evident at every turn as of late.

Already the construction of the United States of Antichrist is far advanced. Although the individual regional entities that comprise the quickly evolving global-governing power to come are in constant flux, the skeleton that will soon take on prophesied end-times flesh is in view today. Here is how it looks at a quick glance:

- European Union[3]
- North American Union[4]
- South American Union[5]
- African Union[6]
- Mediterranean Union[7]
- Eurasian Economic Union[8]
- Gulf Cooperation Council (Arab states of the Gulf)[9]
- South Asian Association[10]

3. "European Union," Wikipedia, http://en.wikipedia.org/wiki/European_Union.
4. William F. Jasper, "Obama Presses 'North American Union' with Mexico, Canada," *New American*, February 24, 2014, http://www.thenewamerican.com/usnews/constitution/item/17705-obama-presses-north-american-union-with-mexico-canada.
5. "Russian Diplomats Attend Union of South American Nations Summit," *Sputnik International*, December 5, 2014, http://sputniknews.com/latam/20141205/1015524408.html.
6. "Cooperation with Africa Must Occur at Earliest Signs of Crisis, Ban Tells Security Council," UN News Centre, December 16, 2014, http://www.un.org/apps/news/story.asp?NewsID=49622#.VJX17F4APA.
7. "Union for the Mediterranean," Wikipedia, http://en.wikipedia.org/wiki/Union_for_the_Mediterranean.
8. "Eurasian Economic Union," http://en.wikipedia.org/wiki/Eurasian_Economic_Union.
9. Jasim Ali, "Awaiting the Final Push towards a GCC Customs Union," *Gulf News*, December 13, 2014, http://gulfnews.com/business/opinion/awaiting-the-final-push-towards-a-gcc-customs-union-1.1425948.
10. "South Asian Association for Regional Cooperation Wikipedia," http://en.wikipedia.org/wiki/South_Asian_Association_for_Regional_Cooperation#Members_and_observers.

- Asia Pacific Union[11]
- Caribbean Community[12]

Peace, Prosperity, and the Coming Holocaust

Dave Hunt once wrote in a stunning book called *Peace, Prosperity, and the Coming Holocaust* that things would look rosy on the surface for a time. There would be a time of relative peace — in this nation, at least — and the economy would seem to provide a prosperous time for the United States.

He said through many scripturally based thoughts that it was all a ruse — smoke and mirrors — meant to deceive and lull into deadly complacency. The inevitable "holocaust" would come when the deception had achieved its venomous, desensitizing effect.

I am of the prayerfully studied opinion that the "peace" and "prosperity" eras of Dave's Holy Spirit-directed warnings are nearing their end. The very fabric of civilization, itself, is observably coming apart. The swift development of the United States of Antichrist — the ten toes of Nebuchadnezzar's dream-image as fleshed out in Revelation 17:12–13 — means the seven years of Tribulation must be on the very cusp of prophetic initiation. The greatest of all holocausts is about to come upon a sinful world of anti-God rebels.

That means that the Rapture of the Church — when Jesus Christ calls all born-again believers in a millisecond to be with Him — is even at the door of this generation.

Europe in Upheaval

Europe today is in dynamic upheaval, struggling to stand on the feet and toes that will give the eventual Antichrist system its balance, its equilibrium. But just as Daniel foretold, the feet and toes are not made of purely a metal of strength. The EU is made partly of the governmental strength that was the ancient Roman Empire, but also is constructed of weakness intrinsic within the governments of contemporary times. This makes the whole structure that is the final form of all worldly economic-governmental power subject to crashing to final collapse. This is exactly what Daniel foresaw as given in Daniel 2:44:

---

11. Mireya Solis, "East Asia Forum. China Flexes Its Muscles at APEC with the Revival of FTAAP," November 24, 2014, http://www.eastasiaforum.org/2014/11/23/china-flexes-its-muscles-at-apec-with-the-revival-of-ftaap/.
12. "Carribean Community," Wikipedia, http://en.wikipedia.org/wiki/Caribbean_Community.

And in the days of these kings shall the God of heaven set up a kingdom, which shall never be destroyed: and the kingdom shall not be left to other people, but it shall break in pieces and consume all these kingdoms, and it shall stand for ever.

Paul wrote of the economic reality that drives the world toward God's judgment and wrath:

But they that will be rich fall into temptation and a snare, and into many foolish and hurtful lusts, which drown men in destruction and perdition. For the love of money is the root of all evil (1 Timothy 6:9–10a).

Rushing Toward the End

Certainly, the truth of God's Word frames what is happening at this time in history and where it all is heading as the rulers of this fallen sphere grasp for the wealth of this world and strive to cast off the bonds of governance God wisely placed upon the would-be masters of planet earth.

Go to now, ye rich men, weep and howl for your miseries that shall come upon you. Your riches are corrupted, and your garments are motheaten. Your gold and silver is cankered; and the rust of them shall be a witness against you, and shall eat your flesh as it were fire. Ye have heaped treasure together for the last days. Behold, the hire of the labourers who have reaped down your fields, which is of you kept back by fraud, crieth: and the cries of them which have reaped are entered into the ears of the Lord of sabaoth. Ye have lived in pleasure on the earth, and been wanton; ye have nourished your hearts, as in a day of slaughter. Ye have condemned and killed the just; and he doth not resist you (James 5:1–6).

It looks like we are in the end of the age era of the toes of Nebuchadnezzar's night vision. The Roman Empire, thought long defunct, is about to strike back!

This means that Rapture Ready . . . or not, Christ will soon call all believers to Himself.

CHAPTER 12

WHO IS THAT MASKED MAN ON A WHITE HORSE?

Reason #12: The fact that the Antichrist spirit is front and center each and every day in culture and society constitutes a major reason I believe this is the generation that will be left behind.

The first time I saw a television show was around 1950. Our neighbors, an older couple, invited me in each afternoon and allowed me to sit in their living room, with the grandmotherly lady, Omie, as I recall her name, serving me home-baked cookies and a "pop" as we called soft drinks in Illinois during those days. It was heaven on earth for those 30 minutes, to a boy of eight.

With the "William Tell Overture" thumping in the background, there galloped a huge, white horse, with his rider, who was wearing an equally white hat and a black mask. He was followed closely behind by a pinto horse with a man in fringed buckskin aboard. That's right. It was Silver and Scout carrying the Lone Ranger and Tonto, his ever-present Indian (guess I should say Native American) companion.

Each program, the masked man would ride to the rescue in one situation or another. I remember always sitting on pins and needles wondering if he would arrive in time, each and every episode. He always did, of course.

In the genre of heroic fiction, the protagonist good guy is frequently depicted as the guy in the white hat — at least symbolically. We hear these heroes referred to in general terms as "the man on a white horse." He rides onto the scene with the purpose of righting all wrongs — setting everything as it should be once again.

In those episodes of *The Lone Ranger,* there was always a terrible situation for him to rectify. They were real nail-biters, even with the buffering of cookies and pop to help alleviate the angst.

The world is presently within a problematic time that will soon lead into an even worse time of trouble. As a matter of fact, the greatest of all prophets — the Lord Jesus Christ — said a time will come that will be the worst time that had ever been on earth to His time at that moment, or that will ever be upon this problem-plagued planet.

He said that it will be a time of "great tribulation." This is the statement from which we get the term that is applied to the seven years immediately preceding the Second Advent of Christ. We have seen thus far that this era is also called Daniel's 70th week. It is the same time frame of those seven years foretold by Jeremiah the prophet as a period of great trouble for God's chosen people, Israel. Jeremiah says the following:

> Alas! for that day is great, so that none is like it: it is even the time of Jacob's trouble, but he shall be saved out of it (Jeremiah 30:7).

This seven years of horror will follow the Rapture of all born-again believers who are living or who died during the Church Age. We have seen that this period will be initiated with the signing of a covenant of false peace by a man. This "prince that shall come" (Daniel 9:26) has come to be called Antichrist.

The prophetic Scripture that speaks most specifically to this coming prince is one with which most students of Bible prophecy are thoroughly familiar:

> And I saw when the Lamb opened one of the seals, and I heard, as it were the noise of thunder, one of the four beasts saying, Come and see. And I saw, and behold a white horse: and he that sat on

him had a bow; and a crown was given unto him: and he went forth conquering, and to conquer (Revelation 6:1–2).

We are given the picture of the first of the four horses of the Apocalypse as they carry their riders across the last seven years of human history just before Christ's Second Coming back to earth. This is the Tribulation.

The first rider on that spectacular white steed is none other than Antichrist. As the prophecy says, he will come forth conquering everything and everyone that is in his path.

Most scholars and students from the fundamentalist camp who are of the premillennial, pre-tribulation view of Bible prophecy believe the bow in this vision indicates that this prince will come in on a peace platform. He has a bow, but displays no arrows.

This is exactly the image the prophet Daniel is given to prophesy:

> And through his policy also he shall cause craft to prosper in his hand; and he shall magnify himself in his heart, and by peace shall destroy many (Daniel 8:25).

A crown is given to him, so, apparently, most of his conquests are like Hitler's at the very beginning of his aggression. In the fuhrer's initial demands, he met almost no resistance. It seems the same might be the case when the future tyrant called Antichrist rides onto the scene.

He will look like a great peacemaker and one who can re-establish order, which will no doubt have been all but totally destroyed. He will even promise prosperity as Daniel's prophecy indicates. He will "cause craft to prosper."

However, he "will destroy many" through his conquests, his "peacemaking," and his "causing craft to prosper." This man on the white horse will be wearing a mask for sure, and his motives and intentions will be nothing like those of my childhood hero on his white horse who wore a mask for noble reasons.

Antichrist's mask will camouflage for a time the greatest deception ever perpetrated on humanity. World conditions will make the deception one for which most everyone will fall, or take the bait, as they say — hook, line, and sinker.

One of the great prophecy scholars of recent times, Dr. David Breese, said of this eventuality:

One can certainly see that, given the mental state of our time, people are looking for a human savior and are willing to enthusiastically respond. Jack Anderson, the columnist, said, "The world is now in such a condition that everyone appears to be waiting for a rider and a white horse to pick them up and carry them off to a splendid tomorrow."

Will there be such a rider on a white horse?[1]

World conditions are indeed building toward crisis at every level. They are all desperately appealing for bringing into existence a new world order — a rant that has been issuing forth throughout our troubling times.

Henry Kissinger: "What Congress will have before it is not a conventional trade agreement but the architecture of a new international system . . . a first step toward a new world order."[2]

Mikhail Gorbachev: "World progress is only possible through a search for universal human consensus as we move forward to a new world order."[3]

George H.W. Bush: "What is at stake is more than one small country, it is a big idea — a new world order . . . to achieve the universal aspirations of mankind . . . based on shared principles and the rule of law. . . . The illumination of a thousand points of light. . . . The winds of change are with us now."[4]

Mikhail Gorbachev: "We are beginning to see practical support. And this is a very significant sign of the movement towards a new era, a new age. . . . We see both in our country and elsewhere . . . ghosts of the old thinking. . . . When we rid ourselves of their presence, we will be better able to move toward a new world order . . . relying on the relevant mechanisms of the United Nations."[5]

---

1. Dr. David Breese, "The Roman Empire's Greatest Caesar," *Raging Into Apocalypse*, William T. James, ed. (Green Forest, AR: New Leaf Press, 1995), p. 89.
2. Dr. Henry Kissinger, "In the Lead Up to Congress being Challenged to Sign onto the North America Free Trade Association (NAFTA)," *Los Angeles Times*, July 18, 1993.
3. Mikhail Gorbachev, "Address to the U.N. Calls for Mutual Consensus," December 7, 1988.
4. George H.W. Bush, State of Union Message, 1991, http://grahamhancock.com/phorum/read.php?2,497435,498033.
5. October 30, 1991, Middle East Peace Talks in Madrid, http://www.apfn.org/thewinds/library/new_world_order.html.

George H.W. Bush: "It is the sacred principles enshrined in the United Nations charter to which the American people will henceforth pledge their allegiance."[6]

President Bill Clinton: "Norman Cousins worked for world peace and world government. . . . Strobe Talbott's lifetime achievements as a voice for global harmony have earned him this recognition. . . . He will be a worthy recipient of the Norman Cousins Global Governance Award. Best wishes . . . for future success."[7]

Egyptian President Hosni Mubarak: "The renewal of the nonproliferation treaty [is] important for the welfare of the whole world and the new world order."[8]

British Prime Minister Tony Blair: "This is a moment to seize. The kaleidoscope has been shaken, the pieces are in flux, soon they will settle again. Before they do, let us re-order this world around us."[9]

Vice President Joe Biden: "The affirmative task before us is to create a New World Order."[10]

History's top champions of building a global order have been quite specific in calling for a superman to head such a one-world state. The following often-quoted statement says it all.

First president of the United Nations General Assembly, Paul-Henri Spaak, who was also a prime minister of Belgium and one of the early planners of the European Common Market, as well as a secretary-general of NATO, declared:

We do not want another committee, we have too many already. What we want is a man of sufficient stature to hold the allegiance of all the people and to lift us up out of the economic morass into

---

6. 1992, Address to the General Assembly of the U.N, http://www.apfn.org/thewinds/library/new_world_order.html.

7. 1993, Strobe Talbott (Bill Clinton's roommate at Oxford) receives the Norman Cousins Global Governance Award for his 1992 *Time* article, "The Birth of the Global Nation" and in appreciation for what he has done "for the cause of global governance."

8. *New York Times,* April 1995, http://www.nytimes.com/1995/04/06/world/clinton-backs-drive-against-nuclear-arms-in-mideast.html.

9. October 2, 2001, Speech at Labour Party Conference, http://www.theguardian.com/politics/2001/oct/03/uk.afghanistan.

10. April 5, 2013, speech for Import Export Bank, http://www.thenewamerican.com/usnews/politics/item/15036-joe-biden-on-creating-a-new-world-order.

which we are sinking. Send us such a man, and whether he be God or devil, we will receive him.[11]

Another top new-world-order leader and self-confessed luciferian, Robert Muller, who also served as assistant Secretary General of the United Nations, once said:

> If Christ came back to earth, his first visit would be to the United Nations to see if his dream of human oneness and brotherhood had come true.[12]

I think it would be a good guess to suppose that when the man in the mask comes riding onto the stage of history atop the shining white steed of Revelation 6, one of his first appearances will take place in front of the gathered delegates of the U.N. Before reaching the status that would place this man on his United Nations pedestal, however, he would first likely have established himself as the man with a plan.

Years ago, my great friend Dave Breese wrote a scenario for how this formative encounter between this special individual and the global elite might take place. I share that with you here with the caveat that such a meeting might already have taken place in our time. My own belief is that it is highly likely that the "plan" has at its center the theme of "climate change."

> With the 50 or so globalists-elite gathered near Chicago, a young man steps to the front of the lectern in a luxuriously appointed dining hall and speaks:
>
> "As we all know, the world is in the midst of a growing set of very serious problems. Dealing with them is already beyond the natural ability of any of us. These problems may, however, be amenable to the mutual, corporate activity of knowledgeable individuals — like those who are here this evening.
>
> "Notice first of all the global economy. The nations of the world that once bore most of the weight of the economies of the world are themselves in serious straits.
>
> "Think with me about the United States for just a moment. Many an optimistic conversation is carried on here about how great the economy is and how wonderful are our future possibilities. The

---

11. http://www.theforbiddenknowledge.com/hardtruth/united_nations_index.htm.
12. Ibid.

facts are the opposite. We are a debtor nation living off the unearned incomes of our grandchildren. Our national debt is many trillions of dollars and growing every day. The global economy indeed is very shaky. So serious is the problem that I think we can say we are being held together by some kind of mysterious force, by faith rather than merely an archaic love of country.

"Ladies and gentlemen, you know all of these things, but I say them to remind us of the need for action that is now upon us. We have all lived lives of relative wealth and convenience, conditions we do not want to discontinue. They will be discontinued, however, unless we move with a new plan to vouchsafe our future. Virtually the same precarious conditions exist in every aspect of life in America and in the world. It is imperative that we produce a new form of world influence, of world control, before our whole elite culture slips away from us. We must find a way to re-establish that pinnacle of power from which we have operated for three or four generations. . . .

"I have called us together to recommend a course of action. The time for our program has come upon us, and if we do not act in these days, we will lose our opportunity to touch the world — yes, to lead it. We are at the place that was well-described by Shakespeare when he said, 'There is a tide in the affairs of men, which, taken at the flood, leads on to fortune; omitted, all the voyage of their life is lived in shallows and in miseries.' Ladies and gentlemen, I promise you fortunes, but if we do not act in these days, it will be shallows and miseries. . . .

We have the opportunity in these very days to expand our thinking and rise to the great occasions that are before us."

[*Author's note:* Dave Breese went on to analyze the conditions of the times in which he wrote the above scenario.]

Things are much, much advanced today in their stage-setting for the coming of Antichrist. Therefore, we can expect to exist con-comitantly in that interesting era of earth two great conditions. The first is the vast expansion of human knowledge and the second is the rise of perilous conditions across the world.

When we read the prophetic Word, we are certainly supposed to ask, "Does that prediction resemble anything that I see on earth today?" We can quickly agree with the close resemblance between the condition of our external world and the teaching of the Word of God. Dozens of other comparisons and individual passages tell us detail after detail of the rise of Antichrist. They will surely promise that they can create a new world order and bring to pass the dawn of a new day. Their plans for the future will not be merely business as usual; their plans will hinge on an exciting dimension that touches every life.

Again, as we are thinking of the convincing messages that they will bring, we cannot help but compare the associates of the Antichrist with today's politicians. Hundreds upon hundreds of such men and women live in Washington, D.C., and thousands more populate the major cities of the world. They are convincing in the presentation of global plans. When needed, they will be able to bring in an army to back up their convincing displays of the organization of the Antichrist.[13]

Even though we can agree that that scenario, written in the early 1990s, is a bit dated, Dr. Breese demonstrated a remarkable degree of foresight in framing developments that would be in place decades later. I believe that the nucleus for such a plan is now in place. As mentioned earlier, I believe that central theme these elitists have chosen for the new globalist order to proceed is *climate change.*

The new world order architects will need one thing in order to convince nations like the United States and others to give up national sovereignty. That will require a crisis of monumental magnitude. This globalist plan cannot come into being without the creation of world conditions that have the populaces of the nations — and the leaders — clamoring for solutions to their unbearable dilemma.

That crisis will be the Rapture of all believers in Jesus Christ. The Rapture will, I believe, bring all of the pent-up economic indebtedness and chaos crashing in upon a world ripe for judgment.

Again, Jesus spoke of this time as recorded in Matthew 24:36–42 and Luke 17:26–30. It will be pretty much business as usual right up until the time Christ catastrophically intervenes by calling His Church home (Revelation 4:1).

---

13. Dave Breese, "Globalists Elite at the Throttle," *Foreshadows of Wrath and Redemption,* William T. James, ed. (Eugene, OR: Harvest House, 1999), p. 220–226.

The world is presently perfectly positioned for that calamitous future event. It will be a wonderful occurrence for those who have accepted Christ as Savior. Sadly, tragically, it will be devastating to those left behind.

If the world is presently as near the time of Rapture as all of this suggests, then the man who will bring total devastation through his satanically powered, tyrannical rule must be very near the time of mounting his white horse.

Perhaps the most noted scholar of our time in the matter of biblical eschatology (the study of end things) was Dr. John Walvoord. I had the privilege to know him, and he contributed to my books on Bible prophecy.

Since it's impossible to improve on Dr. Walvoord's perspective on the topic of the coming Antichrist, I want to again share a brief excerpt from his exposition on the earth's final tyrant.

Walvoord on Antichrist

The Rise of the Antichrist

When false teachers taught the Thessalonian believers that they were already in the day of the Lord, Paul had to correct this. He argued in 2 Thessalonians 2 that they were not in the day of the Lord period after the Rapture because the man of lawlessness had not appeared. Second Thessalonians 2:1–3 states:

"Concerning the coming of our Lord Jesus Christ and our being gathered to him, we ask you, brothers, not to become easily unsettled or alarmed by some prophecy, report or letter supposed to have come from us, saying that the day of the Lord has already come. Don't let anyone deceive you in any way, for that day will not come until the rebellion occurs and the man of lawlessness is revealed, the man doomed to destruction."

His work is further described in 2 Thessalonians 2:4: "He will oppose and will exalt himself over everything that is called God or is worshiped, so that he sets himself up in God's temple, proclaiming himself to be God."

The "man of lawlessness" is another reference to the one who is also called the Antichrist. The word "antichrist" is mentioned four times in the Scriptures (1 John 2:18, 22, 4:3; 2 John 7). As used by John, it applies to anyone who is opposed to Christ and is a false leader. The term has been used to describe the end-time ruler because his activities are so obviously anti-Christ, and he is Satan's substitute for Jesus Christ as King of Kings, Lord of Lords, and God. However, the book of Revelation and other passages of Scripture outside of the Johannine epistles never used the term.

The Antichrist appears on the scene as the conqueror of the ten-nation revival of the Roman Empire. According to Daniel 7:8, a little horn comes up among the ten horns and uproots three of them, which signifies that he has conquered three of the ten countries. From there on, although Scriptures do not explain the reasons, he is regarded as the ruler of all ten nations. In other words, he takes over as the dictator of the revived Roman Empire. From this position he rises to power gradually until finally he becomes the world ruler of scriptural prophecy.

Second Thessalonians 2:14 offers remarkable evidence that the Rapture of the church occurs before the end-time prophecy. Paul is demonstrating that they are not in the day of the Lord as false teachers have taught them, because the man of lawlessness has not appeared. When will the man of lawlessness appear?

His full revelation comes in the middle of this last seven years of end-time prophecy when he claims to be God. But he will be revealed earlier than that, when he makes the covenant of Daniel 9:27 for seven years leading up to the second coming of Christ. In order to have this position of power, he has to be the one who conquers the Roman Empire and becomes the head of the ten countries. This must occur, therefore, more than seven years before the Second Coming. If he has to appear before the day of the Lord can begin, it should be obvious that the Day of the Lord will begin more than seven years before the Second Coming. This automatically disposes of counter-opinions which put the Rapture at the Second Coming or during the Great Tribulation or at the beginning of the Great Tribulation or the beginning of the seven years, for the man of lawlessness will be revealed more than seven years before the Second Coming. Accordingly, the rise of the Roman empire will become a very important factor in determining how soon the Rapture of the church may take place.[14]

---

14. John Walvoord, "Antichrist, Armageddon, and the Second Coming of Christ," *Forewarning*, William T. James, ed. (Eugene, OR: Harvest House, 1998), p. 345–346.

More on the Man of Sin

To instruct further on the man on the white horse of Revelation 6, we consider additional ponderings from a Bible prophecy scholar I greatly respect. Daymond R. Duck is highly regarded as an authority in biblical eschatology.

Several elaborate systems have been developed in an effort to reveal the name of the Antichrist, but they have all been wrong. Some names these systems have come up with are Adolf Hitler, Benito Mussolini, Henry Kissinger, Ronald Reagan, William "Bill" Clinton, and several of the popes. These should be seen for what they are — just wild guesses. Furthermore, trying to identify antichrist is just a waste of time because he will not be revealed until after the Rapture (2 Thessalonians 2:1–12). Dr. Ed Hindson concisely stated it when he said: "Only after the Rapture of the church will the identity of the antichrist be revealed. In other words, you don't want to know who he is. If you ever do figure out who he is, you have been left behind! This is absolutely true." Nothing is more futile than trying to identify the Antichrist before the Rapture. Doing so would be an effort to prove the Bible wrong. That has never happened and it is not going to happen now. All anyone does by trying to identify the Antichrist before the church is taken out is embarrass himself and bring criticism upon Christians.

In connection with this, let me hasten to add that 666 is the Antichrist's number. It is not my driver's license number, my credit card number, my Social Security number or any other number associated with me. Also, it is not any of your numbers. It will not be several billion different numbers for the several billion different individuals on earth. It is his number, one specific number that identifies one specific individual.

[Another] thing we do not know about the Antichrist is whether or not he is already alive as a person. It seems reasonable that he will have to be a full-grown man when he appears. And if the Rapture is as close as most prophetic authorities think, it makes sense to assume that he is not only alive, but already grown. The thing to remember is nobody knows and all a person can do is speculate. . . .[15]

---

15. https://www.raptureready.com/abc/antichrist.html.

The most frequently asked question at prophecy conferences and in Bible prophecy classes — at least in my experience — is: "Is America in Bible prophecy?" The second most asked is: "Do you think Antichrist is alive on earth today?"

These questions are for the most part posed by people in the audiences or classes in general. However, more and more frequently I find these questions being asked by journalists, both print and broadcast. It is interesting to me that I rarely hear a skeptical or scoffing tone in the voices of the media representatives who interview me. I wish that were true when I sometimes mention end-times prophecy to pastors and teachers in churches, from whom there often is a tone of incredulity in their responses.

There seems a sense, even among secular journalists, that perhaps there's something to this Bible prophecy stuff after all.

Don't get me wrong: I'm not sensing a sudden turning to God, or to His Word. However, there is a halting uncertainty there. Like, "Well, maybe I had better be just a bit more serious about the subject, since there is such angst over these strange economic conditions."

Economic Conditions

There is a sense that strange, unexplainable things are happening, and even secular newshounds seem to viscerally understand that Bible prophecy has something to do with the increasingly troubling issues and events of our time. U.S. leaders — I use that term loosely — have seemingly thrown caution to the wind. It's like, as I heard one Bible prophecy broadcaster say the other day, those who are supposed to be trying to fix the melting financial structure of America have placed the whole shebang on 17 black, and have given the roulette wheel a hope-filled turn. Actually, it is more like they have written trillions in IOUs and put them on 17 black, and have given the wheel a turn.

If the little ball ends up on any number other than 17 black, what then? That is the crux of the crucial nature of this insanity surrounding the American economy as the end of the age approaches. Craziness rules — like when the Federal Reserve reaches into its right pocket and transfers trillions of dollars by IOU to its left pocket to keep the American financial system afloat.

Conditions are ripe for global depression. There is a growing need of economic salvation for America and the world. There is a strong call for a new order that will provide such salvation. We've seen before the call by Henri Spaak for a man to lead the world out of the morass, which even in that earlier time threatened to suck mankind into its inescapable depths.

Can the one who will become Antichrist be on the scene today?

Jesus forewarned that false christs will come on the scene in the latter times. As Dr. John Walvoord's words mentioned previously, the definition of "antichrist" is most often given as the one who will present himself in place of (imitate) Jesus Christ, and will at the same time oppose Jesus Christ. The "beast" is prophesied to be the world's worst tyrant of human history. The prophet Daniel was given the following about this person who is called "son of perdition," "man of sin," and many other names.

> And in the latter time of their kingdom, when the transgressors are come to the full, a king of fierce countenance, and understanding dark sentences, shall stand up. And his power shall be mighty, but not by his own power: and he shall destroy wonderfully, and shall prosper, and practise, and shall destroy the mighty and the holy people. And through his policy also he shall cause craft to prosper in his hand; and he shall magnify himself in his heart, and by peace shall destroy many: he shall also stand up against the Prince of princes; but he shall be broken without hand (Daniel 8:23–25).

We will examine this man who is of legendary proportions, yet who transcends by far any legend. He is not an imaginary monster such as Dracula in the Stoker novel, or Darth Vader as in Lucas's fictional wars among the stars. Antichrist, when he is revealed, will be a real monster, and a most treacherous one, because he will through supernatural deceit appear as a geopolitical and socio-economic savior of mankind. He will indeed at first appear to be that shining knight on the dazzling white horse. Be sure, the beast of Revelation 13 is about to step into the spotlight of history's final act.

The question "Where is Antichrist?" is appropriate for this "time of the signs," as my friend Chuck Missler has phrased his description of these strange days. So many signals are on today's prophetic horizon that one must ask, if he or she knows much about Bible prophecy, "Is Antichrist alive today?"

Those who have looked at the world's issues and events through the prism of God's prophetic Word throughout preceding decades of America's history have heard questions about the leaders of the times. Are presidents like Franklin D. Roosevelt, Ronald Reagan, Bill Clinton, George W. Bush, or non-presidents like Henry Kissinger and others the Antichrist? Now the question is pointed at President Barack Hussein Obama: "Is he the Antichrist?"

This hour is more prolific with end-times signs than any in history. Obama's watch as president marks one particular characteristic that adds, peripherally, to the more substantial signals pervading the news at present. I refer to conditions like Israel's being back in its land and the center of world attention, the Roman Empire seeming to revive in the form of the European Union (EU), and the Gog-Magog coalition of Ezekiel 38–39 forming right before our eyes.

Something Rotten in Denmark — And Everywhere Else

The smell permeates almost every corner of America and the world. It is an odor of things to come. Beyond the political exigencies of this troubling hour is the spiritual atmosphere that has the stench of Antichrist and his father, the devil. The scent was prevalent two thousand years ago, and the Bible prophet John forewarned about its cankering, corrosive qualities, as well as defined it:

> Little children, it is the last time: and as ye have heard that anti-christ shall come, even now are there many antichrists; whereby we know that it is the last time (1 John 2:18).

> Beloved, believe not every spirit, but try the spirits whether they are of God: because many false prophets are gone out into the world. Hereby know ye the Spirit of God: Every spirit that confesseth that Jesus Christ is come in the flesh is of God: And every spirit that con-fesseth not that Jesus Christ is come in the flesh is not of God: and this is that spirit of antichrist, whereof ye have heard that it should come; and even now already is it in the world (1 John 4:1–3).

Denial of Jesus Christ and God's prescription for living godly lives on planet earth saturate this generation. The antithesis of Christ's words is not only carried out in the sinful lives of earth-dwellers; the opposition to the Lord is set in the hardened rebellion of man-made law.

The denial that Christ came to teach God's standards for living on the planet He created is almost imperceptible. Most — even leaders of every conceivable religious sort — often agree that Jesus was a great teacher of good. But when Jesus is held up as the only way to God the Father (John 14:6), the shrieks emanating from the spirit of Antichrist come from every dark direction of this fallen sphere.

During the present hour, there are even claims that Jesus taught that it is the mother's right to choose whether her baby lives or dies. It is held among a growing number of clergy that Jesus Himself gave blessing to those who chose homosexuality over heterosexuality. And the point has now been reached in America that the Supreme Court of the United States has usurped the throne of God, in effect, by saying God's way for mankind in the matter of marriage is wrong. Now, man can marry man and woman can marry woman. It isn't an abomination, as the Creator would have it. *Same-sex marriage* is even better in some ways to heterosexual marriage, we are to accept.

Antichrist Spirit Rampant

Most worrisome of all, the world is more and more embracing the lie that Jesus only represented the Christ spirit during His time on earth. He didn't die for the sin of man. He didn't resurrect from the dead because He didn't really die at the crucifixion, but feigned death on the cross. He didn't ascend to on high to sit at the right hand of God. He is, therefore, not coming back to rule and reign.

The majority of the world — including many in our government as it is presently constituted — deny that Jesus is God, the second person of the Godhead, the Trinity. Just a cursory examination of the earliest phase of the Obama presidential administration tells the story of this time of the growing Antichrist spirit. The first months following the inauguration brought changes by presidential edict that are diametrically opposite God's will as given in His Word. For example, the president ordered that money of the American taxpayers be used to help with abortion practices in foreign nations, reversing former President George W. Bush's presidential order that no such use of taxpayer money be made. This Obama did, despite the protestation of more than half of the American public.

The United States is being channeled and forced into a mold that looks like the biblically foretold one-world order that will be ruled with a deadly iron fist by the one who is called "the beast." With the stage of history's last act set, for all practical purposes, it is perhaps not far-fetched to suspect that Antichrist is among us even now. He is here in spirit, for sure. Rapture Ready . . . or not, it will happen!

CHAPTER 13

A REALLY STRONG COCKTAIL CALLED ISRAEL

Reason #13: Israel in the center of geopolitical controversy, with anti-Semitism growing worldwide and attempts at forcing a peace covenant demanding that Israel give up its land, constitutes the number one reason, I believe, why this is the generation that will be left behind when the Rapture occurs.

No stronger proof exists that the God of the Bible is the only true God than does the nation He chose through which to manifest Himself to mankind. It is a people, therefore, that the god of this world, the *father of lies,* hates with a vitriol that only a deliberate denier of truth could ignore. We are witnessing in this generation yet another build-up toward an all-out attempt by Satan to destroy Israel.

Iran's mullahs and their governmental underlings are at the forefront of this hatred. Almost daily they call for Israel's destruction. They are but the nucleus of the entirety of the militant Islamists of the Middle East calling for Israel's elimination from being a state — or even a race of people.

Practically all of the United Nations constituency is made up of those who are anti-Israel. Sadly, under the Obama administration, the United

States, too, has demonstrated a desire to, as one administration official said early on, "put space between America and Israel."

It is as if the whole world of diplomats has had blinders placed on its better sense. While the nation, avowed to destroy Israel — and America, too — engages in an all-out attempt to create nuclear weapons, the diplomats only give lip service to intervening to halt the madness. The U.S. Congress is also seemingly impotent to do anything to truly try to stop Iran's getting weapons and the missile systems to deliver them — even to America's heartland.

The mainstream media in America, usually opposed to any sort of nuclear proliferation, only cheers for the American president while he, in my view, aids and abets the Iranian effort to produce weapons that will almost without question one day be used to initiate World War III.

As a matter of fact, those who don't have the blinders on their better sense believe that war has already begun — thus in the same sense that World War II began with the appeasement of Adolf Hitler in Munich when Neville Chamberlain was duped by der Fuhrer with the "peace in our time" agreement the British prime minister waved around after returning from that fateful meeting with perhaps the world's worst tyrant to this time in human history.

End-Time Earth's Cup of Trembling

Zechariah, the Old Testament prophet, provided us the reason for giving this chapter its title. It is a prophecy we have looked at before that only the willfully ignorant of geopolitical realities of our day will deny.

> The burden of the word of the LORD for Israel, saith the LORD, which stretcheth forth the heavens, and layeth the foundation of the earth, and formeth the spirit of man within him.
>
> Behold, I will make Jerusalem a cup of trembling unto all the people round about, when they shall be in the siege both against Judah and against Jerusalem. And in that day will I make Jerusalem a burdensome stone for all people: all that burden themselves with it shall be cut in pieces, though all the people of the earth be gathered together against it (Zechariah 12:1–3).

Israel is, at present, at the center of the turmoil in the Middle East. While there is great concern over the growth of ISIS (Islamic State of Iraq and Syria), with that horde's genocidal rampage against Christians and others in the region, the prime concern continues to be the potential for nuclear war to ignite because of Iran's nuclear aspirations and Israel's determination to defend itself.

Zechariah's prophecy is in view, and the world's diplomats are nervous as they see that *cup of trembling* beginning to reach the brim with Mideast war potential.

Modern Israel, as we who hold to the premillennial view of Bible prophecy consistently say, is the number one signal of where this generation stands on God's prophetic timeline. That nation is, therefore, the best example in the geopolitical arena to use for focusing on details of issues and events shaping the stage-setting for Bible prophecy fulfillment. The student who watches Bible prophecy develop from the premillennial, pre-Tribulational viewpoint has, with clarity others can't see, I think, seen Israel come back into its own land, with its ancient national language restored. It did so following a miraculous rebirth into modernity on a single day, just as prophesied (Isaiah 66:6–9). The intricate details of the amazing rebirth are there to be gleaned by the hundreds, if not thousands.

Pressured in A.D. 135 through genocidal action by Roman Emperor Hadrian to leave their homeland given them by God, the Jews scattered into many nations of the world. God's chosen people never truly found peace; rather, they mostly encountered persecution and death during the intervening centuries leading to coming back in large numbers following the Balfour Declaration of 1917.

Hitler's perpetration of genocide upon the Jews during the time leading up to and through World War II, culminating in the Holocaust, shamed the world into allowing a Jewish state to be reborn. What Satan meant for evil in trying to thwart God's promise to Israel being fulfilled, God turned into good. However, demonic rage by the false religion of Islam continued to fester, breaking into all-out warfare against Israel on numerous occasions. God gave Israel the victory in every instance that nation was attacked.

Now, to look at the clearly observable, detailed kinds of prophetic movement wrought by recent events involving the modern Jewish state. Zechariah the prophet declared the whole world will turn against Israel and Jerusalem, in particular, at the end of human history. Israel's refusal to give in to demands by the Palestinian Authority (PA) — merely the proxy entity for all of Israel's Islamist Arab and Iranian antagonists — has brought condemnation of practically every nation on earth.

We've all watched the anger spew from the U.N. secretary-generals over the years, and from the leadership of practically every nation represented in the U.N. General Assembly. They threaten to grant the PA its request for nationhood, using much of Israel's land, including East Jerusalem, in which to establish the new country's capital. The U.S. presidential administration has thus far, in my estimation, shown little more than token interest in opposing this assault on Israel's sovereignty. As a matter of fact, the Obama administration has indicated that if Israel isn't forthcoming in concessions to the ongoing, so-called peace arrangements that include Israel giving up land, America might withhold support altogether.

Israel's only true friends left on the planet consist mostly of evangelical Christians, particularly those who see with the clarity mentioned above through the premillennial, pre-Trib prism. When the Church — the Body of Christ — is removed from this fallen planet in the Rapture, Israel will be alone, or so it will seem.

But, not so.

At that moment when all seems lost, Michael the archangel will stand for that chosen people (Daniel 12:1). God Himself will deal with and for His chosen people and the city He equates to the apple of His eye. All is shaping into the prophetic picture, with details filling in moment by moment the matters involved in getting to the total fulfillment of every jot and tittle that is foretold. The intricacies of the peace process provide details that fascinate the student of Bible prophecy, for example.

The development of the atomic bomb (an invention of Jewish scientists, incidentally) and the hydrogen bomb, for that matter, has caused a worldwide furor stemming from the Middle East. Israel is at the center of the controversy, of course. Israel has nuclear weaponry and is threatened with extinction — as the Jews always are. They have vowed, "Never again!" Never again will they be subjected to genocide without fighting to the death with those who want every Jew on the planet dead.

Israel continues to be completely surrounded on all but the Mediterranean side by those whose often-avowed intention is just that — to eradicate the Jews, and thus the nation of Israel.

The world knows that the end of the human race through nuclear war could easily begin at Jerusalem. Thus, that city is ground zero for the entire world's attention, just as Zechariah and other prophets foretold. Isaiah prophesied that a peace covenant will be made over this very city. It will be a covenant that will, in fact, be made with "death and hell." It will bring the wrath of God down on the whole world for forcing such an agreement upon His chosen people and upon His most beloved city. (Read Isaiah 28:15, 18.)

America is at the heart of just such a covenant-producing process. The Roadmap to Peace has been a part of world diplomatic jargon for more than a decade now. Jerusalem, with the strong-arming of the diplomatic world to make Israel stop building in that city and with the PA (the Islamist world) demanding that Jerusalem be given over to them, is at the epicenter of the coming earthquake of wrath as foretold by God Almighty through His prophet, Zechariah.

> And this shall be the plague wherewith the LORD will smite all the people that have fought against Jerusalem; their flesh shall consume away while they stand upon their feet, and their eyes shall consume away in their holes, and their tongue shall consume away in their mouth (Zechariah 14:12).

Every examination of prophecy about the very end of the Church Age that deals with the nations and their individual and collective fates/destinies must begin and end with Israel. Therefore, we continue looking at details of modern Israel as juxtaposed against all nations — thus to determine how the minute elements of ongoing developments in geopolitics are setting the prophetic stage for Christ's return.

We looked at how Israel and Jerusalem are at ground zero for the diplomatic world. The international community correctly sees this as the place on earth most likely to be the ignition point for World War III. It is intriguing to dissect with the scalpel of Bible prophecy each and every layer of development in the geopolitical issues and events of our time that involve the modern Jewish state. Iran is a most fascinating case in point.

Persia, as we have looked at many times, is listed as a key player that assaults Israel in the Ezekiel 38–39 Gog-Magog prophecy. Modern Iran is at the center of what was ancient Persia, as we know.

With Iranian Shah Mohammed Rezā Pahlavi being in power through most of the 1970s, Israel didn't have to be overly concerned about neighbors to that section of its north. One reason was because America's military, particularly the U.S. Air Force, worked closely with the Shah's air force in training and maintenance missions. I can report this from more-or-less personal secondhand information, because my own father-in-law was in charge of all aircraft maintenance for American-made military aircraft in Iran's arsenal through 1976. The shah was America's friend, even if sometimes being beastly in treatment of his own people, and looking down his nose at Israel to his south.

The point is, Bible prophecy students were hard pressed to see how the Gog-Magog force could ever be formed with this arrangement in place. We know what happened, as we think on how quickly things have fallen in place one event after the other since the shah's fall in 1979.

America, under the Carter administration, was run out of town, literally, with the coming of the Iranian Revolution, as the Islamists came to power under the Ayatollah Ruhollah Khomeini. Iran became increasingly bellicose against the West, and, of course, became blood-lust determined to erase Israel and every Jew off the map. We've almost lost count of how many times the Iranian political leaders and mullahs have declared they intend to destroy the Jewish state. Every day the chant rings in our ears: "Death to America! Death to Israel!" America is declared "the great Satan." Israel is declared "the little Satan."

Russia and the present Iranian regime have become working partners at many levels, the most troubling being at the nuclear level. The Gog-Magog nucleus has formed between Russia, Iran (Persia), and Turkey (Togarmah) within an amazingly short period of time.

It's also prophetically astonishing to watch a most-asked question among prophecy students in the process of being answered by the flood of developing issues and events. Why is America not mentioned in Bible prophecy? It is the most powerful nation ever to exist. . . . Again, it is intriguing to consider that America was instrumental in all of these developments — as one would expect the most powerful nation ever to exist to be, I suppose.

America "defeated" the Soviet Union through tactics involving Cold War attrition — and the heart of that antagonist became again "Russia." This territorial rearrangement aligns almost precisely with the ancient geographical area called "Rosh," the leader of which the prophet Ezekiel foretold will be "Gog" of the Gog-Magog war against Israel.

The United States has slipped from its ultimate superpower status since that time of the Reagan-led peaceful defeat of the Soviet Union. Under the Obama administration, America's economic standing, thus its fiscal hegemony over the other nations of the world, has declined, many agree, precipitously. Prophecy students of the premillennial, pre-Trib perspective can point with a certain amount of credibility to the fact that America's slippage coincides closely with this nation's bringing pressure on the Israeli government to give in to demands that they give up land for peace with their Islamist neighbors.

At the same time, China, which most students of the premillennial, pre-Trib viewpoint of Bible prophecy believe is the chief nation that will make up the "kings-of-the-east" force that will one day kill one-third of the world's population, is draining U.S. economic power while buying up American assets. America is, in effect, funding the development of the awesome military force predicted in Revelation 9:16. This would have been flabbergasting to even consider during those Reagan years, and that hasn't been that many years ago.

China, of all nations on earth, has perhaps provided, at least to a degree, the answer to the question: Why is America not mentioned in Bible prophecy?

The United States can also be seen as instrumental in the details of developing Bible prophecy regarding the region that is foretold to spawn the world's most despicable dictator.

As we have seen before in this volume, Daniel the prophet said that the "prince that shall come," and will emerge from the people that "destroy the city and sanctuary." This means, many believe, that Antichrist will come from the area of Rome — from Europe, in general — as the Romans destroyed Jerusalem and the Jewish Temple in A.D. 70. Again, the viewpoint is important to recognize, because the premillennial, pre-Trib view — in almost every instance of examination of prophecy yet future — provides logical placement, thus explanation, of what we have watched develop in world headlines, especially since Israel became a nation again May 14, 1948.

America's influence has been absolutely profound in bringing the modern Jewish state into prominence. My book, *The American Apocalypse: Is the United States in Bible Prophecy?* (Harvest House, 2009) details the intricacies of America's part in that rebirth. The United States' influence in bringing modern Europe into prophetic configuration is only slightly less profound.

With much of Europe in shambles because of the destructiveness of World War II, there was real danger of depression even worse than that of the 1930s. While Europe suffered, America was ascending toward super power status. Its military and industrial might soared, with military personnel returning to a nation that was burgeoning with a roaring economy and full employment.

The United States implemented the Marshall Plan to save Europe and avert humanity-destroying disaster.

The Marshall Plan (officially the European Recovery Program, ERP) was an American initiative to aid Europe, in which the United States gave $13 billion (approximately $120 billion in current dollar value) in economic support to help rebuild European economies after the end of World War II. President Harry S. Truman signed it into law April 3, 1948. The plan was named after Secretary of State George C. Marshall.

Interestingly, it was Marshall who, a month later, threatened to resign if Truman supported the rebirth of Israel. Truman did so anyway, and Marshall didn't follow through on his threat.

America's intricate linkage to the return of Israel as a nation, in its own homeland, with its own language restored, is a truly prophetic intervention by the hand of God, it should be obvious to anyone who will examine that history honestly.

Israel's Destiny

Some time ago I was asked by a Jewish Israeli publication to write an essay presenting my view of what the Bible says about Israel and its future. That presentation is as true at this moment as it was when I wrote it.

> Israel is the one nation in human history that the Creator of all things chose to be "a people unto himself":

>> For thou art an holy people unto the LORD thy God: the LORD thy God hath chosen thee to be a special people unto himself, above all people that are upon the face of the earth (Deuteronomy 7:6).

> Jehovah made promises to the patriarchs Abraham, Isaac, and Jacob that are staggering in their implications. He promised to bless those who bless the nation that would spring from the loins of these men, and warned about His curse for those who cursed those people. God said to Abraham:

>> Now the LORD had said unto Abram, Get thee out of thy country, and from thy kindred, and from thy father's

house, unto a land that I will shew thee: And I will make of thee a great nation, and I will bless thee, and make thy name great; and thou shalt be a blessing: And I will bless them that bless thee, and curse him that curseth thee: and in thee shall all families of the earth be blessed (Genesis 12:1–3).

Certainly, this promise can easily be verified as coming true throughout recorded history. The modern record, as a matter of fact, is contemporary proof of the veracity of the Almighty and His prophetic promises. Historians — except those blinded by the great deceiver, Lucifer — concede, sometime reluctantly, that Israel's history in ancient times was a record of greatness. David and Solomon's exploits and accomplishments are legendary, but built upon archeological facts. Israel has achieved greatness among the nations of this earthly sphere.

One point over which secularist historians at the minimum raise eyebrows of skepticism is that man received laws and moral codes through Moses, the son of Abraham. Most give Hamarabi's Code that honor. But, those who believe that God is who He is know the great human deliverer of the chosen people came down from Sinai with rules for living life, given by the God of Heaven to His creation called man. Particularly, the Ten Commandments were meant for Israel to follow as fealty to their God, and as example to the rest of the world.

God's promise to make Israel a great nation and to bless all other nations through His chosen people has come true. The United States, for example, has the Ten Commandments upon its walls within government buildings, including the Supreme Court. America, despite the anti-God forces who want to destroy the nation's moral underpinnings, continues to lead the world in most areas of improvement of the human condition. This is due to the Ten Commandments' influence upon American ethics and achievement. But, it goes profoundly deeper.

Much of America's successes in technological, medical, and every other category of progress have been contributed by members of the Jewish race. We don't have to look far to find them. I'll just mention the most obvious: Albert Einstein, the German-born, genius physicist who became an American citizen. No more than a cursory study will show, indelibly, that God's Word is true, when He followed through on the promise to make the people of the book the head of all peoples:

> And the LORD shall make thee the head, and not the tail; and thou shalt be above only, and thou shalt not be beneath; if that thou hearken unto the commandments of the LORD thy God, which I command thee this day, to observe and to do them (Deuteronomy 28:13).

Then what about the maltreatment, the genocide against the Jewish race down through the millennia, particularly during the 20th century? This doesn't appear to be God making Israel the head of all nations. Here is where God placed some conditions upon the people He chose as destined to become the head of all others. Note the last of the above promise: "if that thou hearken unto the commandments of the LORD thy God, which I command thee this day, to observe and to do them."

God will make Israel the head of all nations, if that people will listen to His instructions and commandments. Not only is that where the nation Israel has strayed; this is where those who say that God is through with Israel — that the Jewish race is no longer God's chosen — have also strayed. God's Word says that ALL have sinned and come short of the glory of God. All have strayed — both Jews AND Gentiles.

Israel's detractors within Christianity say the Jews rejected their Messiah in His first visitation. Therefore, they say, Jehovah has written off the Jews and the nation Israel. The Israel in the land surrounding Jerusalem since May 14, 1948, is not the Israel of the promises, the detractors say. Modern Israel is but an imposter, and God considers it no more within His prophecy for future national or racial greatness than He considers any of modern Israel's blood-vowed enemies.

Absolutely nothing could be further from the truth. It is true that the Israel of Jesus Christ's day rejected Him as Messiah. It is equally true that those of His own race, the Jews, cried "Crucify him!" the hierarchy of which convinced the Romans to crucify

Jesus. But God's Word says that every person is a sinner. We are born into sin — thus because Adam, the physical father of mankind, disobeyed God in the Garden of Eden. Again, God's Word says that "all have sinned and come short of the glory of God."

The Jews, as a race, are no guiltier than my race, which is Gentile. We all, as the human race, put Jesus Christ to death on the cruel Roman cross. He came to earth, sent by His Father, the God of heaven, to offer himself as the lamb slain from the foundation of the world. Jesus the Christ — the Jews' Messiah — came to fulfill all Mosaic Law, the Ten Commandments. In Christ we can now believe, and our sins are cleansed, washed away by Christ's sacrifice for all eternity. Through His shed blood, we ALL — Jew and Gentile — are in the family of God forever.

But, each individual human being must accept this grace gift that replaced the sacrificial system of blood from innocent lambs of the physical sort. We must accept Christ as Savior, as Lord one-on-one with God, because He gives each person the free will to accept or reject His grace offer of salvation.

Now, I must come to the sad part — the tragic part of this essay, really — in which I have been asked to address your nation's prophetic destiny.

The Bible foretells that the Jewish race as a whole, Israel as a nation, will continue to reject their Messiah, the one who came to them more than two thousand years ago. This rejection will continue to result in God's promises being delayed until the moment Jesus returns to put an end to mankind's final war called Armageddon.

Israel was scattered after the A.D. 70 destruction of Jerusalem and the Temple atop Mount Moriah. This was exactly what Jesus predicted in the Olivet Discourse (Matthew 24, Mark 13, and Luke 21.) Jesus prophesied that not one stone of the Temple would be left upon another. Titus and the Roman legions saw to the fulfillment of this prophecy.

The Jews lost their temple, their city, and, following Hadrian's purge in A.D. 135, their geographical homeland area, plus their common language (Hebrew) as a cohesive link to one another as a distinct people. Yet God's Word foretells that Israel will be a nation again at the end of days — the time just before Christ returns.

Again, tragically and sadly, you are back in the land for a time that will be worse than any ever experienced by any people. The prophet Jeremiah foretold this:

> Alas! for that day is great, so that none is like it: it is even the time of Jacob's trouble; but he shall be saved out of it (Jeremiah 30:7).

It will be a time of horrors beyond anything even Adolf Hitler dreamed about perpetrating upon the Jewish race. Can we see a build-up toward that time? Let us consider the words of the prophet Zechariah, and put his prophecies as a template over today's headlines:

> The burden of the word of the LORD for Israel, saith the LORD, which stretcheth forth the heavens, and layeth the foundation of the earth, and formeth the spirit of man within him.
>
> Behold, I will make Jerusalem a cup of trembling unto all the people round about, when they shall be in the siege both against Judah and against Jerusalem. And in that day will I make Jerusalem a burdensome stone for all people: all that burden themselves with it shall be cut in pieces, though all the people of the earth be gathered together against it (Zechariah 12:1–3).

The peoples of the earth are gathering against Israel. Even some leaders within the U.S., governmental and religious, want Israel to give away land for peace. The "Zionists" are seen as the problem.

Israel is basically isolated today, so far as true allies are concerned. The United States stands almost alone as your friend. However, it hurts to say that support is eroding, while some within recent American diplomatic efforts seem to want to exclude your nation from talks involving the small territory you now occupy — territory, incidentally, which is but a fraction of the land the Lord your God granted you through Abraham, Isaac, and Jacob. These negotiators join the so-called international community in wanting to placate Israel's hate-filled enemies.

This Neville Chamberlain-like, "peace at any cost" maneuvering is not lost on those who want Israel wiped off the map. It is creating

a perception of weakness that will tempt them to act on their satanically driven hatreds.

Ezekiel the prophet foretold of a time at the end of days when
a coalition will invade from the North (all biblical direction is given
from Jerusalem). There is not space here to go into detail, but excellent scholarship has determined the chief attacker will be Russia,
joined by many surrounding peoples. This attack will include forces
from the area of ancient Persia, which encompasses all of Iran, and
considerable surrounding geographical areas. This coalition, I am
convinced today's news headlines indicate, is gathering now. This
will be the God-Magog assault described prophetically in Ezekiel
chapters 38 and 39.

The one bright prospect, and it is a bright spot, indeed, is that
the God of Israel will never let Israel be destroyed; we have His
Word on that:

> This is what the Lord says, He who appoints the sun to
> shine by day, who decrees the moon and stars to shine by
> night, who stirs up the sea so that its waves roar — the Lord
> Almighty is his name: "Only if these ordinances vanish
> from my sight," declares the LORD, "will the descendants
> of Israel ever cease to be a nation before me" (Jeremiah
> 31:35–36; NIV).

The bottom line is that Israel, the Jewish race, is again destined
to become hated and persecuted — this time with satanic vitriol
that will make Hitler's Holocaust look somewhat less terrible by
comparison.

Antichrist, the long-foretold, sometime spoofed, but 100 percent Bible prophecy guaranteed to come on the world scene tyrant,
will implement genocidal policies against the Jewish race that will
go far beyond Draconian.

I didn't make up this prediction. God's Word, the Bible, does say
it. I accept that Word as the only truth there is. I, and other Christians who know Jesus Christ as Lord, love, or should love, the Jewish
people — the nation Israel. God loves you; so must we. You are His
chosen. However, I, and they, can't change what God has prophesied
to take place, I'm convinced, in the relatively near future.

But, I, and they, are charged with showing individuals within Israel the way to escape the coming time of Antichrist's regime of horror. Accept Christ now. He is Messiah. And one day, perhaps very soon, He will call His people — Jews and Gentiles who accept Him as Savior — to be with Him forever. This will be the Rapture. (That stunning event, in which millions of people will vanish from planet earth, can be found in 1 Thessalonians 4:13–18 and 1 Corinthians 15:51–55. Jesus spoke of it in John 14:1–3.)

The Rapture will take place before that time of horror — the era Jesus called "great Tribulation" (Matthew 24: 21).

The people of the nation Israel who are unrepentant (the remnant, for most will die in this last holocaust) will accept Christ at the last moment.

Here's what that future remnant's Messiah says:

> And it shall come to pass in that day, that I will seek to destroy all the nations that come against Jerusalem. And I will pour upon the house of David, and upon the inhabitants of Jerusalem, the spirit of grace and of supplications: and they shall look upon me whom they have pierced, and they shall mourn for him, as one mourneth for his only son, and shall be in bitterness for him, as one that is in bitterness for his firstborn (Zechariah 12:9–10).

Israel will then be made the head of all nations, with the resurrected King David ruling as coregent with the Messiah, the Lord Jesus Christ, atop Mount Zion at Jerusalem for one thousand years — the Millennium! Believe it or not, that is your nation's great God-promised destiny.[1]

We who love Israel pray that you will believe.

Zola Levitt on God's People

My dear friend Zola Levitt (*Zola Levitt Presents*) was a champion for support of Israel. He was perhaps the best-known Jewish-Christian voice from the premillennial, pre-Trib view of Bible prophecy. He wrote the following (as excerpted).

---

1. Terry James, "Israel's Destiny," Rapture Notes, http://www.rapturenotes.com/israelsdestiny. html.

Israel started out as one nation under Jewish leadership thirty-five centuries ago! History and archaeology show this to be Jewish land from the Mediterranean to past the Jordan River, and from the deserts of the south to northern borders that exceed the Galilee and Golan Heights on the north. But even though the formal boundaries of Israel are about half the size of what they were in biblical times, world leaders, and especially Arab leaders, demand that even this small area be cut in half again and an equal portion be given to those who have sworn to drive Israel into the sea.

"It Is Written"

Why is all this happening to Israel? The best of all reasons is that prophetic Scripture says it will happen. While the world press dithers over Israel's supposed intractability with the peace process or bad treatment of the Palestinians or a wrong-headed prime minister, the real reason is that Israel must be maneuvered into a position where it will be "hated of all nations" (Matthew 24:9). It is well to remember that close to 100 percent of end-times prophecy concerns that tiny nation, and the biblical signs of the end pertain especially to Israel. The Olivet Discourse of our Lord and His answer to the disciples' question, "What will be the sign of Your coming and of the end of the world?" (Matthew 24:3), details phenomena that are global in scope but of particular concern to those in the Holy Land. The Lord addresses His disciples as Israelites in particular when He observes, "He that shall endure unto the end, the same shall be saved" (verse 13). It is the Jewish people gathered in Israel at the time of Armageddon who must endure "unto the end" — that is the Second Coming of the Lord — to be saved. At the time, "they shall look upon me whom they have pierced, and they shall mourn for him as one mourneth for his only Son. . . ."

We know that the start of the Tribulation period is signaled by the Antichrist's peace covenant with Israel, and it is obvious that we are being prepared for such news day by day. The "peace process" has conditioned the world to imagine that there is some drastic situation in Israel that badly needs some international agreement to settle it. To look at the world objectively, it is clear that peace covenants are needed much more in other trouble spots where there are real conflicts going on and not in Israel, which is suffering from

Rapture Ready ... or Not?

something more like a common ghetto problem. But to satisfy the prophecy, world opinion is being manipulated to where the Antichrist's seven-year offer will be most welcome. Even the Israelis, I think, will sign that covenant in a hopeful spirit out of necessity at the time it is offered. (The necessity will not be the need to make peace, but simply pressure from the United Nations and certain powerful members to come to some accommodation with the Arabs.) The media will immediately trumpet the idea that peace has at least been achieved in Israel only to be proved as wrong.[2]

2. Zola Levitt, "Israel on the Spot," *Foreshadows of Wrath and Redemption*, William T. James, ed. (Eugene, OR: Harvest House, 1999), p. 138–140.

CHAPTER 14

ARMAGEDDON LINEUP FOR THE SUPER BOWL OF WAR

Reason #14: Wars and rumors of war threaten world peace.
All nations of the world being in prophetic configuration, and
pushing God out of culture and society, is a strong reason to
believe this is the generation that will be left behind.

Armageddon! The term evokes mental pictures of the almost unthinkable. The end of the world; nuclear holocaust; the destruction of the human race — these are images that come to mind. It is a term that has been bandied about throughout history, so much so that it has almost lost its true identification. Arnold Fruchtenbaum, one of the foremost experts on the subject from a biblically prophetic viewpoint, refocuses our understanding on this terrifying word.

> While the term "Battle of Armageddon" has been commonly used, it is really a misnomer, for more than one battle will be taking place. For this reason, many prophetic teachers have stopped employing that term and are using the term "Campaign of Armageddon." . . . But this, too, is a misnomer because there will be no

fighting in Armageddon itself; all of the fighting will take place else-where. A more biblical name for this final conflict is found in the closing words of [Revelation 16] 14: *the war of the great day of God, the Almighty.* This is a more accurate description of the nature and extent of this final conflict.

The train of thought is now interrupted by a parenthetical state-ment [Revelation 16:] (v. 15) containing a message of comfort and hope to the believers living at this point in the Great Tribulation. They are encouraged to continue in the faith, for when they see the gathering of the armies together, then they can know that the Second Coming of Jesus the Messiah is just around the corner.

The train of thought is picked up again in verse 16, which names the place where the allies of the Antichrist will be gathered: *Har-Magedon.* As the ASV [American Standard Version] text shows, the word is a combination of two Hebrew words which mean, "the Mountain of Megiddo." Megiddo was a strategic city located at the western end of the Valley of Jezreel, guarding the famous Megiddo Pass into Israel's largest valley. One can see the entire Valley of Jezreel from the mount upon which the city of Megiddo stood. So what is known as the Valley of Armageddon in Christian circles is actually the biblical Valley of Jezreel. The term *Armageddon* is never applied to the valley itself, but only to the mount at the western end. Here, in this large valley of Lower Galilee, the armies of the world will gather for the purpose of destroying all the Jews still living.

It should be noted that the passage says nothing of a battle in this valley, for no fighting will take place here. The Valley of Jezreel, guarded by the Mountain of Megiddo, will merely serve as the gather-ing ground for the armies of the Antichrist. Armageddon will play the same role that England played in the closing stages of World War II. The allied forces gathered their armies together in England, but that is not where the final battle took place. The final conflict began on the beaches of Normandy, France, on D-Day. Armageddon will also serve as a gathering place, with the battle beginning elsewhere.[1]

Armageddon, then, is a place rather than a war, as Dr. Fruchtenbaum has told us. Without meaning to diminish the seriousness of the matter, I liken

---

1. Arnold G. Fruchtenbaum, "The Campaign of Armageddon and the Second Coming of Jesus the Messiah." http://www.raptureready.com/rr-armageddon.html.

it, for the purpose of our chapter's title, to one of the great cities where the Super Bowl is played annually — in which the fans and teams gather — rather than to the stadium where the game/battle will actually take place. But it is indeed a war — a campaign of the fiercest sort — that will lead all combatants to this Mideast staging area for earth's last attempt to stop God's plan to install His Son, Jesus Christ, upon the throne of David in Jerusalem for His thousand-year (millennial) reign.

We see this attempt to thwart God's plan again as represented in the following Scripture.

> Why do the heathen rage, and the people imagine a vain thing? The kings of the earth set themselves, and the rulers take counsel together, against the LORD, and against his anointed, saying, Let us break their bands asunder, and cast away their cords from us. He that sitteth in the heavens shall laugh: the LORD shall have them in derision. Then shall he speak unto them in his wrath, and vex them in his sore displeasure.
>
> Yet have I set my king upon my holy hill of Zion. I will declare the decree: the LORD hath said unto me, Thou art my Son; this day have I begotten thee. Ask of me, and I shall give thee the heathen for thine inheritance, and the uttermost parts of the earth for thy possession. Thou shalt break them with a rod of iron; thou shalt dash them in pieces like a potter's vessel (Psalm 2:1–9).

The history of mankind demonstrates an unending proclivity for waging war. It is rebellion of the most egregious sort against the God of heaven. Its purpose is satanic. The intention is to murder as many of God's creation called man as possible, thus to gain personal power. This truly reflects the desire of Lucifer the fallen one, who still intends to put himself above the throne of the Creator.

The influence and intervention by the wicked serpent is most visible when thinking upon the wars waged against God's *chosen people,* the Jews. One would think that this ages-long genocide would have come to its climax when Adolf Hitler and his Nazi murderers tried to carry out the "Final Solution." This resulted in more than six million being slaughtered, simply because they were of the Jewish race.

However, this rage against God's plan to put Christ on the throne for all eternity has yet to come to culmination. That's why Jeremiah the prophet calls

that future three and one-half years — the last half of the seven-year Tribulation — "the time of Jacob's trouble" (Jeremiah 30:7). The beast of Revelation
13 will do his best to complete the Final Solution Hitler failed to finish.

Antichrist will wage war on the Jewish race — and against the whole
world — in fashion and fury that would, according to Jesus, cause the end
of all flesh upon the planet (Matthew 24:21) if He, Christ, didn't intervene
at Armageddon.

In effect, all the wars of human history have been part of the campaign
called Armageddon. The general waging this constant campaign is Lucifer.
As we look at the world around us today, particularly in the Middle East,
can there be any doubt that Satan and his wicked minions have ramped up
the murderous effort to inflict as much death and carnage as possible?

However, it is scheduled to get much, much more violent. As the title of
this chapter implies, the campaign of Armageddon will be the Super Bowl
of war. The final movement toward the terminus-battlefield of this history-
long conflict will be the most bloody ever waged by the raging warriors
that will be the most advanced of all time, with the most technologically
devastating battle gear ever used in war.

Although the greatest numbers killed by these end-times forces will take
place during the Tribulation, we can see preparations being made at this
very moment to soon wage all-out war. The war that began in centuries past
will take on unparalleled dimension near the beginning of that seven-year
era. John the Revelator was given the symbolic view of the horrendous war
to come when the heavenly being directed him to watch as the seal of the
scroll was opened.

> And when he had opened the second seal, I heard the second
> beast say, Come and see. And there went out another horse that was
> red: and power was given to him that sat thereon to take peace from
> the earth, and that they should kill one another: and there was given
> unto him a great sword (Revelation 6:3–4).

Jesus Forewarns of War

Jesus Christ, the Lamb whom John saw take the second sealed scroll and
open it, showing the unleashing of the rider on the red horse of war, is the
same Jesus that prophesied about the rage of man throughout history and
leading up to the time of His return. Jesus said the following in that regard.

> And ye shall hear of wars and rumours of wars: see that ye be not
> troubled: for all these things must come to pass, but the end is not yet.
> For nation shall rise against nation, and kingdom against kingdom:
> and there shall be famines, and pestilences, and earthquakes, in divers
> places. All these are the beginning of sorrows (Matthew 24:6–8).

War has been a continuing plague within human interaction since the day
Cain slew Abel. Rumors of wars are always with us because, as James wrote:

> From whence come wars and fightings among you? Come they
> not hence, even of your lusts that war in your members? (James 4:1).

The world's concept of peace is never true peace, but merely a lull between
episodes of warfare. When so-called peace is enforced, threats of wars and
murmurings of hostilities bubble just below the surface of civility. Jesus, in
His Olivet Discourse on final prophecies, however, was talking about warfare that will come with greater frequency and ferocity the closer the end of
this earth age comes. Wars, followed by rumors of wars, will come much like
contractions increase for a woman who is about to give birth.

We do not have to go back very far in the historical record to document
that we live in an age of such convulsive activity. Wars on a global scale are
the ultimate manifestations of man's fallen nature, which cannot find peace
apart from Christ's atonement. Natural man harbors violence capable of
producing great destruction. One-on-one violence, families warring against
each other, gang warfare in our cities, ethnic group against ethnic group —
all these confirm that ours is a generation witnessing one of the key final
prophecies foretold by Jesus Christ.

The frightening fact that mankind now possesses, through nuclear
weaponry, the capability to destroy all life on earth is proof that God's prophetic Word is truth (see Mark 13:20). Can there be any doubt that John
was given a look at nuclear weaponry in that Revelation 6 foretelling of the
rider on the red horse? That frightening rider was given a "great sword," and
that "sword" will indeed be used in a massive way before human history has
run its course.

Today, all of the Middle East and much of the rest of the world look
with trepidation at Iran as it works on its nuclear program. The American presidential administration, it is charged, has made a potentially deadly
agreement to let that regime go ahead with its development, trusting Iran to

ultimately not produce a nuclear bomb. The concern is well founded. The mullahs and the government leaders — all of the violent, militant, Islamist variety — have threatened to destroy Israel at first opportunity. They shout "Death to America!" on a daily basis, as we have looked at previously.

Not only do these tyrant-led governments seek nuclear capabilities, but they already possess warheads that can contain biological agents such as anthrax and other virulent, life-threatening microentities; nerve agents of great destructive potential; and other agents even more deadly that could be unleashed at any moment.

Because Iran will almost without any doubt soon produce a nuclear weapons capability, its Middle Eastern neighbors are now openly saying they will seek to become nuclear as well — for defensive purposes.

It is well known that Iran wants the oil fields of Saudi, and wants to exert hegemony over the whole region. The Saudi family won't sit still for this to happen. It has the funds to purchase nuclear weapons off the shelves of such nations as Pakistan, and says it will do so.

Rather than limit the proliferation of such weaponry, as the Obama administration has promised, there now will almost certainly be unleashed a nuclear arms race among some of the most volatile geopolitical actors on the planet. To add to the angst, a nuclear-armed North Korea continues to make threats to America and its neighbors. It isn't yet very good at it, but it continues to launch missiles to develop its capability.

With Iran and North Korea avowed to destroy those with whom they disagree, and with Iran in particular truly capable of developing ICBMs that can reach America's heartland, there is good reason to believe that we are well into the beginning of the time of wars and rumors of war predicted by Jesus. Only the staying hand of God has thus far prevented wars of world-ending proportions. There is coming a time when God will remove His restraining hand and mankind's love affair with war and killing will bring the human race and all other flesh to the point of extinction. Remember, Jesus said that if He did not return, "no flesh should be saved" (Mark 13:20).

Thankfully, God Almighty will not permit His creation to be utterly destroyed by man. The Lord Jesus Christ will intervene and put an end to the violence. All who harbor murderous, warring intentions within their hearts will be locked forever in outer darkness when Christ judges and rules. True peace will at last permeate the planet as the Lord of lords and King of kings sits upon the throne of the millennial earth.

Meantime, though, inhabitants of earth face frightening things in the future, as foretold by Jesus and the Old and New Testament prophets.

Spirit World at War

One of the prospects not much touched on even by Bible prophecy scholars is the spiritual dimension of the wars that rage throughout history, right up to the final gathering of all earthly military forces at Armageddon. At least two such scholars have written on the matters involved, however.

> All of this [spiritual influence in human war-making] has significance for Christ's second coming and the battle of Armageddon, when Jesus returns at the end of the tribulation period with the unseen armies of heaven. The battle of Armageddon will really be a war between the armies of the earth and the armies of heaven led by the Lord Jesus Christ (Revelation 19:11–19). The powerful weapons of mankind will not work in a war with beings from the spirit world.
>
> It does not score points in the secular court of public opinion, but most Christians are aware of the fact that the Bible teaches that supernatural beings are influencing the human race. Most Christians know that a fallen angel, Satan, appealed to the lusts of two vulnerable human beings, Adam and Eve, and caused the corruption of the entire human race (Genesis 3:1–7). Most Christians believe the church began when the Holy Spirit came to baptize people into the body of Christ (Acts 2:1–4). It may not be fashionable in the secular world to believe in the Holy Spirit, fallen angels, demons, and other such beings, but the Bible says they are real and they have a vested interest in what goes on in this world. Although many educated people scorn the idea, it is important to understand that the war-producing struggle between good and evil in the heart of man is actually the result of a greater struggle between forces in the supernatural realm. The Bible even teaches that this struggle will heighten as we approach the end of the age. The apostle Paul said, "The Spirit speaketh expressly, that in the latter times some shall depart from the faith, giving heed to seducing spirits, and doctrines of devils" (1 Timothy 4:1). Seducing spirits have caused a lot of trouble in the world, but they

are going to be an even greater problem in the days to come. The prophet Daniel actually called this struggle between supernatural forces in the unseen world "a great war." He had been fasting and praying for three weeks when he had a vision of Christ, fell into a deep sleep, and was touched by a good angel from the supernatural realm. The good angel told Daniel that he had been trying to reach him, but the prince of Persia had prevented him from getting through. He said he made it only because another angel named Michael helped him.

He also said he would have to go back and fight against the prince of Persia. Then the prince of Greece would come (Daniel 10).

Daniel's vision means there was a literal king of Persia who ruled in the physical realm. It also means there was a demonic prince of Persia who ruled in the spiritual realm. The same thing can be said for Greece: a physical king of Greece ruled in the natural realm and a demonic prince of Greece ruled in the spiritual realm. Furthermore, God had assigned an angel named Michael to rule over Israel in the spiritual realm, and he assisted the good angel in his struggle against the demonic prince of Persia. This provides conclusive evidence that Satan has a spiritual kingdom that includes a group of fallen angels called demons. It does not mean that Satan has demons behind every door or under every bed, but it does mean that he has fallen angels who are real and often influence the natural world in a negative way. Their evil effect on the vile passions of man is often responsible for war.

This is consistent with the teachings of Jesus, who spoke of Satan's kingdom and referred to him as the prince of this world (John 12:31, 16:11; Matthew 12:22–29). It is also consistent with the teachings of Paul. He said, "We wrestle not against flesh and blood, but against principalities, against powers, against the rulers of darkness of this world, against spiritual wickedness in high places" (Ephesians 6:12). The apostle called Satan the prince of the power of the air (Ephesians 2:2) and the god of this world (2 Corinthians 4:4). Many of the world's best scholars understand this to mean that Satan has a kingdom governed by a system of powerful fallen angels who influence the lusts of people on this earth. Their evil influence on the lusts of unregenerate man fuels the fires of war.[2]

The late Dr. John Walvoord, when he served as Dallas Theological Seminary chancellor, wrote on the spiritual influences surrounding the time of history approaching Armageddon:

The Final World War

The term Armageddon, which appears in Revelation 16:16, is the Aramaic translation of the Mountain of Megiddo located in the northern part of the plain of Esdraelom, later called the plain of Jezreel, and a place frequently mentioned in the Old Testament as important to military events (see Joshua 17:16; Judges 4:7, 5:21; 1 Samuel 31:1–3; 1 Kings 18:40; 2 Kings 9:27, 23:30; 2 Chronicles 35:20–24; Zechariah 12:11). Most expositors recognize that Armageddon is the Aramaic form of the Old Testament Megiddo.

Megiddo is designated the Tell El Mutesellim in the Plain of Esdraelom. At one time it was a city with massive fortifications and an important center for the Canaanites until Israel took it over about 1100 B.C. It was one of the chariot towns of Solomon (1 Kings 9:15, see also 10:26–29). At one time it included huge stables for horses, a governor's palace, and a complicated water system. In modern times it has been subject to many excavations to uncover the historic past. It is important in prophecy as the central marshaling point for the great armies that participate in Armageddon, the final war leading up to the second coming of Christ. From the mountain itself, which is not a high mountain, the Mediterranean can be seen to the west and the Valley of the Plain of Esdraelom stretches out some twenty miles to the east and opens up into several other important valleys. This is where millions of people will be centered in the great war before the second coming, though the armies are actually two hundred miles north and south over the whole land of Israel and stretching out all the way east to the Euphrates River. Revelation 16 mentions Armageddon as the important center for the great battle that follows the sixth bowl of the wrath of God, which permits the

---

2. Daymond R. Duck, "Wars and Rumors of War," *Foreshadows of Wrath and Redemption*, William T. James, ed. (Eugene, OR: Harvest House, 1999), p. 54–56.

kings of the east to cross the Euphrates and descend upon Israel for the final battle.

Satanic Influence on the Battle

A strange paradox exists in the situation. Revelation 16:13–14 describes demons as three unclean spirits like frogs that come out of the mouth of the dragon, the beast and the false prophet, enticing the kings of the world to gather for the battle which is called "the battle of the great day of God Almighty." Less than three years before, the devil had deceived the world into accepting the Antichrist as the world ruler (13:7). Under those circumstances, if the devil had united the world under the world dictator, why does he now encourage the nations to rebel against him? The answer is found in subsequent Scriptures which indicate the satanic purpose to gather all the armies of the world together in view of the fact that at the second coming the army of heaven would descend with Christ to take charge of the earth. Satan wanted all the armies available to fight the army from heaven. Ultimately, this proves to be a complete failure. When Christ comes He destroys the armies with a word (19:15), and no battle ever takes place between the army of heaven and the armies of earth.

The Old Testament mentions Megiddo often but principally in connection with the death of Josiah, the king who attempted to oppose the king of Egypt (2 Kings 23:29, 30; 2 Chronicles 35:20–24). The extent of the future conflict at Armageddon is made clear by the fact that two hundred million soldiers alone crossed the Euphrates River from the east adding to the millions already there (see Revelation 9:16). It is by all odds the greatest war of all history. Because such an army seems impossible, some people believe they are actually demons, though there is no proof for that interpretation. The Orient with more than one billion people in population could provide such an army.

Though it is common for Bible teachers of prophecy to picture this war as one of nuclear character, most of the evidence points to traditional warfare with the armies sweeping north and south across Israel (see Daniel 11:40–45). Zechariah 14 pictures house-to-house warfare, which is not compatible with nuclear war. The king of the south, namely the African forces, opposes the king of the north, who apparently is the Antichrist (and includes all the military power of Europe and the former Soviet states). But the battle is not resolved until the day of Christ's second coming.

Other Events Preceding Armageddon

Preceding the second coming are a number of other world events. Revelation 17 chronologically precedes the events of Revelation 16 and pictures the world church as a harlot astride a scarlet-colored beast. The beast is the ten-nation group led by the Antichrist, and the harlot is the world church movement — devoid of all true Christians and guilty of putting genuine Christians to death (Revelation 17:3–6). Revelation 17 pictures her rise to fame and power and at the same time mentions her ultimate destruction by the ten kings under the Antichrist, who are declared in Revelation 17:16 to hate her. The ten kings will destroy her and burn her with fire, the purpose being to clear the deck entirely so that the final form of world religion in the great tribulation can be the worship of Satan and the worship of the Antichrist.

The Destruction of Babylon

Also in the period leading up to Armageddon, and somewhat simultaneous with it, is the destruction of Babylon. Some identify Babylon with Rome and the city of Rome but obviously Babylon has another historic location. In Revelation 18 it is described as a great commercial city, which it is not now. Though there is dispute as to its actual part in the end times, it seems that Babylon or the site of ancient Babylon could be the capital of the final world government that has been transformed into a commercial city. Many prophecies, however, have held that Babylon would be ultimately destroyed just prior to the second coming and that it will never be inhabited again. Though the prophetic picture is somewhat complicated by the predicted attacks on Babylon already fulfilled when the future is declared in Isaiah 13:20 (for instance, "she will never be inhabited or lived in through all generations"), it goes on to speak how it would be a waste without population (Isaiah 13:19–22; Jeremiah 50:2, 3, 39–46, 51:37–48). This has never happened in history and indicates the necessity of this ultimate destruction just before the second coming. Jeremiah 50:1–51:8 provides a complete picture of this future destruction and ultimate desolation of the city.

The Final Bowl Judgment

While the battle of the great day of God Almighty is underway (Revelation 16:12–16), the final bowl of wrath is poured out, consisting of a gigantic earthquake that destroys all the cities of the world except for Israel (Revelation 16:17–21). Mountains and islands disappear, and the earth will be pelted with huge supernatural hailstones weighing one hundred pounds each. It is a final act of terrible destruction on the earth with a great loss of life and property that just precedes the second coming of Christ.[3]

Earth's Armageddon Powers Line Up for End-Game

Frequently today, pundits that are hired by broadcast and cable networks to analyze potential for war to erupt are saying bluntly that the Middle East, in particular, is a powder keg. I have had such people — retired military people with expertise in these areas — personally tell me that war could explode there at any second. It is almost miraculous, they seem to be of the consensus opinion, that war hasn't already begun.

Of course I am of the unshakable belief that it is absolutely the mighty hand of God that has prevented any such eruption to this point. But, Bible prophecy foretells that such restraint will one day be lifted.

The situation that looked so ominous between Russia and its former hostage client-state, Ukraine, is also a volatile potential ignition point for war that has been put on hold by God Himself.

The major power spheres of the world seem caught in a vortex of the winds of history. Powerful currents push one sphere against another as the globe grows smaller due to the burgeoning technologies. The exponential growth of every aspect of electronic instrumentality development has practically eliminated the buffering element of time that once was vital to the diplomatic process — i.e., whenever crises developed between nations (such as during the Cuban missile crisis of 1962) there was, because of slower

---

3. John Walvoord, "From Armageddon to the Millennium," *Foreshadows of Wrath and Redemption*, William T. James, Ed. (Eugene, OR: Harvest House, 1999), p. 346–349.

communications, time for each antagonist to ponder the situation and give nuanced responses. Kennedy and Khrushchev thus had a natural time factor that allowed for measured words.

Today, the diplomats might still carve out time necessary to make nuanced decisions, but behind the scenes there are instantaneous, electronic inputs that can't be fully monitored or controlled by those on the front lines of dealing with any given crisis. We think of the computer hacking by Chinese operatives that infamously stole personnel data from U.S. government agencies, which everyone was apparently powerless to stop, or even know about for months, in some cases.

The Western world is concerned with what goes on in the Middle East in guarding against disruption of petroleum availability and acts that might adversely affect prices and movement. Middle Eastern nations watch their neighbors because of the constant frictions between the various Islamist sects. Sunnis hate Shiites, who hate them in return. All are turned against Israel with millennia-long antagonisms that threaten at all times to erupt into conflict.

All of Asia watches China warily because of the dragon nation's build-up of its military that has been funded by China's economic siphoning of America's wealth. North Korea looks always to be itching for reigniting the conflict with the south.

The thaw of the Cold War appears to be on the verge of turning relations frigid again. Putin moves the Russian military toward the super power status it enjoyed under the Soviet regime. Russia and China are making nice with each other in joint military maneuvers. Iran is coming closer every hour to acquiring nuclear weapons. Israel has said they will never let that occur.

America, with an administration that seems oblivious to any danger posed by the likes of Cuba, South and Central America, or by Mexico, refuses to see fanatic Islam as a problem, while pushing Israel away in diplomatic gestures of disdain.

The Armageddon lineup for the Super Bowl of war is about ready to take the field at Jezreel.

CHAPTER 15

THE GREATEST COMEBACK OF ALL TIME!

Reason #15: Rebellion, with evil growing at every level,

is a primary reason Christ is about to return and this is

the generation that will soon be left behind when Christ

calls the Church into heaven.

Those of us who follow sports of various sorts are excited by great comebacks in the sporting events involved. The Apostle Paul used sporting analogies on occasion — like when he referred to completing the course, running the race, receiving the rewards at the bema (judgment seat), etc. The Roman Empire, which was in power at the time Paul was spreading the gospel, reveled in sporting events and gave great accolades to the winners. Paul took advantage of this intense interest in sporting events among many of those to whom he spoke to draw parallels between pursuing things of God and trying to excel at sports of the time. It was a teaching method that was God-inspired and quite effective. No greater man ever taught God's Word than Paul.

So, in my opinion, great comebacks of sporting teams, by way of analogy, are legitimate fodder for talking about the most important event that will ever occur in the earth's future.

We have all heard of Muhammad Ali (formerly Cassius Clay), who had his heavyweight championship taken away from him because of his refusal to enter the military draft. He later won the championship back at a time that boxing fans recognize as an age past one's prime for boxers. His is considered a great comeback.

Some remember many football games in which teams made great comebacks, as when Boston University's quarterback Doug Flutie led his team to a last second victory with the famous "Hail-Mary Pass."

As parents and fans of those who play on hometown teams, we are excited when our players and teams overcome scores that looked like they were about to spell defeat. A great comeback is always part of life's high points, whether in sports or in observing the human condition in general.

Likewise, watching people come back from adverse circumstances in any endeavor is usually uplifting to our own spirits. There is scheduled for the biblically prophetic future a comeback that will be magnificent beyond all imagination for some, and stunningly devastating to others.

The comeback was predicted in an astonishing announcement. It was a promise straight from the throne room of heaven. It was delivered by special messengers.

Jesus' closest associates — the disciples who had been with Him throughout His ministry and who had watched Him be crucified and buried, and who then had been with Him after His Resurrection from the dead — stood flabbergasted at the sight before them. Jesus had just talked with them, instructing them on what to do in carrying out their mission on heaven's behalf. Their eyes must have been wide and blinking, their mouths opened in utter amazement at the scene before them.

> And when he had spoken these things, while they beheld, he was taken up; and a cloud received him out of their sight. And while they looked stedfastly toward heaven as he went up, behold, two men stood by them in white apparel; which also said, Ye men of Galilee, why stand ye gazing up into heaven? this same Jesus, which is taken up from you into heaven, shall so come in like manner as ye have seen him go into heaven (Acts 1:9–11).

Christ's Second Advent (Second Coming) was promised by the God of all creation. As a matter of fact, Jesus Christ IS the very God of heaven. He said that He and His Father are one. He said that if you have seen Him, the Son, you have seen the Father. The Bible says that God cannot lie. What He has prophesied is 100 percent guaranteed to come to pass.

The world, led by Lucifer, the god of this fallen sphere and *prince of the power of the air,* supposed they had rid the planet of Jesus, whom they executed like a common criminal. The world denied and continues to deny that He arose from the dead and now is at the right hand of God the Father. The world of rebels continues to mock and scoff at the prophecy that He will return, while they do what is right in their own eyes and the world gets worse and worse. Planet earth's rebellious unbelievers hold that Jesus was defeated at the Cross and will never come back. He is dead and gone. One observer of these days in which anything godly is mocked has written the following.

Mockers are the Seal of God's Coming Judgment

There are two criteria for a society to fulfill which seals its destruction from God. The first is to legalize iniquity while the second is to mock God and those that warn of the coming judgment for sin.

God clearly lays out in the Bible what are the conditions for triggering His righteous judgment on a nation. America is now almost completed these requirements and is ready for judgment. . . .

The United States now is enacting, by both customs and laws, the ordinances of the Amorites; therefore the nation is defiled before the Holy God of Israel and faces His judgment. By promoting homosexuality, America has become like the ancient pagan Amorites and has now come under the direct judgment of God.

America promotes homosexuality by custom with events such as Gay Pride Day, Gay Awareness Month (June), Gay Day at Disneyland, Gay Day at sporting events and events like Southern Decadence in New Orleans. There are gay clubs in high school and colleges. The political parties are pandering to the homosexuals for their votes. By custom, homosexuality has woven into the fabric of America. It is an ordinance.

America is continually making ordinances to advance the homosexual agenda. They can legally "marry" now in all states. Homosexuals are now able to adopt children and gain custody of children during a divorce. There are now numerous hate speech laws which are being used to silence opposition to the homosexual agenda. Both federal and state courts are declaring that homosexuality is a "right."

America is a long way down the road to enacting all the ordinances of the Amorites.

The Bible warns of God judging a nation that enacts these ordinances. When the corporate attitude of a nation is friendly toward homosexuality then at this point the iniquity is full. It is apparent that "the cup" of America's sin is rapidly filling up. Americans hardly blush anymore at fornication and adultery.

The nation kills over one million babies a year with up to fifty-five million killed "legally" since 1973. The legalizing of abortion was an additional "Ordinance of the Amorites/Americans." . . .

The last act before judgment is that the people are so hardened in sin, they mock God, His Word, and those that warn of the impending doom (2 Chronicles 36:15–16).[1]

One of God's most prominent men of faith has said: "Our world is filled with fear, hate, lust, greed, war, and utter despair. Surely the Second Coming of Jesus Christ is the only hope of replacing these depressing features with trust, love, universal peace, and prosperity."[2] Israel's rejected Messiah, and the much-maligned Lamb, "slain from the foundation of the world that takes away the sins of that world," will one day, during earth's darkest hour, break through the black clouds of Armageddon and make the most spectacular comeback ever.

And I saw heaven opened, and behold a white horse; and he that sat upon him was called Faithful and True, and in righteousness he doth judge and make war. His eyes were as a flame of fire, and on his head were many crowns; and he had a name written, that no man knew, but he himself. And he was clothed with a vesture dipped in blood: and his name is called The Word of God. And the armies which were in heaven followed him upon white horses, clothed in fine linen, white and clean. And out of his mouth goeth a sharp sword, that with it he should smite the nations: and he shall rule them with a rod of iron: and he treadeth the winepress of the fierceness and wrath of Almighty God (Revelation 19:11–15).

---

1. John McTernan, "Warning: Mockers in the Last Days," www.raptureready.com, "Newest Articles."
2. Karen Ridder, "Jesus Is Coming Soon? 7 Billy Graham Quotes about Second Coming," Newsmax.com, http://www.newsmax.com/FastFeatures/jesus-is-coming-soon/2014/11/16/id/606797/.

Last-Days Scoffers

As presented above, this generation is full of scoffers, mocking the prophesied return of Jesus Christ to the earth. This is as the great Apostle Peter foretold it would be at the end of the age of grace (Church Age):

> Knowing this first, that there shall come in the last days scoffers, walking after their own lusts, and saying, Where is the promise of his coming? for since the fathers fell asleep, all things continue as they were from the beginning of the creation (2 Peter 3:3–4).

God's prophecies are 100 percent accurate, so it doesn't surprise in the least that there is the scoffing and mocking today, exactly as one of God's prophets said there will be as time nears the Lord's return. We have covered in this book the many signals that are occurring simultaneously, and with phenomenal frequency and intensity, pointing to where we are on God's prophetic timeline. Chief among these are all of the geopolitical dynamic intrigues surrounding the nation Israel — God's prophetic timepiece. The sneering at the thought that there could possibly be a Rapture just throws fuel on the fire of the end-of-days deluge — the end that is coming in with a flood of last-days indicators as foretold by Daniel the prophet:

> And after threescore and two weeks shall Messiah be cut off, but not for himself: and the people of the prince that shall come shall destroy the city and the sanctuary; and the end thereof shall be with a flood, and unto the end of the war desolations are determined (Daniel 9:26).

Daniel was foretelling what would happen from the time the Messiah, Jesus Christ, would die for the sins of mankind until the very end of human history at Armageddon. Great, convulsing, prophesied issues and events would, near the very end of the age, he forecast, gush through the generation alive at the time like a flood.

Daniel's End-Time Flood

It is obvious that one of those predicted manifestations of the end-time flood is the level of anger that is presently coming against believers who proclaim that one of the most stupendous events of all human history will one day — perhaps very soon — take millions upon millions from the earth's surface in a fraction of a second.

I receive in my email each week any number of messages declaring that the truth we champion regarding Bible doctrine and prophecies — particularly the pre-Tribulational Rapture of the Church — are everything from ludicrous to heretical. This criticism gets especially intense whenever our raptureready.com website is written or spoken about in a major media outlet. That is to be expected, because there can be no spiritual discernment among those of the lost world. Believers in Jesus Christ can understand, while those who do not belong to God's family through belief in His only begotten Son cannot understand:

> For what man knoweth the things of a man, save the spirit of man which is in him? even so the things of God knoweth no man, but the Spirit of God.
>
> Now we have received, not the spirit of the world, but the spirit which is of God; that we might know the things that are freely given to us of God. Which things also we speak, not in the words which man's wisdom teacheth, but which the Holy Ghost teacheth; comparing spiritual things with spiritual. But the natural man receiveth not the things of the Spirit of God: for they are foolishness unto him: neither can he know them, because they are spiritually discerned (1 Corinthians 2:11–14).

Defense of Rapture to Lost and Saved

Trying to explain or defend the Rapture to the world of the lost is, therefore, fruitless. There is just no way they can understand or believe this doctrine, unless and until they repent, ask for — and accept — God's grace gift offer of salvation through Jesus Christ's sacrifice on the Cross at Calvary nearly two millennia ago. We can go through the vast body of scriptural text, laying out the Bible facts as we are confident God's Word presents truth about the Rapture. But unless one is capable of spiritual discernment from the Holy Spirit, a person, no matter how intellectually brilliant, can never come to believe those facts. He or she might even come to understand the facts in a purely cerebral sense, but never truly comprehend them to the point of knowing that the Rapture is a cataclysmic event in the future of one particular generation of earth's inhabitants.

So our efforts to explain the Rapture will meet with quite limited results, seeing as how there is a great spiritual discernment disconnect, when explaining to those who don't know Christ for salvation. This we accept, and thus can move ahead with limited frustration in putting the truth about prophecy and the Rapture before these as best we can.

Dealing with the Body of Christ — all born-again believers — is quite another thing, when it comes to our frustration meter. It becomes a bit more disconcerting when our efforts to put out truth about prophecy and the Rapture in particular are met with the same arguments, no matter how thoroughly and how cogently we organize and present what God's Word has to tell His children about these matters.

Hard-Shell Rapture Detractors

There are, of course, the die-hard preterists (believing that most all prophecy has been completed or should be spiritualized) and the reform replacement theological enclaves (those who declare that God's promises have been taken from Israel and given to the Church). These make their livings throwing mud balls — usually with stones at the centers — at those of us who proclaim the truth that Jesus will come for His Church BEFORE the Tribulation era. These who refuse to see two programs of God's dealing with mankind, Israel, and the Church — these two dovetailing into one magnificent prophetic culmination — castigate us who believe that God deals with His creation called man dispensationally (the ages of Adam, Noah, Moses, Abraham, David, the Church, Tribulation, Millennium, etc.). Sometimes it seems fruitless to try to break through the thick spiritual iron wills of these in trying to present truth about the Rapture. But these are not the most troubling that seem to fit the 2 Peter 3:3–4 description, so far as scoffing is concerned. The more concerning are those who, despite being given, time after time, the same tremendously in-depth explanation from God's Word about the Rapture and the truth that it will be a pre-Tribulational one, continue to come to us with the same arguments to the contrary. This, despite the fact that they visit the Rapture Ready website and can read more than 15,000 articles on matters of God's truth, many dealing specifically with eschatology.

These are Christians who just seem to have it in their determination that they must go through the Tribulation, the time about which Jesus foretold the following:

> For then shall be great tribulation, such as was not since the beginning of the world to this time, no, nor ever shall be (Matthew 24:21).

The Tribulation, if we can imagine, will be worse than the concentration camps, torture chambers, crematoriums of Hitler, or the most terrible days of the Inquisitions with all of the devilish methods of torture. Yet, there seems to be a need — they deludedly think — for some Christians to go through that time, during which Antichrist will do his dead-level best to kill every person who refuses to worship him.

Anti-Rapture Example

I've chosen one letter from such a Christian. It is a simple and mild letter; no mud-ball throwing. But, it represents the most troubling of all of the critics of the Rapture of the Church. It is most troubling that these types think as they do, because it shows an almost willfulness against accepting God's promises, summed by this passage:

> For God hath not appointed us to wrath, but to obtain salvation by our Lord Jesus Christ (1 Thessalonians 5:9).

Here is what she wrote, in part:

> I know that the Tribulation is going to be extremely bad and even worse than I can imagine but I sincerely believe I along with you and other Christians that are living at the time, will be going thru the bad. I am prepared mentally and will do whatever comes my way to either get thru or stand up and say no when needed. If I am one that is to [be] beheaded then so be it. I know GOD will be holding my hand and whatever comes my way, HE will see me thru.
>
> If I can be of any use to GOD to help save people then I am prepared to do as HE wants. I have many family members that are not believers now and pray daily that will change. I do believe that many souls will be saved. I know that I am a sinner and do not like verses of the Bible taken out of context.
>
> The whole book or at least the chapter needs to [be] read and understood not just a verse here and now to prove a theory that did not even come into being until a couple of hundred years ago. How is every eye going to see JESUS return if HE comes back in secret. Just don't believe any are going to be "raptured away." The Bible states that HEAVEN will be coming down here not us going up there.

Tragic Unscriptural Misconceptions

The Christian sister makes a number of statements of misconception that are dealt with through hundreds of the thousands of articles on the Rapture Ready website. This is my problem. Many criticisms of us who hold to the pre-Trib Rapture are issued forth by those who obviously have never mined the rich resources available to them, before making their criticisms/argumentations.

She writes that she is sure that she will be going through the Tribulation in order to stand for Christ and help God save people out of that horrendous time. She charges that she has disdain for those who twist Scripture out of context, with those (like us, I presume) using scattered and sporadic Scripture passages to make our points.

She, at the same time, provides no Scripture for any of her criticisms of the Rapture "theory," as she puts it. However, most who make this charge do so, using Scripture from Revelation that they declare shows saints in the middle of that time of Tribulation. Thus, they conclude, the Church is right there, taking the brunt of Antichrist's rage and God's wrath.

Dispensational Discernment Required

Indeed, believers will populate that era by the millions. It will, many who study that period believe, be a time of the greatest coming to Christ in the history of man. What the writer of this letter — and others — fails to recognize or even consider is that God deals with man, including His children, in dispensations.

There are saints of the Church Age at present, and there will be saints during the Tribulation. Neither will be together in the same dispensation.

Jesus told us that He would build His Church upon the gospel message the Apostle Peter had just given, telling Jesus that he believed Jesus was the Christ, the Son of the Living God:

> And Jesus answered and said unto him, Blessed art thou, Simon Barjona: for flesh and blood hath not revealed it unto thee, but my Father which is in heaven.
>
> And I say also unto thee, That thou art Peter, and upon this rock I will build my church; and the gates of hell shall not prevail against it (Matthew 16:17–18).

Do you see that? The gates of hell — Satan — will not prevail against the Church. That's all about the Church Age saints.

The Revelation tells quite another story for God's saints. The following Scripture is speaking, of course, about Satan's great tyrant, Antichrist, during the Tribulation era:

> And it was given unto him to make war with the saints, and to overcome them: and power was given him over all kindreds, and tongues, and nations (Revelation 13:7).

The Church will not be "overcome" by Satan, because it won't be here. The Tribulation saints (those who accept Christ after the Rapture) will be overcome to a large extent — lose their physical lives for the cause of Christ.

Myth-Making Against Rapture

Our Christian critic-friend proves that she has at least done some study, but not from God's Word. She has read the books and literature of those who incessantly and speciously claim that we who believe in the pre-Trib Rapture have learned our "false" doctrine from a 19th-century witch who somehow influenced John Darby to later perpetrate the hated Rapture theory.

The most ludicrous of the criticisms is that we base our view that there will be a Rapture upon Margaret MacDonald's vision in the 1800s. It makes me almost nauseous to have to even address this — for the thousandth time — when, if the critics would just read what is already written on the subject on the site, it should quell their proclivity to make such ridiculous claims. But I will briefly answer again for those who are so intellectually and spiritually lazy.

The Rapture, the "catching up" (Greek: *harpazo*) was revealed by Paul the Apostle. It is a mystery he gave us through Holy Spirit inspiration, as recorded in 1 Corinthians 15:51–55 and 1 Thessalonians 4:13–18. The Rapture was not the concoction of John Darby, who picked up this teaching and gave it improved order of presentation centuries after the doctrine was believed and taught by the early church fathers (first two centuries A.D.).

The Rapture isn't built on one or two verses, but on the entire body of Scripture. When viewed in totality, and in context, the doctrine flows with prophetic signals we observe occurring in the world today — i.e., the world isn't getting better and better as the "kingdom-now" people believe (that the Church will make the world better until Christ can return to set up His throne). The pre-Trib Rapture view puts forward that the world will grow worse and worse. The Church will be removed from earth, then God's judgment will begin to fall on rebellious earth-dwellers.

Which do we see happening today? The world getting better and better? Or are things looking worse and worse for planet earth? Read the daily headlines or watch the hourly news, and you will have your answer.

Two Phases of Second Coming

Again, Paul shows us the mystery — he reveals the mystery of the Rapture in 1 Corinthians 15:51–55. The mystery he is expanding upon is the wonderful promise Jesus made as shown in John 14:1–3. Jesus is coming for us — before God's wrath must fall.

A foreshadowing of that principle is seen in Genesis, chapter 19, when God said that He could do nothing in the way of sending judgment upon Sodom and Gomorrah until Lot was first removed. Lot represented the only righteousness God recognized. It was Lot's faith — as puny as it was — that kept him and the other few believers of his family from the time of God's wrath — again, Revelation 3:10.

Our critic asks how all eyes can see Christ return, if He comes secretly in some Rapture. She declares she just doesn't believe anyone is going to be raptured away, and she states that Christ will be coming down to earth, not Christians going up to Him. Again, she and those who fill her head with anti-Rapture rhetoric fail to, or willfully refuse to, see God's dispensations in dealing with man. In the case of the return of Christ, Scripture makes it clear there are two separate returns. These are at least seven years apart, one from the other.

Jesus will return at some unknown time in the Rapture. Jesus, Himself, likens that coming to a thief-in-the-night experience for those on earth. They won't know what has happened, and certainly won't see Christ. Paul says it is a moment in time when all believers (the Church) will meet Jesus in the air:

> For the Lord himself shall descend from heaven with a shout, with the voice of the archangel, and with the trump of God: and the dead in Christ shall rise first: Then we which are alive and remain shall be caught up together with them in the clouds, to meet the Lord in the air: and so shall we ever be with the Lord (1 Thessalonians 4:16–17).

Jesus will come the second time, following at least seven earth years, at the close of the Tribulation era, known also as "Daniel's 70th week." This time He will come all the way to the planet, and every eye will behold Him. There will be absolutely no doubt about this re-entry and landing:

> And I saw heaven opened, and behold a white horse; and he that sat upon him was called Faithful and True, and in righteousness he doth judge and make war. His eyes were as a flame of fire, and on his head were many crowns; and he had a name written, that no man knew, but he himself. And he was clothed with a vesture dipped in blood: and his name is called The Word of God.
>
> And the armies which were in heaven followed him upon white horses, clothed in fine linen, white and clean. And out of his mouth goeth a sharp sword, that with it he should smite the nations: and he shall rule them with a rod of iron: and he treadeth the winepress of the fierceness and wrath of Almighty God (Revelation 19:11–15).

Scriptural Proof Required

As stated before, each of these things intended to deny the validity and credence of pre-Trib Rapture are dealt with at great length, and in tremendous depth throughout the raptureready.com website. All opposing views are carefully dissected, and with Scripture given at every point along the way in addressing any and every question. But, it DOES take determined research to seek out truth found in the articles — truth that is God's Word, not merely ours.

Here is the main crux of this dear lady's problem in not discerning truth about Christ's coming for the Church. She presents not one Scripture to back up any of her assertions, declarations, or suppositions/postulations. She simply parrots things critical of the Rapture doctrine she has read or heard from those who mock, without anything of spiritual substance to back her/their criticisms. My intention is not to pick on her. I want only to use her method of criticism — a method used in almost every instance by those who listen to the anti-Rapture crowd — as an example to show there is no foundation to her/their argument/denial that the Rapture is a doctrine taught in God's Word. This is our answer to such critics. Study the Word of God. Make your criticisms from His Word — as the dear woman says — not from just a Scripture here or there, but from the whole context of the matter, whatever the matter happens to be.

I have studied most all of the positions and variations thereof involved in these arguments for decades — which gives away my age, I guess. The pre-Trib view of prophecy yet future is absolutely the only one that makes sense in the totality of scriptural context, and in terms of what we see unfolding today in things of geopolitics, global socio-economics, and religion.

Salvation and Rapture Inseparable

The Rapture is an issue incontrovertibly linked to salvation — something Jesus did on the Cross, which puts us in God's family when we truly believe. That faith keeps us from the time of God's wrath — both in the coming Tribulation and in eternity. Wrath and judgment must fall upon rebellious mankind, because of sin. Jesus paid the price for that sin. He said on the Cross, "It is finished." Sin was forever paid for at that moment, for those who would accept His sacrifice — the only sacrifice that God will accept — the precious blood of His Blessed Son.

We are told that we as Christians, while in the flesh, will have tribulations (troubles). Certainly Christians have had troubles down through the years — persecutions, genocide, martyrdom, etc. These horrors are still happening in some places around the world. But this was not, and is not, God's wrath and judgment, but was, and is, satanic rage against God's people. The Tribulation will include satanic rage, but it will be within the horrific storm of God's wrath and judgment.

Christians (those who have been, as our critic says, saved following the Rapture) will certainly suffer satanic rage, but not God's wrath. Many will be martyred, as in the times of the early persecutions — like Christians are being martyred in some nations today. But, we are told that we (Paul denotes the difference between Christians of the Church Age and those who aren't in God's family by the use of pronouns) aren't appointed to wrath, but to salvation through our Lord Jesus Christ. We who know Christ for salvation are told by Paul to "comfort one another with these words" — not look to fear, but to comfort (read 1 Thessalonians 4:18 and 5:9–11). We will be kept out of "the time of testing" (the Apocalypse or Tribulation), John was told by Jesus (Revelation 3:10).

Rapture Ready or Not . . .

Now, you might not agree, and that's fine. If you know Christ, you are going instantly to Him anyway, when Jesus says "Come up hither," as He did to John in Revelation 4:1–2. You will have no other choice, if you are in God's family. But, please don't ever think — or claim — that there are only scattered verses here and there, or that there is no tremendously deep body of scriptural evidence and proofs beneath the truth of the pre-Trib Rapture.

Again, you can disagree, but please don't accuse us of not knowing about the other views, and don't just blindly accept what opponents falsely say when they lie, proclaiming that we just believe in something a 19th-century Englishman said, or that we follow some woman who dabbled in the occult. That isn't true, and you should look more deeply into the evidence upon which we base these understandings than just to take the word of those who make such shallow and deceptive accusations.

Put this Scripture in a place you can memorize it — and make it your model truth for avoiding the pitfalls of intellectual and scriptural laziness:

> Study to shew thyself approved unto God, a workman that needeth not to be ashamed, rightly dividing the word of truth (2 Timothy 2:15).

Greatest Comeback Ever!

The King of all kings is on His way back from heaven to claim victory in the age-long contest between good and evil. His victory will, if I may again use Paul's sports analogy, be accomplished in two rounds — to use boxing or golf as example — or in two halves, if thinking in terms of football.

The first part of the victory will be won at the end of the Church Age (Age of Grace) when Jesus Christ calls all born-again believers to Himself in the Rapture. The final part of the victory will be achieved when He breaks through the darkness and destruction of Armageddon to put an end to rebellion against God (Revelation 19:11).

Rapture Ready . . . or not — the first phase of Christ's spectacular comeback is about to occur!

ON BEING RAPTURE READY

M y heart stopped the third time and I was once again instantaneously in the middle of the young, jubilant throng of heavenly beings. Their beautiful, sparkling eyes pierced into my soul, their faces framing laughter of the most joyous sort. They thrust their hands skyward while we ran effortlessly toward some unfathomably wonderful destination.

These were, I'm absolutely certain, the "cloud of witnesses" of Hebrews 12:1–3.

They were, among other reasons, cheering approval of this very book you have now almost finished reading. *Rapture Ready . . . Or Not? 15 Reasons Why This Is the Generation That Will Be Left Behind* is one reason I was brought back into this life. There is no other matter more important to the heavenly realm at this critical moment than the truth that the Lord Jesus Christ is at the very gates of heaven, ready to call His Church home in the Rapture.

The Lord of creation knows that I don't write this to take unto myself any glory or honor. I deserve, in my own self-effort, death and hell like all others of fallen mankind. It is only in Christ that I am found acceptable to God the Father. He alone deserves all honor and glory and worship.

For His own reasons, He commissioned me to present this volume for the reader who willingly seeks Him in these closing hours of the age. Time is very, very short.

Planet earth is at the very end of the Church Age — this present dispensation of grace. I believe that there is no doubt that the indicators we have examined are powerful reasons to conclude that the present generation is that which is on the verge of being left behind when the Rapture takes place.

Being left behind will mean all people on the earth will be subjected to horrendous events unlike any experienced in human history. Again, the Lord Jesus Christ said:

> For then shall be great tribulation, such as was not since the beginning of the world to this time, no, nor ever shall be (Matthew 24:21).

The whole purpose of producing this book is because the Lord of heaven doesn't want anyone to suffer this terrible time of judgment and wrath. Simply answering the Holy Spirit's call to one's own spirit will assure that the person will go to be with Jesus Christ when He says "Come up here!" (Revelation 4:1).

Genuinely accepting this call of God to salvation will forever grant His pardon for all sin, past, present, and future — based upon His Son's sacrifice on the Cross at Calvary nearly two thousand years ago.

Once again, here is the scriptural call of the Holy Spirit to the spirit of each and every person alive today.

> That if thou shalt confess with thy mouth the Lord Jesus, and shalt believe in thine heart that God hath raised him from the dead, thou shalt be saved. For with the heart man believeth unto right-eousness; and with the mouth confession is made unto salvation (Romans 10:9–10).

Believe in the Lord Jesus Christ, and you will be saved. It's just that simple. God loves you, and implores you to accept His offer of forgiveness. Accept His offer, and you will instantaneously become a part of His eternal family — a child of the Living God.

Rapture and Reasons Reviewed

Although those many indicators that this generation is at the very end of the Church Age have been looked at in depth, we will summarize the prophetic symptoms that infect these, what I believe to be the last of the last days.

"How near do you think the Rapture might be?" This or similar questions issue from people, both believers in Christ and nonbelievers. The queries come over the Internet, during question-and-answer sessions at prophecy conferences, and from those such as my History Channel interviewer during filming for the aforementioned series of documentaries on prophecy (*The Nostrodamus Effect*).

Despite innate skepticism, even within believers, one senses that there flows just beneath the surface of decorum in posing the question a visceral trepidation that there will be such a thing as "the Rapture." While those who attend prophecy conferences and secular media types seem genuinely to want an opinion on how near the Rapture is, there is almost zero interest in that great event within Christ's Church in general. This singular reality is, by itself, a factor worth examination while contemplating the question of when the Rapture might occur. More about that in due course.

Strange Goings-On

To begin considering matters involved, the question can't be adequately entertained to any degree of understanding without once again analyzing our strange times — this bordering-on-bizarre generation that Jesus Himself was most likely prophesying in the Olivet Discourse and other places in Scripture.

America presently has a collective nervous twitch. Worry about the diseased economy is the instigator of the societal surface spasms. Uncertainty about movement into the radical changes President Barack Obama has brought about (as promised) has, rather than put minds at ease, caused a form of national schizophrenia. The schism separates Americans in crucial areas of politics and morality, which are in most aspects inextricably linked.

Those divisions threaten to raise the national temperature to a fever pitch. There is a sense that, as radio talk-show host Glenn Beck — and others — say, a powerful crisis event lurks in the immediate future. It will be the crisis, these believe, that will cause government to snap its voracious, all-consuming, lust-to-control jaws shut on liberty.

So it is more than a matter of curiosity that leads me to think upon the many issues and events swirling about this generation that seem almost certainly of biblically prophetic significance. This, while there is the obvious disconnect of the Church of the Lord Jesus Christ, for the most part, from those foreboding issues and events that are everywhere we look.

Money Worries and Changing World Order

In secular (non-spiritual) terms, pocketbook issues almost always lead the way with the adult American citizen. This is a fact, whether talking about those who produce income or those who don't. And, therein lies much of the division in America today. The great political — and cultural — schism, like it or not, is provably engendered and perpetuated by those who work, pay taxes, and contribute to the nation's economic progress, versus those who don't work, but receive the taxpayer-funded largesse of growing government that is devoted to taking care of and growing exponentially its voter base from cradle to grave. This is not to say society — particularly private charity — should neglect the truly needy, those who can't work because of physical or mental incapacity.

Cynical? If so, it is cynicism steeped in provable statistics, the presentation of which isn't the thrust of this book's conclusion. Such thought — at least in a general sense — is necessary, however, in order to understand the role the riches of this fallen world play in setting up today's prophetic alignment and the nearness of the Rapture.

The wallet issue that is front and center — most intensely focused on — is the "healthcare for everyone" debate. Universal coverage so that no person will go without healthcare was the proclaimed great concern the politicians paraded over and over before the sycophantic mainstream media microphones and cameras. But in the cabals of behind-the-scenes power politics, it is ever-increasing governmental control — not equitable healthcare for all Americans — that many within government seek. Congressional leaders, as we know, have not been leading the way en masse to give everyone the same premium healthcare system they themselves enjoy.

Control, then, is the operative word in thinking on the question of the nearness of the Rapture. Control of economy is the thrust that impels human leaderships within government toward the time of absolute power that will corrupt absolutely. The Antichrist regime is the ultimate government that lurks in the dark haze of the prophetic future.

In the Twinkling?

Many economic gurus — especially those on the blogs of the Internet — although they haven't a clue of what will be the true paradigm shift that will fling open the gate to enslavement, are on the mark in sensing that there hovers an unprecedented moment of crisis somewhere just ahead. That crisis just might be created in the twinkling of an eye, as a matter of fact!

The Rapture will, with unbelievable swiftness, sweep everyone left behind on earth into its vortex of soul-rending calamity.

Love of Money Key to Satan's Scheme

"It's the economy, stupid!" is the infamous slogan spewed first by Democrat operative James Carville as a rallying cry for Bill Clinton's presidential bid. The declaration was picked up and echoed, seemingly with glee, by mainstream news pundits and other media types. The electorate's almost total absorption with money matters, as those matters affect their day-to-day lives, continues to plague attempts at bringing about consensus in America that we come together as one mind, one people.

Money is the central point of interest, but it is also the societal element that most widely separates we the people. Therein lies the nucleus of the problem for Lucifer's plot to usurp the throne of God. He knows it isn't possible to usurp the heavenly throne, but he observably has a blueprint for ruling on earth. Jerusalem and Mt. Moriah are his ultimate objectives in this regard, but more about that later.

Humanism is at the heart of Satan's plot for achieving the installment of his man, Antichrist, on that earthly throne. He will succeed in doing so for a very brief time. To accomplish this, economy is the ingredient within the human condition that must be brought into governance under Lucifer's authority in order to close the great schism that monetary chaos has produced and continues to perpetuate. The chasm must be breached — not in order to make life better for humanity, but to give Satan a system of buying and selling that will enslave ALL mankind.

> And he causeth all, both small and great, rich and poor, free and bond, to receive a mark in their right hand, or in their foreheads: And that no man might buy or sell, save he that had the mark, or the name of the beast, or the number of his name (Revelation 13:16–17).

To avoid any misunderstanding, I am not saying that the people and their obsession with pocketbook issues is a good thing in order to throw the proverbial monkey wrench into Satan's plans to rule on earth. The love of money is the root of all kinds of evil, the Bible tells us, and Americans are obsessed, probably more than any culture that has ever existed, with money and the deadly materialism with which it infects this generation. The point is, monetary intrigues will power the engine of humanistic drive from this point forward as never before. Anyone with any sensibility to look at what has been happening over the past months and years with regard to the economic dynamics shaping things in America and the world should be able to know that doing business has forever changed. The economy of the United States continues to be deliberately dismantled — and I believe it is being supernaturally accomplished — by forces determined to restructure the world for setting up the ten-kingdom governance prophesied for the time just before Christ's return to earth.

> And the ten horns which thou sawest are ten kings, which have received no kingdom as yet; but receive power as kings one hour with the beast. These have one mind, and shall give their power and strength unto the beast (Revelation 17:12–13).

One-World Economic Order

In considering the question of how near the Rapture might be, I view the rush toward one-world economy almost the equivalent in order of importance to Israel being front and center on the end-times stage. A flood of other end-times-type issues only slightly less consequential than those two mentioned rage through this generation. It is difficult to prioritize them for purposes of determining their order of importance in looking at how near might be Christ's call to the Church as prophesied in 1 Corinthians 15:51–55 and 1 Thessalonians 4:13–18. I believe, however, that one prophetic symptom of our day has developed that stands out as being almost equivalent to Israel and the drive for one-world economic order in pointing to the nearness of the Tribulation hour: the mesmerized church.

Church Deluded

Despite the claims that the Church is rising to meet the challenges of this troubled age, one is hard-pressed to document any such massive movement. It seems just the opposite. Anti-God movements are growing, aided and abetted by news and entertainment media. Rather than opposing things going on that run counter to God's Word, there have developed entertainment-oriented, mega-church organizations that do their best to emulate the world's glitz and glamour. They teach and preach a feel-good, do-good pabulum that surely makes the Lord of heaven want to retch. As a matter of fact, God said it would be just this way as the time of Christ's return nears:

And unto the angel of the church of the Laodiceans write; These things saith the Amen, the faithful and true witness, the beginning of the creation of God; I know thy works, that thou art neither cold nor hot: I would thou wert cold or hot. So then because thou art lukewarm, and neither cold nor hot, I will spue thee out of my mouth (Revelation 3:14–16).

Antichrist Spirit Pandemic

The Antichrist spirit is alive and infecting everything in today's world system. No big surprise, right? But the demonstrable fact that it is alive and well at this very moment within so-called Christian church organizations across America is a staggering reality to consider.

Here's what John the Apostle, through divine inspiration, had to say two thousand years ago:

Beloved, believe not every spirit, but try the spirits whether they are of God: because many false prophets are gone out into the world. Hereby know ye the Spirit of God: Every spirit that confesseth that Jesus Christ is come in the flesh is of God: and every spirit that confesseth not that Jesus Christ is come in the flesh is not of God: and this is that spirit of antichrist, whereof ye have heard that it should come; and even now already is it in the world (1 John 4:1–3).

End-Times Church Sickens God

The Laodicean church is symbolized as the church that will at the very end of the Church Age (Age of Grace) literally make the God of all creation sick to His stomach. The Lord describes through John that organization's true character, and why He is sickened:

Because thou sayest, I am rich, and increased with goods, and have need of nothing; and knowest not that thou art wretched, and miserable, and poor, and blind, and naked (Revelation 3:17).

Jesus spoke to the very things that mark the Laodicean church in foretelling the end of the age. The prophecy is prominent — is, as a matter of fact, the very first characteristic Jesus lists in His Olivet Discourse for the time just before His return:

> And as he sat upon the mount of Olives, the disciples came unto him privately, saying, Tell us, when shall these things be? and what shall be the sign of thy coming, and of the end of the [age]? And Jesus answered and said unto them, Take heed that no man deceive you. For many shall come in my name, saying, I am Christ; and shall deceive many (Matthew 24:3–5).

Only one who denies that God's Word is truth can miss the importance of the Lord's words here. Jesus is speaking to the deception that will be tied up in false teachings and false prophesying at the time just before He returns. Please understand that I'm not meaning that all large churches, even megachurches, are evil. Some still adhere to Bible truth in their preaching and teaching. However, the "if-we-can't-beat-'em-we-will-join-'em" false religionists of recent years have expropriated the Church's personnel and presented a compromised message before the senses of the glitz-mad American public. The tactic has worked. The megachurch super-complexes under whose roofs the masses continue to swell mark this generation, almost certainly, as the Laodicean church. I believe these church entities are organizations or multiple levels of organizations filled not with the Holy Spirit, but with the spirit of Antichrist.

A primary tactic chosen by most of these organizations to draw the masses is to give people an entertainment spectacle every time they sit in the plush theater pews. There is nothing wrong with being physically comfortable while sitting, but to be always spiritually comfortable sitting under preaching and teaching that should point to the more abundant life conviction of the Holy Spirit is devastating to the soul. The compromise is in the "Let's talk about it," feel-good, do-good message of "God loves you, and would never condemn you to a hell, which in any case, doesn't exist." God DOES love us — so much so that He sent His only Son, Jesus the Christ, to die as the once-and-for-all sacrifice for the sin in which we are otherwise lost forever.

The thesis-antithesis-synthesis psychobabble theologizing — "Let's talk about it" compromise — is proof that these organizations of religiosity deny that Jesus Christ is the only way to salvation — to reconciliation with God the Father. They are of the Antichrist spirit. These believe they are indeed "rich, and increased with goods, and think they have need of nothing; and know not that they are wretched, and miserable, and poor, and blind, and naked," in God's holy view.

True Church's Willful Ignorance Breaking God's Heart

Troubling as these unredeemed types of churches are in these fleeting days of this age, the overt, deliberate ignorance of things of God's prophetic Word in those true Christian churches who still adhere to Jesus as the only Way must be heart-wrenching to the Lord of heaven. Most Christians are without any understanding of the times in which we find ourselves.

To those who study the times in light of Bible prophecy, the seminaries, pastors, teachers, and Christians in the pews of America are observably, for the most part, happily ignorant of the astonishing fact that Israel is being put in the position of Zechariah 12:1–3 — that the Jewish state is being forced toward a peace from which will come Antichrist and the Tribulation.

Christians, by and large, have no idea that the European Union is shaping to be the matrix out of which Antichrist will come, that the Russian/Iranian/Turkey/other nation alignment is configuring for the Gog-Magog war of Ezekiel chapters 38 and 39.

Today's church can't discern that powerful spiritual as well as geopolitical dynamics are forcing the economies of America and the world into a one-world mold that will eventuate in the ten-kingdom rearrangement of Revelation 17:12–13. They don't see that we are in the "perilous times" of Paul's forewarning in 2 Timothy, chapter 3. They don't understand that this nation and the world are filled with the spirit of Antichrist, and that God's judgment and wrath must be near.

As they go through their routines of life, Christians today are doing anything and everything except heeding the words of forewarning of our Lord:

And what I say unto you I say unto all, Watch (Mark 13:37).

He said also:

When these things begin to come to pass, then look up, and lift up your heads; for your redemption draweth nigh (Luke 21:28).

A Big Surprise Coming!

Jesus said another thing. He forewarned that a great many believers will be caught by surprise at the time of His return in the Rapture:

Be ye also ready: for in such an hour as ye think not, the Son of man cometh (Matthew 24:44).

Seems to me we are in such a "think not" time at present.

Lately, emails and articles I've been receiving are trending toward the thought that Christians who are not living exemplary lives as believers will miss being taken in the Rapture of the Church, should they not be fully "repented up" and ready to go. These will be "left behind," as the LaHaye and Jenkins novel series title puts it. First, it is perhaps best to consider what is meant by the "exemplary life" in terms of prerequisites for making it to heaven in the Rapture.

Those who insist that one must be living the exemplary life usually frame that as "living a life of holiness" or "living righteously." By this, I presume they mean for the most part that one must be doing "good works" rather than living life in the "broad way" along which the pedestrian world moves. I would, of course, agree that the born-again believer in the Lord Jesus Christ should be doing exactly that every day. There's no question that God's Word calls us to that model for life while upon this fallen planet.

However, the question is now raised — and it is closely akin to the question raised whenever the declaration is made that one can lose one's salvation: at what point does one "lose" his or her salvation? What particular "sin point" is reached that causes the salvation meter in heaven to go "TILT," removing the sinner's name from the Lamb's Book of Life? Or, for our purposes here, at what point does one sin enough to be taken off the list of those who hold tickets into heaven, who will be lifted to be with Jesus Christ in that millisecond of time known as the "twinkling of an eye" when Jesus calls: "Come up hither!" (Revelation 4:1–2)?

Those who believe that the names of the redeemed can be removed from the Lamb's Book of Life, of course, use the following Scripture as one that proves their position is true:

> He that overcometh, the same shall be clothed in white raiment; and I will not blot out his name out of the book of life, but I will confess his name before my Father, and before his angels (Revelation 3:5).

This is proof, say the "conditional security proponents," that one's name can be removed from the Book of Life. But let's have a closer look to examine whether this is true.

Those who hold that believers' names can be erased from this blessed Book of Life insist that the born-again must "overcome" sin. In their belief dictionary, this means we must stay sin free — that is, either live above sin or stay continually "repented up" in order to keep our names in the Book.

They miss the point entirely as to who actually does the overcoming. It isn't the believer who overcomes all sin, but the Lord Jesus who died in order to take sin away from those who believe, so that we are no longer separated from God the Father in the eternal sense. This is seen, for example, in the following:

> For whatsoever is born of God overcometh the world: and this is the victory that overcometh the world, even our faith. Who is he that overcometh the world, but he that believeth that Jesus is the Son of God (1 John 5:4–5)?

It is simple belief in the Savior who takes away the sins of the world that makes us overcomers. We still sin and come short of the glory of God, but His precious blood shed at Calvary covers all of our sins — past, present, and future. We overcome the world, the flesh, and the devil — all sin in this earthly sphere — only by belief in the only begotten Son of God (John 3:16). Our overcoming is only through God's great grace, through faith. We can never overcome by our own power.

When we sin, we break fellowship with our Lord, but we never break the eternal, family relationship. We do the following to take steps toward making right the sinful break in fellowship that we have caused. First, we must realize and admit that we are not sinless, because repentance cannot truly be made unless we confess that we have sinned. Upon such confession and repentance there is given blessed remedy:

> If we say that we have no sin, we deceive ourselves, and the truth is not in us. If we confess our sins, he is faithful and just to forgive us our sins, and to cleanse us from all unrighteousness (1 John 1:8–9).

God's Word shows us that our salvation and our ability to overcome are totally based on what Christ did for us and our faith in Him alone. This brings us to the matter of the title of this conclusion, "On Being Rapture Ready."

Going to Christ when He calls, as Paul outlines in 1 Corinthians 15:51–55 and 1 Thessalonians 4:13–18, and given by John in Revelation 4:1–2, is a salvation matter. We know that from the overall gospel message and from the total context of God's dealing with His family. Remember when Jesus prayed that beautiful prayer to His Father, as the Lord faced the Cross (John chapter 17)? Read it again, and you will see that it is absolutely clear that born-again believers are forever secure in the Father's hand, based upon what Jesus did on the Cross.

We know with absolute certainty that we are once and forever in God's family because of the words of the One who created all that exists:

> My Father, which gave them me, is greater than all; and no man is able to pluck them out of my Father's hand (John 10:29).

Paul confirms that the Rapture is a salvation matter as follows:

> For God hath not appointed us to wrath, but to obtain salvation by our Lord Jesus Christ, who died for us, that, whether we wake or sleep, we should live together with him. Wherefore comfort yourselves together, and edify one another, even as also ye do (1 Thessalonians 5:9–11).

The Rapture will be Christ keeping us from the hour of temptation or Tribulation (read Revelation 3:10). The Tribulation is the time of God's wrath — to which Paul tells us we are "not appointed." However, there are many who insist that Christians who haven't properly confessed their sins will go through that time of God's wrath (and the entire seven years of the Tribulation will be God's judgment and wrath). They use the following verse to make their case:

> Watch ye therefore, and pray always, that ye may be accounted worthy to escape all these things that shall come to pass, and to stand before the Son of man (Luke 21:36).

The key word they hold forth as relevant here is the word "worthy." Does this word not mean that we as born-again believers must be good enough to stand before Jesus in that raptured throng? Does this word not mean, therefore, that if we fail to live up to God's standards while on this earth, we will (at some point in God's holy view of what it takes to fall from being Rapture ready) lose our ticket in that translation moment, thus not be taken when the shout is heard, "Come up hither!"?

Like in examining the issue of salvation, in looking at the term "overcoming," we now look at the word "worthy." What does it mean to be "worthy," as given in this Rapture example? Again, the answer is wrapped up in the same name as before: "Jesus." Jesus is the only person "worthy," in God's holy eyes, to be in the heavenly realm.

Remember what Jesus said to a man who addressed Him as "Good Master"?

> And Jesus said unto him, Why callest thou me good? none is good, save one, that is, God (Luke 18:19).

Jesus, the second person of the Godhead, was not seeking to chastise the man for addressing Him in this way. The Lord was confirming through this question that He is indeed God, the only good, the only righteousness. Righteousness is the only ticket to heaven — either through the portal of death, or through the Rapture. Only through Jesus — being born again into God's family through belief in Him — can a person enter the heavenly realm.

Jesus spoke to this all-important matter by addressing Nicodemus:

> Jesus answered and said unto him, Verily, verily, I say unto thee, Except a man be born again, he cannot see the kingdom of God (John 3:3).

God's Word says about fallen mankind:

> As it is written, There is none righteous, no, not one (Romans 3:10).

And it also says:

> For all have sinned, and come short of the glory of God (Romans 3:23).

So Jesus is the only person "worthy" to enter heaven. It is through Him that any of us are worthy to stand before Him in that heavenly realm. That is the truth found in the Scripture in question.

On a less magnificent scale (one more earthly,) the word "worthy" in this passage means that we should be in a constant mindset of prayerful repentance. We should always want to be found "worthy" — cleansed of all unrighteousness, as stated in 1 John 1:9, so that we will hear our Lord say to us on that day, "Well done, good and faithful servant" (Matthew 25:23).

This is what is meant by the term "Rapture ready." To be IN Christ is to be worthy, or Rapture ready. If one is born again, he or she is in Jesus Christ — thus worthy in God's holy eyes.

At the same time, to be worthy means to be carrying on life in an exemplary fashion at all times. The believer should be conducting himself or herself in such a way as to please their Lord.

> And now, little children, abide in him; that, when he shall appear, we may have confidence, and not be ashamed before him at his coming (1 John 2:28).

All of this said, the born-again child of God will go to be with Jesus Christ at the Rapture, whether his or her walk in this life has been exemplary or not. That child can never for any reason be removed from God's eternal family.

For the person who hasn't accepted Jesus Christ, it is a frightening prospect for the future he or she faces at this critical time in history. All the reasons we have examined point to the reality that Christ is about to intervene into this darkening world. He is preparing to call God's family home in the Rapture. God's children will, from that moment, and throughout eternity, experience ever-increasing joyfulness and pleasure beyond any ever known while in mortal bodies on earth.

> But as it is written, Eye hath not seen, nor ear heard, neither have entered into the heart of man, the things which God hath prepared for them that love him (1 Corinthians 2:9).

Rapture ready . . . or not, life on planet earth is about to forever change in one, electrifying moment. Don't be left behind.

Terry James' commentaries and in-depth articles on issues and events as they pertain to Bible prophecy appear on what is traditionally the most visited Bible prophecy website on the Internet.

www.raptureready.com

Author Biography

William T. (Terry) James

Terry James is author, general editor, and co-author of numerous books on Bible prophecy, hundreds of thousands of which have been sold worldwide. James is a frequent lecturer on the study of end-time phenomena, and interviews often with national and international media on topics involving world issues and events as they might relate to Bible prophecy.

He is an active member of the PreTrib Research Center Study Group, a prophecy research think-tank founded by Dr. Tim LaHaye, the co-author of the multi-million selling "Left Behind" series of novels. He is a regular participant in the annual Tulsa mid-America prophecy conference, where he speaks, and holds a Question and Answer series of sessions on current world events as they might relate to Bible prophecy.

He is partner and general editor in the www.raptureready.com website, a site that is the attraction of national and international media, and was recently rated as the #1 Bible prophecy website on the Internet. The site has received attention from CBS, ABC, NBC, BBC, *Time Magazine*, *The Rolling Stone*, *The New York Times*, *The Los Angeles Times*, *The Chicago Tribune*, and many other broadcast venues and publications across America, and the world. James writes a weekly column for the site, Nearing Midnight, and contributes in-depth articles on a continuing basis. His book *Heaven Vision: Glimpses into Glory* can be purchased on Amazon.com.

Terry James and his wife, Margaret, live near Little Rock, Arkansas.